How Much Should a
Person Consume?

How Much Should a Person Consume?

Environmentalism in India and the United States

RAMACHANDRA GUHA

UNIVERSITY OF CALIFORNIA PRESS

Berkeley   Los Angeles   London

University of California Press, one of the most distinguished university presses in the United States, enriches lives around the world by advancing scholarship in the humanities, social sciences, and natural sciences. Its activities are supported by the UC Press Foundation and by philanthropic contributions from individuals and institutions. For more information, visit www.ucpress.edu.

Copublished with Permanent Black, Delhi, India
Not for sale in South Asia

University of California Press
Berkeley and Los Angeles, California

University of California Press, Ltd.
London, England

Cataloging-in-Publication data is on file with the Library of Congress.

ISBN-13 (cloth): 978-0-520-24803-8
ISBN-10 (cloth): 0-520-24803-1
ISBN-13 (paper): 978-0-520-24805-2
ISBN-10 (paper): 0-520-24805-8

Manufactured in the United States of America

15   14   13   12   11   10   09   08   07   06
10   9   8   7   6   5   4   3   2   1

This book is printed on Natures Book, which contains 50% post-consumer waste and meets the minimum requirements of ANSI/NISO Z39.48-1992 (R 1997) (Permanence of Paper).

In memory of C.V. Subbarao

Contents

I was forced to admit, at the end of thirty years' devotion to the Cause, that I was never made for it. I was born condemned to be one of those who has to see all sides of a question. When you're damned like that, the questions multiply for you until in the end it's all questions and no answer. As history proves, to be a worldly success at anything, especially revolution, you have to wear blinders like a horse, and see only straight in front of you. You have to see, too, that this is all black, and that is all white.—**Eugene O'Neill**

Preface

This book is a comparative history of environmentalism which draws upon more than two decades of research in India and the United States. These are two large, complex, ecologically and culturally diverse countries, albeit at very different stages of economic development; they are also the two countries I know best. Beyond that, they may perhaps be taken as representative of the North and the South. Both are democracies, with vibrant traditions of activist protest and intellectual work. One has arguably the most influential environmental movement in the North Atlantic world; the other certainly has the most vigorous environmental movement in the non-Western world.

In the course of this work I have accumulated numerous debts. Many are acknowledged in the first chapter; of those that are not, I would like especially to thank the Society for Promotion of Wastelands Development, New Delhi, and the John D. and Catharine T. MacArthur Foundation, Chicago, for grants which allowed me the time and space to complete this book.

Two chapters of the book have been previously published more or less as they appear here. Chapter Six was published as "Lewis Mumford: The Forgotten American Environmentalist—An Essay in Rehabilitation," in David Macauley, ed., *Minding the Earth: Philosophers of Ecology* (New York: Guilford Press, 1995). Chapter Four appeared under the title "Prehistory of Community Forestry in India," in *Environmental History*, vol. 6, no. 2, 2001.

Some of the material in other chapters was earlier presented in the form of lectures: parts of Chapter One as the Walker–Ames Lecture at the University of Washington, Seattle, 2001; a part of Chapter Two as the Ranjan Roy Memorial Lecture, Department of Physics, St Stephen's College, Delhi, 1999; another part as the J.R.D. Tata Oration at the Xavier Labour Relations Institute, Jamshedpur, 2001; parts of Chapter Four as the Manley Memorial Lecture, University of California, Santa Barbara, 1989; parts of Chapter Five as a keynote address at a seminar on National Parks in Developing Countries organized at the Centre for Development and Environment, University of Oslo, 1996; parts of Chapter Nine as the Tirath Gupta Memorial Lecture at the Indian Institute of Management, Ahmedabad, 2002. I am grateful to these institutions for allowing me the opportunity to first present ideas and arguments which appear in revised and, I hope, refined form in this book.

As regards individuals, I wish once more to honor and remember the dedicatee of this book. Some knew C.V. Subbarao as a gifted economist; others knew him as a devoted teacher; yet others as a well-known writer in his native Telugu. And in the history of modern India he will be remembered as a central figure in the nurturing of the democratic rights movement. I knew and admired his public role; but for me, personally, he was also a friend and moral compass. For the first ten years of my writing career it was his judgment that I most anxiously awaited, his approval I most craved. That was not always forthcoming; in particular, he thought I wrote far too much for the public prints. But he was not disappointed by my early essays on the history of environmentalism. These were published in 1992 and 1993; tragically, he died shortly after. Now, when I write for the newspapers, I keep his memory at a distance, but when I write something more substantial I always ask myself before sending it out into the world: "What would C.V. Subbarao have thought of this?"

When I began research on environmentalism I did so as a sociologist, a Marxist, and an Indian who had never left his homeland. Twenty-five years later these self-descriptions have changed without being completely overturned. In method and temperament I am a historian nowadays, though I probably look out more for patterns and relationships than do those who formally study history as a discipline. My political orientation is now somewhat removed from Marxism, but my scholarship is not entirely uninfluenced by it. And while I live in India and retain an Indian passport, this document is stamped with evidence of frequent travel overseas. Whether these transformations have made me any wiser is not for me to say. But I think they have made me humbler.

CHAPTER 1

History *sans* Chauvinism

chauvinism: exaggerated or aggressive patriotism . . . excessive or prejudiced support for one's own cause, group, or sex—*Oxford English Dictionary*

T he Berkeley Nobel laureate George Akerlof once remarked of his fellow economists that if you showed them something that worked in practice they would not be satisfied unless it was also seen to work in theory. This insight explains much about the dismal science, including why, as late as 1980, the MIT economist Lester Thurow could so magisterially write: "If you look at the countries that are interested in environmentalism, or at the individuals who support environmentalism within each country, one is struck by the extent to which environmentalism is an interest of the upper middle class. *Poor countries and poor individuals simply aren't interested.*"[1]

Thurow could write as he did because of the theory that environmentalism was a full-stomach phenomenon. In the West, the rise of the green movement in the 1960s was widely interpreted as a manifestation of what was called "post-materialism." The consumer societies of the North Atlantic world, wrote the political scientist Ronald Inglehart, had collectively shifted "from giving top priority to physical sustenance and safety toward heavier emphasis on belonging, self-expression, and the quality of life."[2] A cultivated interest in the protection

[1] Lester Thurow, *The Zero-Sum Society: Distribution and the Possibilities for Change* (New York: Basic Books, 1980), pp. 104–5, emphasis added.

[2] Ronald Inglehart and Jacques René-Rabier, "Political Realignment in Advanced Industrial Society: From Class-based Politics to Quality-of-Life

of nature was thought possible only when the necessities of life could be taken for granted. As for the poor, their waking hours were spent foraging for food, water, housing, energy: how could they be concerned with something as elevated as the environment?

Now, contrast Thurow's remarks with a signboard that I came across some years ago in an oak forest near the Himalayan town of Shimla. The sign, put up by the Himachal Pradesh state's Forest Department, proclaimed in Hindi:

Kehte hain Ved Puran, bina Vriksh ke nahi kalyan.

Roughly translated, this might read:

The Hindu sacred books say there's no happiness without trees.

The nine words on that signboard contain the seeds of an alternative theory of the origins of environmentalism. They suggest—contrary to what modern historians might say—that the ancient Hindus were the first environmentalists. A precocious ecological consciousness was manifest in their myths, folklore, and ritual practices, where gods played with animals, where humans attained salvation in the forest, and where lowly plant and insect species were treated with reverence. It is further argued that this feeling for nature has persisted into the present. According to this view, where the Western world has succumbed to godlessness and materialism, and deracinated Indian intellectuals have followed it down that polluted path, the environmental wisdom of the Hindus is still embedded in the living practices of peasants in the countryside.[3]

Thurow's claim that environmentalism is a phenomenon of the developed world alone is an expression of what I shall call *disciplinary*

Politics," *Government and Opposition*, vol. 21, no. 4, 1986; cf. also Inglehart, *Culture Shift in Advanced Industrial Societies* (Princeton: Princeton University Press, 1990).

[3] Representative statements include Banwari, *Pancavati: Indian Approach to Environment*, translated from the Hindi by Asha Vohra (Delhi: Shri Vinayaka Publications, 1992); Vandana Shiva, *Staying Alive: Women, Ecology, and Development* (New Delhi: Kali for Women, 1988). The historian Mukul Sharma, of the University of Delhi, is completing a book on the various dimensions of this "Hindu" environmentalism.

chauvinism—the belief that social and cultural changes are the simple byproduct of economic changes. Such is the theory; the practice, as it happens, is all too different. For Thurow did not look very closely around the globe. Seven years before he wrote his lines the Chipko movement had decisively shown the entry by the poor into the domain of environmentalism. Here, a group of illiterate peasants in the Himalaya threatened to hug trees in order to stop them being felled by commercial loggers. Nor was Chipko unique: the 1970s saw a slew of popular movements in defense of local rights to forest, fish, and water resources, as well as protests against large dams. These movements took place in India, Brazil, Malaysia, Ecuador, and Kenya, among peasants, pastoralists, and fisherfolk: that is, among communities even economists could identify as poor.[4]

On the other hand the slogan in the Himalayan forest was an expression of what one might call *cultural* chauvinism. This is as blinkered, and as oblivious of the diversity of human experience, as the chauvinism of the economist. No culture has a monopoly on environmental consciousness, nor on environmental depletion either. The episode of the Khandava forest in the Mahabharata—where the killing of animals and the burning of woods is celebrated in epic verse—and the clearing of the Indo-Gangetic plain in recorded times suggest that there were periods when Hindus thought the forests fit only for destruction. That Hindus are somehow natural environmentalists is also daily contradicted in contemporary India by peasants who pump pesticides into the soil.

Although the chain of influence is hard to establish, I doubt that Hindus would have begun thinking of themselves as environmentalists had it not been for an essay written as recently as 1967 by a Western scholar: I refer, of course, to Lynn White Jr's "The Historical Roots of Our Ecologic Crisis," first published in *Science* and reprinted countless times since.

As is common in such cases, more people knew White's thesis than his work. In the form in which it seeped into popular consciousness the thesis ran as follows: the Book of Genesis says that Man shall dominate

[4] An illuminating comparative analysis of these movements is contained in J. Martinez-Alier, *The Environmentalism of the Poor* (London: Edward Elgar, 2004).

Nature; Christians have taken this to heart and been uniquely irresponsible in their use of nature and natural resources. Or, to simplify further: Christianity is principally responsible for the environmental crisis.[5]

White's essay may very well be the most influential ever written by a historian. It has spawned a massive secondary literature—thousands of books and articles written explicitly to contest, approve, or amplify his thesis. Christian theologians claim that White misrepresented their scriptures; that, in fact, the ethic of "stewardship" is as important a motif in the Bible as the idea of domination. On the other side, those with a vested interest in Eastern religions have seized with glee on White's apparent denunciation of Christianity.[6]

It took a generation for these ideas to gain common currency. But when they did, the original provocateur was wholly forgotten: the copywriter of the Himachal Pradesh Forest Department had never heard of Lynn White. Nor have the other Hindus who now claim their culture is somehow superior to all others in the matter of environmental ethics. Likewise, the Buddhist literature on the subject is a product of the past two decades. Now, we are told, the Buddha was the first environmentalist for he was born in a *sal* forest and attained enlightenment under a *ficus* tree and came to preach the philosophy of ecological restraint, also known as the Middle Way. But how is it that claims such as these were never current before 1967?

I do not know how White would have reacted to this competitive chauvinism. Whose side would he be on? Perhaps it doesn't matter

[5] See Lynn White, Jr, "The Historical Roots of Our Ecologic Crisis," *Science*, March 10, 1967. Actually, White's thesis was somewhat more complex. He did not suggest that Christianity was somehow intrinsically "anti-ecological;" rather, that historical conditions were making it so. In his view, as new technologies of production and communication were invented, European man began to feel more in command of his surroundings. Thus, while earlier calendars and pictures showed man in a position of subordination to nature, from the early medieval period these works tended to place man in a position of domination.

[6] And the literature is still growing. Some years ago, the Worldwide Fund for Nature commissioned a series of popular pamphlets on the subject; *Hinduism and Ecology, Islam and Ecology*, etc. More recently, the Divinity School of Harvard University has organized a series of international conferences on the same lines, whose proceedings have been appearing in book form.

much, for the real roots of environmental destruction (and conservation) lie not in ancient religions but in *secular* processes of the *modern*
world.

Believers and theologians will go on tracing the roots of environmental crises in human departures from scriptural mandates, and
therefore identifying the prospects of environmental reform in a
renewed adherence to them. For the historian, however, environmentalism is principally a product of and reaction to the Industrial Revolution. The industrialization of Europe, and later of North America,
rested on the discovery of new resources—fossil fuels, pre-eminently—and on new ways of extracting, transforming, processing, and
consuming them. Putting these resources to use spawned novel technologies of production, transport, communication, and storage. When
colonialism followed industrialization, the scale of resource flows
between and within societies hugely increased. In the eighteenth and
nineteenth centuries the invention of new technologies within, and
the colonization of new lands without, together led to a massive expansion of the resource catchments owned by Europeans.

What we gloss as the Industrial Revolution was actually four revolutions in one: the revolution in industry (properly so called); the
concomitant revolution in agriculture, which now witnessed a great
augmentation in its productivity because of the new resources and
technologies; the revolution in transport and communication caused
by such inventions as the steam engine and the telegraph; and the
demographic revolution, whereby advances in sanitation and health
greatly reduced human mortality and led to a steady increase in the
population of Europe. Scrupulous historians would probably add a
fifth and sixth revolution to this list. Both occurred in the political
realm: the fifth being the advent of democratic and socialist ideas within Europe; the sixth being Europe's political conquest of the rest of the
world.

There is, then, a whole array of transformative processes lurking
within the familiar if somewhat misleading term "Industrial Revolution." A one-sentence summary of these processes might read: "More
people, producing more, traveling more, consuming more, and excret-
ing more." The social changes these activities wrought have generated
a huge library of scholarly works; environmental changes, which also

accelerated hugely through the devastation of forests and habitats and by the fouling of the air and waters, have not generated a scholarship nearly as voluminous.

There had certainly been human induced ecological changes in the premodern world, but they had been localized. A tribe of hunter-gatherers may have hunted a species of bird to extinction, but there were other edible species for the tribe to harvest. A community of peasants may have exhausted the fertility of their soil, but there were other soils to which the peasants could move. However, with industrialization, there was for the first time in human history a perception of a generalized—one might almost say *civilizational*—environmental crisis. The damage to nature was unprecedented in both scale and intensity. This alarmed some writers and thinkers, who began to search for ways to stem, and in time reverse, these new processes of environmental degradation. Thus was born the "environmental movement."

There was no environmentalism before industrialization; there were only the elements of an environmental sensibility. For every tribe of hunters that pursued a species to extinction, there was a tribe that harvested its prey prudently so as not to deplete prey populations in the long run. There were peasants who used the land carelessly, and other peasants who designed sophisticated systems of water and soil management. And, as the classical literatures of West and East demonstrate, there were poets and playwrights who wrote with insight and empathy about the natural world. All this might be said to constitute the prehistory of environmentalism, though not environmentalism itself. For, neither peasant nor poet transcended their locality to offer any systemic vision of reorganizing nature. *That* needed the Industrial Revolution, widespread environmental degradation, and the response we term "environmentalism."

It is that suffix "ism" which is decisive. With it, the preservation or conservation of natural resources is no longer a matter of intuitive feeling, but a wide-ranging social program.

As far as I know, the first historian to point to the organic links between industrialization and environmentalism was the Cambridge scholar G.M. Trevelyan. In a now-forgotten lecture of 1931 he observed that the "love of nature in its most natural and unadulterated form has grown *pari passu* with the Industrial Revolution. James Watt and

George Stephenson were contemporaries of Rousseau and Wordsworth, and the two movements have gone on side by side ever since, each progressing with equal rapidity." One movement furthered the appreciation and understanding of natural beauty; the other movement intensified the rate at which nature was destroyed. As Trevelyan noted: "No doubt it is partly because the destruction is so rapid that the appreciation is so loud."

This sense of nostalgia was made more marked by the conditions of city life—the conditions of the vast majority of English people. Their separation from the natural world, enforced by urban living, fostered the yearning to return periodically, for short spurts, to nature. "And for that reason, if for no other, the real country must be preserved in sufficient quantity to satisfy the soul's thirst of the town dweller."

Illustrative here was the change in the English perception of the Alps and the Scottish Highlands—once regarded as hostile, but, by the time Trevelyan wrote, as the epitome of what was wild and therefore beautiful. This change in attitude toward mountain scenery, remarks the historian, "is almost identical in time and progress with the march of the Industrial Revolution, and has, I think a certain causal connection with it." He believed that the

> modern aesthetic taste for mountain form, is connected with a moral and intellectual change, that differentiates modern civilized man from civilized man in all previous ages. I think that he now feels the desire and need for the wildness and greatness of untamed, aboriginal nature, which his predecessors did not feel. One cause of this change is the victory that civilized man has now attained over nature through science, machinery and organization, a victory so complete that he is denaturalizing the lowland landscape. He is therefore constrained to seek nature in her still unconquered citadels, the mountains.[7]

Two points are crucial here. The first is that by the end of the nineteenth century few parts of the world were unaffected by European

---

[7] G.M. Trevelyan, "The Calls and Claims of Natural Beauty" (the Rickman Godlee Lecture for 1931), in *An Autobiography and Other Essays* (London: Longmans, Green and Co., 1949), pp. 92–106. A fine recent work on this subject is Robert Macfarlane, *Mountains of the Mind: A History of a Fascination* (London: Granta Books, 2003).

industrialization: colonialism had made sure of this. Thus, the new technologies were used, and abused, far from their original homes. The railway, for example, came to India less than two decades after its invention in Britain. By 1900 there were more than 30,000 miles of track in the Indian subcontinent, to build and maintain which thousands of square miles of forests were destroyed, and acres and acres of land mined for coal. Again, with colonialism came the modern factory system, the chemicalization of agriculture, and the growth of urban centers, all bringing in their wake myriad forms of ecological degradation. These radical transformations of the environment prompted an array of critical responses from those who sought to contain the damage or protect unspoilt areas from contamination.

Here, environmentalism can profitably be compared with three other great movements of the modern world: the *democratic* movement, which asked that ordinary, unprivileged folk also be given a political voice; the *socialist* movement, which wanted the fruits of economic growth to be distributed equitably; and the *feminist* movement, which urged that women be granted political and economic rights equal to those enjoyed by men.

Wherever there is autocracy there are dissenters asking for democratic rights. Where there is capitalism, socialists will rise to oppose it. Where there is patriarchy, there will be women who resist it. The form, shape, and intensity of these protests varies; the oppositional impulse remains constant. So, one might say, wherever there is industrialization, there is environmentalism.

The interpretation of environmentalism offered here challenges both the post-materialist hypothesis and the several versions of the Lynn White thesis. It suggests that one does not have to wait for a society to be fully industrialized for an ecological critique to manifest itself. It argues that the relationship between religion and environmentalism follows rather than precedes industrialization. Once the evidence of environmental degradation becomes widespread, writers and activists seek solace as well as solutions in practices of the past: thus the search for elements of an environmental ethic in the scriptures; thus also the rehabilitation of folk practices of conservation such as sacred groves and community irrigation systems. Over the past few decades much energy and ink has been expended on understanding what religion and custom offer us in countering or moderating the ecological excesses of the present day. The irony is that this return to tradition is itself a product of, indeed is only made possible by, the onset of modernity.

Like the other great movements of the modern world, environmentalism is not unified or homogeneous. We speak of difference feminism and identity feminism, of agrarian socialism and Marxism; likewise, modern environmentalism comes in many shades and strands, several of which are explored in some detail in this book. At the same time, as contemporary with these other movements, environmentalism has engaged in a lively dialog with each of them. The environmental movement has been influenced by, and has in turn influenced, struggles for socialism, feminism, and democracy.

The study of environmentalism worldwide has been beset by different kinds of chauvinism. Two I have already alluded to: those caused by allegiance to a particular academic discipline and to a particular religious faith. But there are other chauvinisms that have been as damaging. These include the phenomenon of nationalism, well studied in so many contexts but not really in the context of environmentalism. There is also the chauvinism caused by partisan adherence to a particular sect or ideology within the environmental movement itself.

Within the scholarly community, the form of chauvinism most widely prevalent is the *disciplinary*: the belief that one's academic discipline provides richer or deeper insights than any other. Within the public at large, the form of chauvinism most common is the *religious*: the dogma that the faith one is born into, or which one embraces, provides a uniquely privileged vantage point into the existential dilemmas of individual human beings, and indeed of humankind.[8] And within the environmental movement, the chauvinisms most obviously in operation are the *national* and the *ideological*, these often operating in conjunction.

[8] I include, within this characterization, secularism and atheism, belief systems sometimes upheld with as much fanaticism and zeal as those based on religion.

The American writer Jonathan Franzen has recently remarked of his country's environmental movement that it is "a constituency loudly proud of its refusal to compromise with others."[9] This characterization alas, is true not merely of American environmentalism as a whole but also of the different sects within it. Deep ecologists will not compromise with bioregionalists, who themselves fight with the votaries of eco-efficiency, while none of the above will talk to gung-ho modernizers or religious zealots. Nor is the American experience unique in this regard. Environmentalists in other lands are likewise implacably hostile to modernizers and developers, and likewise deeply divided among themselves.

This book can be read as a historical analysis of these various forms of chauvinism, but also as a personal attempt to escape and transcend them. For the most part, its later chapters suppress my own voice in favor of the voices of those I write about.[10] The remainder of the present chapter, however, is cast in an autobiographical vein. My intention is not to draw attention to myself but to try and sense, through my own intellectual evolution, some of the wider currents of politics and scholarship as these relate to the history of environmentalism.

II

In 1980, the year Lester Thurow so comprehensively rejected the idea of an environmentalism of the poor, I began a PhD in sociology at Calcutta. I was surrounded by Marxists, for the state of West Bengal and its capital, Calcutta, had lately under come under the rule of a coalition of Communist parties. The finest intellectuals belonged either to this "Left Front" or were further to the left of it. There were, as I recall, no credible liberals around, and naturally no conservatives were visible at all.

To a young middle-class Indian, Marxism had great intellectual and emotional appeal. This is a philosophy that flourishes in conditions of scarcity and inequality; recall that the European and American

[9] Jonathan Franzen, "Reflections: My Bird Problem," *The New Yorker*, August 8 and 15, 2005.

[10] Partial exceptions to this are Chapters Seven and Eight herein, where my assessments of the work of Chandi Prasad Bhatt and Madhav Gadgil combine historical analysis with personal recollection.

intelligentsia turned sharply leftward after the Great Depression, when poverty was pervasive, capitalism seemed in the grip of a general crisis, and revolution seemed round the corner. Likewise, in the India of the 1980s only Marxism, it seemed, could provide a convincing analysis of why some Indians were rich and so many so poor.

There was also a pyschological reason for the attractions of Marxism: it allowed everyone to participate in the conviction that they were ultimately going to be part of the winning side. In 1980 History had not Ended; the Soviet superpower was alive, while—at any rate in ex-colonial countries like India—the Vietnamese, Chinese, and Cuban revolutions had not lost their romantic sheen. In Calcutta, Marxism's appeal was enhanced by the fact that there was no single party line. Within and outside the ruling coalition there were in fact many varieties of Marxism, each drawing inspiration in varying degrees from the several founders of the faith. All admired Marx and all worshipped Lenin; but some venerated Trotsky while others detested him. A figure of great interest, as well as controversy, was Mao Zedong, the lately deceased leader of the socialist revolution in India's great civilizational neighbor, China.[11]

As we saw, for the economist environmentalism was a post-materialist phenomenon restricted to affluent sections of the developed world. For the Marxist, on the other hand, environmentalism was a bourgeois deviation from the class struggle. Classical Marxists believed that the destruction of capitalism and its supersession by socialism would create a resource-abundant utopia in which "Man, the Sovereign of Nature" (as Marx characterized our species) would bend the natural world wholly to his will.[12] Shortly after the victory of the Bolsheviks in Russia, Trotsky argued that "the proper goal of communism is the domination of nature by technology, and the domination of technology by planning, so that the raw materials of nature will yield up to mankind all that it needs and more besides." In Trotsky's characteristically arrogant view:

[11] For a personal, anecdotal account of Calcutta Marxism in the 1980s, see the title essay of my book *An Anthropologist Among the Marxists and Other Essays* (Delhi: Permanent Black, 2001).

[12] Marx used the phrase in one of his essays on India, contrasting what man was and should be with regard to nature with the (in his view, contemptible) worship of monkey gods and cows by Hindus.

The present distribution of mountains and rivers, of fields, of meadows, of steppes, of forests and seashores, cannot be considered final. Man has already made changes in the map of nature that are not few nor insignificant. But they are merely pupil's practice in comparison with what is coming. Faith merely promises to move mountains; but technology, which takes nothing "on faith," is actually able to cut down mountains and move them . . . Through the machine, man in socialist society will command nature in its entirety . . . He will point out places for mountains and passes. He will change the course of the rivers, and he will lay down rules for the oceans. The idealist simpletons may say that this will be a bore, but that is why they are simpletons . . .[13]

In a theoretical sense, Indian Marxism has always been imitative. And on this subject, as on so many others, the views of the classical Marxists were energetically reproduced by their comrades in the subcontinent. Thus, Indian environmentalists were suspect in the Left for asking critical questions of modern science and technology, and for suggesting that modern industrialization might face ecological limits. Greens who opposed large dams and nuclear power plants were dismissed as a bunch of reactionary Luddites; it was also suggested that they were not merely foolish but dangerous for they played into the hands of the American imperialists, who did not wish to see India emerge as a strong and self-reliant power.[14]

At any rate, environmentalism was not a subject that figured in my curriculum at Calcutta, or in the seminars I attended, or in the coffee house conversations in which I participated. Listening to these an aspiring sociologist would have concluded that there were really only two proper subjects of scholarly enquiry: class conflict in the countryside between landlord and laborer; and class conflict in the cities between capitalist and worker.

Some months after I had begun my PhD I attended a lecture by a visiting scholar, Jayanta Bandyopadhyaya, then of the Indian Institute of Management, Bangalore, who spoke about the relevance of

[13] Leon Trotsky, quoted in C. Wright Mills, *The Marxists* (Harmondsworth: Penguin Books, 1963), pp. 278–9.

[14] Cf. Biplab Dasgupta, "The Environment Debate: Issues and Trends," *Economic and Political Weekly*, Annual Number, 1978; Subrata Mitra, "Ecology as Science and Science Fiction," *Economic and Political Weekly*, January 30, 1982.

Schumacherian notions of "appropriate technology." At a reception afterwards I got talking to the visitor. Professor Bandyopadhyaya asked me where I was from (the sub-Himalayan town of Dehradun was the answer), and then asked what topic I intended to pursue for my dissertation. I said I was torn between studying steel workers in Jamshedpur and peasants in Bihar. "If you're from Dehradun," said the professor, "why don't you work on the sociology of the Chipko movement?"

At the time, Chipko was relatively obscure—far from being the global symbol of popular environmentalism it has since become. Now there are tree huggers in California, but back then this protest movement in the Garhwal Himalaya was not very well known even in India. However, the past winter Professor Bandyopadhyaya had met the Chipko leader Sunderlal Bahuguna and been deeply impressed. He had visited Bahuguna's ashram and traveled around some Garhwal villages with him.

For Professor Bandyopadhyaya these encounters with Chipko had confirmed and consolidated his own move away from the Marxist path. Brought up in Calcutta, he had imbibed its socialist air, but his later travels around India and his own studies of the degrading effects of much that passed for modern technology had led him to the Gandhians and their search for more humane and eco-friendly technologies. These were based on a critical appreciation of indigenous peasant and artisanal practices rather than a wholesale rejection of them. His trips around Garhwal with Bahuguna had been, for him, the final nail in the Marxist coffin.

When Bandyopadhyaya suggested I work on Chipko he did so with the invigorating zeal of the convert-turned-missionary. Here was an active, alive, social movement still in the process of being made. But there hadn't been any scholarly studies of it. My home town was at the edge of Chipko country, and I spoke Hindi, a language most Garhwalis understood. And I was a sociologist who had to write a dissertation on an original and unresearched subject. Why look further?

After my first year of course work, I returned to Dehradun for the summer. To explore the Chipko idea I wrote to the two leaders whose names I knew, Sunderlal Bahuguna and Chandi Prasad Bhatt. I got no answer from Bahuguna but Bhatt wrote back inviting me to his home town, Gopeshwar. (That visit is described in some detail in Chapter Seven of this book.) I was charmed by his presence and moved by his work. Two days with him convinced me that I must indeed follow Bandyopadhyaya's advice and write a dissertation on Chipko.

I returned to Calcutta after the vacation and ran the subject past my teachers. Kamini Adhikari, my dissertation supervisor, was a widely traveled woman of cultivated interests. Her main concern was that I should find a meaningful way of relating my theme to debates in sociology. She had studied in Holland, lived in France, and knew Alain Touraine, the French sociologist of social movements. Chipko, she suggested, could be seen as an Indian variant of a "new" social movement—to be distinguished from the "classical" social movements of workers and peasants.

Dr Adhikari was of a different generation, some three decades older than myself. Closer in age and temperament was Anjan Ghosh, a sociologist trained at that redoubt of intellectual Marxism, Jawaharlal Nehru University (JNU) in New Delhi. But unlike the typical JNU product, Anjan recognized that there were other social theorists as great as Marx. In the classroom he introduced me to Max Weber and Emile Durkheim, while outside it he introduced me to the circle of anarcho-Marxists who hung around Samar Sen, the legendary editor of a radical weekly, *Frontier*.

Anjan Ghosh was, for all practical purposes, my guru. Under his close and almost daily guidance I worked my way through the classics of Western social theory and Indian anthropology. His intellectual generosity was remarkable: when I told him I wanted to work on Chipko, he put me on to Shiv Visvanathan, who, he said, knew more about such things than he did.

Visvanathan is a sociologist of science who was then teaching at the Delhi School of Economics. I already knew him; in fact, when I wanted to change fields and cities after my master's degree in economics Visvanathan had advised me to study with Ghosh in Calcutta. Now I had been sent back to him, to be guided through the canonical works of the modern environmental debate. Visvanathan made me read Lynn White on religion and environmental ethics, Garrett Hardin on the tragedy of the commons, and Barry Commoner on the links between modern technology and environmental degradation.[15] Visvanathan

---

[15] The White and Hardin essays I first read in R. Clarke, ed., *Notes for the Future* (London: Thames and Hudson, 1971), while the work by Commoner that most impressed me was *The Closing Circle* (New York: Alfred Knopf, 1971).

may have been the only Indian who had read these writers; through him I became perhaps the second. He also introduced me to pioneering environmental thinkers likewise unread by other Indians: for example, Patrick Geddes and Lewis Mumford, both of whom feature later in this book.[16]

Looking back, these disciplinary transgressions must have been encouraged by the fact that, within India, the discipline of sociology had been far more accommodative of other disciplinary traditions than was the case in Europe and, particularly, the United States. In his withering attack on American sociology C. Wright Mills had written of how it alternated between two poles: "Grand Theory," the formal elaboration of concepts without regard to how people actually lived; and "Abstracted Empiricism," the mere accumulation of statistics and numbers with little regard to their social and historical context.[17] The leading Indian sociologists, in contrast, were engaged in a lively dialog with history and anthropology. They were also keenly immersed in public affairs, in the painful yet deeply interesting transformation of their hierarchical, caste-and-kin bound society into a modern, secular, democratic nation-state. And unlike their American counterparts they did not believe that sociology and elegant prose were necessarily at odds.[18]

III

By the beginning of 1982 my dissertation was taking shape. It was to be an ethnographic study of Chipko. My field material related to the sociology of social movements and the environment-development

[16] Shiv Visvanathan's published work includes *Organizing for Science: The Making of an Industrial Research Laboratory* (New Delhi: Oxford University Press, 1985), and *A Carnival for Science* (New Delhi: Oxford University Press, 1997).

[17] C. Wright Mills, *The Sociological Imagination* (Harmondsworth: Penguin, 1963).

[18] The two Indian sociologists I read with most interest and profit in those years were M.N. Srinivas and André Béteille. To be fair, there were also some American sociologists who engaged with history and wrote elegant English. The two I learnt from were Wright Mills and—to invoke a name from the other side of the political spectrum—Robert Nisbet.

debate. To that end I planned a preliminary trip to Mandal, the village in the upper Alakananda valley where the first Chipko protests had taken place in March–April 1973.

At the time I was living in Dehradun's Forest Research Institute (FRI), where my father worked. He was a paper technologist who ran a laboratory which tested the suitability of various woods for pulping. He had never been near a forest himself. But the FRI was India's flagship institute of forestry education and research. Its history went back to 1906; the collection in its library went back further still.

The FRI library was housed in a gloomy white building located a hundred yards from my house. I spent the weeks before I went to Garhwal in its cavernous corners, reading documents untouched for a hundred years: forest working plans, reports of forest conferences, runs of authoritative journals such as *Indian Forester*. These were the foundational texts of forestry in the subcontinent. They told the story of how and why the Forest Department had come to be India's biggest landlord, with more than a fifth of the country's land in its possession. Through the texts I scoured one could exhume the logic—economic as well as political—of state intervention, and of the scientific (or, as I was to argue, pseudo-scientific) basis of forest management. These narratives, sometimes somber and at other times heroic, all originated with high officials of the British Raj, but within their interstices one could read signs of subaltern resistance.

I finally left Dehradun to go to the home of Chipko. Here, one of the first people I met was Alam Singh Rawat. He had been headman of Mandal village in 1973, when the Chipko movement was born there. Naturally, he had vivid memories of protests against the Forest Department. The early writings on Chipko tended to interpret the movement as a response to tropical deforestation and the global environmental crisis. To my surprise, Alam Singh saw the struggle, rather, in the context of the very local and specific history of the Garhwal Himalaya. Chipko, he told me, was not the first time the peasants of the region had asserted their forest rights. Decades earlier, when India was still a colony, a British Conservator of Forests had come to Mandal village to convert its woodland into state property. The villagers surrounded him, blackened his face with a cattle iron, and ran him out of the district.

After some weeks of trying, I found a file in the National Archives at Delhi which confirmed the tale, in essence if not fine detail. An *Indian* conservator had indeed been attacked, not in British Garhwal but in the princely state of Tehri Garhwal which lay to the west. However, the sentiments were exactly those expressed by Alam Singh. As the secret report on the disturbance put it, the villagers "had taken exception to the reservation of these forests;" indeed, they "objected to any state interference with forests over which they claimed *full* and *exclusive* rights."[19]

By now I had acquired a real taste for the archives. Those weeks in the FRI library and that thrilling printed confirmation of Alam Singh's oral history were the beginnings of what was to become a lifelong addiction. Much of my work was done in the National Archives and the Uttar Pradesh State Archives in Lucknow. Here lay the rich records of the Forest Department. These were records that provided a privileged window into India's rural social history, conveying the relations between a ubiquitous arm of the state and millions of peasants, tribals, pastoralists, and artisans. These were records that had not previously been seen by scholars—a lacuna that delighted me no end. For what can please a historian more than finding documents that no other historian is aware of?

My first exposure to serious research had been deeply satisfying. And there was more to come. On my way back to my institute in Calcutta, I stopped for some days in Delhi. As it happened my visit coincided with a conference on a new forest act being proposed by the Government of India. A draft of the act had been leaked and come to the notice of social activists. To their dismay the new legislation would further strengthen the hands of the state and lead to a further diminution of the rights of peasants and tribals.

In the modern history of India there have been two landmark forest conferences. The first was held in 1875 in the imperial summer capital, Simla (now spelt Shimla). Those attending the conference were senior colonial officials. Their brief was to put in place a legislative apparatus for the state to effectively administer forests. Its most tangible outcome

[19] Cf. Ramachandra Guha, *The Unquiet Woods: Ecological Change and Peasant Resistance in the Himalaya* (Berkeley: University of California Press, 1990), pp. 71–2.

was the Indian Forest Act of 1878, a far-reaching and hugely influential piece of legislation whose impact was felt well beyond India.[20]

Over the summer in Dehradun I had found and studied the proceedings of that Simla conference. Now, more than a century later, I was able to attend a rather different kind of forest conference. It was held at the Indian Social Institute, a place run by Jesuits but hospitable to dissenters of all kinds. For this occasion the dissenters turned out in strength, many coming from parts of India where forests still remained. Here were Gandhian reformists from Garhwal, Maoist revolutionaries from Chandrapur in Maharashtra, Jesuits and lapsed Jesuits from Dhule near Bombay and from Chaibasa in Jharkhand—all people who, unlike me, had "declassed" themselves. But there were also some real subalterns, activists from an *adivasi* or tribal background. Also in attendance were some sensitive members of the intellectual elite such as the newspaper editor B.G. Verghese.

The word most used in their discussions was "draconian," which the new legislation undoubtedly was. Speaker after speaker condemned its provisions for facilitating not forest conservation but the oppression of the forest dweller. For forests were crucial to the sustenance of the rural economy: as the source of wood for agricultural implements, pasture for goats and cattle, rope and bamboo for artisans, herbs for local healers, not to speak of a hundred other users and uses. Under the new laws the collection of many kinds of forest produce was deemed a crime. On the enforcement side, forest officers were given the right to arrest without a warrant.[21]

As subsequent research showed, the bill was not only draconian, it was also colonial. It had taken over, wholesale, 81 of the 84 sections of the 1878 Forest Act which rested on a more or less strict notion of state ownership. One would have expected that Indian independence would have led to a new forest act, more sensitive to local needs and

[20] Cf. D. Brandis and A. Smythies, eds, *Report of the Proceedings of the Forest Conference held at Simla, October 1875* (Calcutta: Government of India Press, 1876); R.S. Troup, *Colonial Forest Administration* (Oxford: Clarendon Press, 1940).

[21] The proceedings of the Delhi meeting were published as Walter Fernandes and Sharad Kulkarni, eds, *Towards a New Forest Policy* (New Delhi: Indian Social Institute, 1983).

more conducive to democratic participation. To the contrary, a colonial act of 1878 continued to guide forest policy more than three decades after independence. And now the attempt finally being made to change it was in the direction of greater state control rather than less.

In the forefront of the opposition to the draft act was the Peoples Union for Democratic Rights (PUDR). This was (and remains) a remarkable institution run by volunteers—many of them students and teachers from the University of Delhi—working on a less-than-shoe-string budget. The PUDR had just published a forceful critique of the act and was beginning to work on other aspects of natural resource management as well.[22] Its members met every Saturday in a room of Triveni Kala Sangam, an artists' enclave in central Delhi. As a researcher in the field of forest policy I was encouraged to attend, and there I gained a great deal from the experiences of PUDR members.

At about this time I also made my acquaintance with two other groups of great energy and promise. One was the Centre for Science and Environment (CSE), a brainchild of the engineer turned campaigning journalist Anil Agarwal. The other was Kalpavriksh, a group of school and college kids deeply committed to a sustainable future. Both groups were also involved in the campaign against the new forest act.[23]

A future historian of Indian environmentalism will have to write at some length on the contributions of the PUDR, the CSE, and Kalpavriksh. India's debt to these groups is enormous; so too is mine. Conversations with their members helped me sharpen my understanding of the environment debate, thus to more effectively link past with present, academic research with public policy.

IV

Looking back it appears that my academic career was determined by a series of lucky accidents. Had I not met Jayanta Bandyopadhyaya I would never have thought of working on Chipko. Had I not lived in

[22] Peoples Union for Democratic Rights, *Undeclared Civil War* (New Delhi: PUDR, 1982).

[23] This draft act was dropped, then reintroduced in even more stringent form in 1994, sparking another pan-Indian debate which was, once more, successful in getting the legislation shelved.

the FRI I would never have seen those forgotten documents on the history of forestry. Had I not seen them, or had I not been in Delhi in April 1982, I would not have attended that famous meeting against the new forest bill.

The first of these accidents introduced me to the environment debate; the second and third, seen in conjunction, helped me overcome the barriers between history and sociology. In India these barriers were formidable. Historians did archival research and worked on the period before 1947, the year of Indian independence; sociologists did fieldwork and studied the ethnographic present. But, as I was finding out, both forest policy and peasant discontent were oblivious of these divides. To properly understand Chipko one needed to study its prehistory; and this meant going back to the colonial past and digging in the archives.

I found it easy to become methodologically promiscuous, for my teachers were encouraging, and I saw that I much preferred archival research to fieldwork in any case. Disciplinary boundaries I could comfortably breach. Somewhat harder to transgress were the boundaries of ideology. From the time I went to Calcutta I had been calling myself a Marxist: a non-party Marxist, perhaps, but still a Marxist. Given that ecology was regarded by all varieties of Indian Marxists as a bourgeois fad, how could I reconcile my faith with my chosen topic of research?

I tried hard, and was not entirely unsuccessful. I noted that one of Marx's first published articles was on the theft of wood; although one could never be sure—I was reading him in an English translation done in Russia from a German original which was convoluted enough in the first place—he seemed to be saying that Rhineland peasants in the nineteenth century had a prior right to forests later claimed by the state, just as had their Garhwal counterparts a hundred years later. The first deprivation was a consequence of capitalism; the second of capitalism *and* colonialism. Those two "c" words provided the analytic grid of my first published essay, which examined the continuities in Indian forest policy through an unmistakably (and, in retrospect, crudely) Marxist lens.[24]

[24] See Ramachandra Guha, "Forestry in British and Post-British India: A Historical Analysis," *Economic and Political Weekly*, 2 parts, October 29 and November 5–12, 1983.

I moved away from Marxism as a consequence of two conversations I had in Delhi, *circa* 1983–4. The first was with a friend who had been an undergraduate with me in Delhi. He had since joined the Communist Party of India (Marxist), which was then, as it is now, the Big Brother among Left parties in India. When I explained to this friend what I was working on, he said that, if it opposed the felling of forests, the Chipko movement was on the side of reaction. For forest felling fueled the paper industry, wherein labored the advance guard of the working class who would lead the proletarian revolution of the future. From the point of view of Marxist catechism his logic was irrefutable. But it left me uncomfortable. How could a man of such manifest sincerity and social commitment as Chandi Prasad Bhatt be, even "objectively speaking," a reactionary?

The other conversation was with the historian Basudev "Robi" Chatterji, then just back with a PhD from Cambridge. Chatterji was to Indian history what Shiv Visvanathan was to Indian sociology—without question the best-read scholar of his generation.[25] At the time, I was enchanted by the school of British Marxist historians whose leading members included Eric Hobsbawm and E.P. Thompson. Chatterji advised me to read the French as well. The British historians, he said, were insensitive to geography, whereas in the *Annales* school geography was integral to history. At his suggestion I read the classic works of Lucien Febvre and Marc Bloch, scholars who were "environmental historians" before the existence of environmental history.[26]

Chatterji also persuaded me of the necessary distinction between political faith and scholarly practice. It was all right to be a Marxist in

[25] Basudev Chatterji is the author of *Trade, Tariffs and Empire* (New Delhi: Oxford University Press, 1990), and editor of the three-volume anthology *Towards Freedom: Documents on the Movement for Independence in India, 1938* (New Delhi: Oxford University Press, 1999).

[26] See, especially, Lucien Febvre, *A Geographical Introduction to History*, English translation (London: Routledge & Kegan Paul, 1950); Marc Bloch, *French Rural History: An Essay on its Essential Characteristics*, English translation (London: Routledge & Kegan Paul, 1978). Both books were originally published before the Second World War. After the War, the works of the second-generation *Annales* historians—Fernand Braudel, Georges Duby, Emmanuel Le Roy Ladurie, and others—also emphasized the impress of the natural environment on human life. For an overview, see Peter Burke, *The French Historical Revolution: The Annales School, 1929–89* (Oxford: Polity, 1990).

one's personal life, he said, to march in demonstrations and even behead a landlord if one thought this would aid the revolution. But when it came to historical research it was not wise to declare oneself a Marxist in advance. For the archives told their own various, complex, contradictory stories which did not always fit into a neat theory.

I was won over by Chatterji's argument. I was still a Marxist (though that too was to change), but no longer a Marxist *historian*. I am grateful for my early exposure to Marx, who taught me that inequality was not natural but rooted in institutions created by men. Marxist historians, especially E.P. Thompson, also made me look out for resistance to authority by those at the bottom of the heap. But I am glad I stopped calling myself a Marxist for it allowed me to learn from alternative traditions of historiography and listen to the archives before asking questions of them.

V

In August 1985 my wife went to Yale University to study graphic design; in January 1986 I joined her because of accident no. 4 in my life. At the American consulate in Calcutta I had found a Yale catalog which listed departments and professors. I recognized two names: James C. Scott, whose work on peasant protest I had read; and W.R. Burch, Jr, whose work on environmental sociology I had heard of. I wrote to both.

Scott answered that to his regret Yale had no program in South Asian studies. Burch, on the other hand, had just been made Director of the Tropical Resources Institute (TRI) at the School of Forestry and Environmental Studies. The Mellon Foundation had awarded the TRI a grant to develop courses in tropical ecology. Yale had no one to teach them. It was at this point that I happened to present myself: a sociologist with environmental interests from the tropics asking to be able to join his wife in a faraway land.

Had Yale's TRI been headed by a soil scientist or silviculturist they would have called in one of their kind. I was fortunate that the TRI Director was a sociologist, and that he had once been to India. Back in 1969 Bill Burch had visited the Gir forest and noticed the simmering conflict between pastoralists and the Asiatic lion. After Gir he stopped in the town of Surat where he met an eminent Indian sociologist who was, as it happened, a Marxist. When Burch suggested that the conflict in the Gir merited closer study he was told ecology was a Western fad. Almost two decades later, the Director of the TRI welcomed my letter as evidence of a belated awakening within the sociological profession in India.

I was to spend eighteen months in Yale, teaching, talking, traveling. My students were outstandingly good. The Forestry School there had the reputation of being the most international place in New Haven (it was; and apparently it still is). Many of its students were former Peace Corps Volunteers with experience in Asia and Africa. There were a handful of Asian and African students as well. And they were all just a few years younger than me—a couple, in fact, were older. Several are my friends still.[27]

On the faculty I was to forge close friendships with Bill Burch and Jim Scott. Burch was that American exception—a sociologist who wrote uncommonly well. He had written a marvelous book on environmental attitudes in America, but was now more interested in policy questions, the restoration of urban environments, and community forestry in the tropics.[28] Scott was also in his own way an exception, an American political scientist who had never crunched a number and whose real interests were history and anthropology. When we met he had just published what I regard as the best of his many books, this one based on eighteen months' fieldwork in a Malay village.[29] Scott and Burch were both catholic in their interests and genuinely internationalist in their outlook. And both were left wing without being of any particular sect or party.[30]

---

[27] Among them, Michael Meyerfeld Bell, now Professor of Rural Sociology at the University of Wisconsin, Madison, whose works include *Childerley: Nature and Morality in an Country Village* (Chicago: University of Chicago Press, 1994), and *An Invitation to Environmental Sociology* (Santa Barbara, California: Pine Forge Press, 2000).

[28] William R. Burch, Jr, *Daydreams and Nightmares: A Sociological Essay on the American Environment* (New York: Harper & Row, 1971).

[29] James C. Scott, *Weapons of the Weak: Everyday Forms of Peasant Resistance* (New Haven: Yale University Press, 1985).

[30] Among the younger faculty at Yale there was Timothy Weiskel, an anthropologist trained in Oxford and France whose work was on the ecological history of West Africa. He published some fine essays but was perhaps at his best in the classroom. Among the students he inspired was William Cronon, whose book

Through Yale I was introduced to the field of American environmental history, which in the mid-1980s was truly coming into its own. Trading on my novelty—there were then not too many Indians doing history in America, and none at all doing environmental history—I wrote to the stars and got back encouraging letters. I went several times to see Donald Worster, then at Brandeis. At a meeting of the American Society of Environmental History held at Duke University I met the ecofeminist scholar Carolyn Merchant and the "materialist" historian Samuel Hays who, like all the others, were unfailingly generous with their time.[31]

I was impressed by the vigor of American environmental history (some 170 scholars attended the Duke meeting), by the quality of the scholarship—in particular its engagement with the natural sciences—and by the intensity of its debates. Here, as in India, scholarship was not always to be distinguished from partisanship. Historians were taking sides: for native Americans against colonists, for conservationists against capitalists, for nature against humans.

Emblematic were the works of that evocative writer Donald Worster. Behind his first book, published in 1977, lay a much older debate between the utilitarian forester Gifford Pinchot and the preservation-oriented naturalist John Muir. Thus, Worster's history of ecology was based on the opposition between "Arcadian" scientists, who, like Muir, thought that nature had an intrinsic value apart from human needs—and "Imperial" scientists, who, like Pinchot, wanted only to put natural resources more efficiently to human use. Worster's later works moved from intellectual to social history while retaining their

---

Changes in the Land bears the impress of Weiskel's teaching. See William Cronon, *Changes in the Land: Indians, Colonists, and the Ecology of New England* (New York: Hill and Wang, 1983). Cronon too was at Yale, and also became a friend. Weiskel now runs a widely acclaimed program in environmental ethics at the Harvard Divinity School.

[31] While I am in the business of paying my dues to American scholarship, I must also mention the Rutgers historian Michael Adas (author of *Machines as the Measure of Men* and other works) and the Berkeley sociologist Louise Fortmann (a pioneer of agroforestry studies), both of whom I got to know in my time at Yale, and whose intellectual example and personal friendship have nourished me since.

moral passion. On the one side there was the exquisite natural beauty of Old America, on the other the destruction unleashed by capitalist agriculture.[32]

The best environmental historians, I found, were moralists too, unambiguously identifying good and evil among individuals and ways of life.[33] The political context is also relevant here. The environmental struggles of the 1960s had led to a series of positive reforms: the creation of the Environmental Protection Agency, the passing of the Endangered Species Act, new legislation to control air and water pollution. But now, in the 1980s, a counter-revolution was taking shape. The American President, Ronald Reagan, was not particularly sympathetic to environmental concerns, while his Secretary of the Interior, James Watt, was positively hostile. The climate was inhospitable to environmental reform and, on that account, most congenial to radical environmental history.

And to radical environmentalism as well. In 1985, just before I reached America, Bill Devall and George Sessions published their book *Deep Ecology*. Before and after the book there was published a series of essays extolling a new environmental philosophy of this name. These essays argued that the philosophy that prevailed in the environmental movement was "shallow ecology," which was to be distinguished from a truer "deep ecology." While the former tinkered ineffectually with the status quo, the latter aimed at nothing less than a cultural and philosophical revolution. Shallow ecology was narrowly "anthropocentric" and thought nature existed only to serve man; deep

[32] Donald Worster, *Nature's Economy: The Roots of Ecology* (San Francisco: Sierra Club Books, 1977); idem, *Dust Bowl: The Southern Plains in the 1930s* (New York: Oxford University Press, 1979); idem, *Rivers of Empire: Water, Aridity and the Growth of the American West* (New York: Pantheon Books, 1985).

[33] They still are moralists, and they still very easily oppose good to evil, sometimes in the same life. Consider Donald Worster's recent essay, "John Muir and the Modern Passion for Nature," *Environmental History*, vol. 10, no. 1, 2005. This combines a presentist reading of John Muir as a proto-feminist and precocious multiculturalist with the (betrayed lover's?) complaint that, in his maturity, Muir abandoned the simple life for the company of capitalists: "Muir no longer made twenty-mile walks with a bag of tea and a loaf of bread tied to his belt; instead, he rode in the substantial comfort of Pullman cars and steamships."

ecology was "biocentric" and had the interests of nature itself at heart. Whereas shallow ecology placed uncritical faith in technocratic solutions, deep ecology believed in spiritual solutions based on a creative reworking of ancient ecological wisdom. Above all, while "reformist" shallow ecologists worked within the scientific and institutional structures of corporations and the state, "revolutionary" deep ecologists were uncompromisingly opposed to the System and all its workings.[34]

The ideas of deep ecology were being carried forward by groups such as Earth First!, militant defenders of the Western wilderness. They came to prominence just as I reached Yale and several of my students were among their sympathizers. Talking to them and reading the literature they passed on to me, I was powerfully reminded of debates among the leftists I had left behind in Calcutta. There were striking similarities in the rhetoric used by radical ecologists and radical socialists. In each case the sharpest attacks were reserved for those closest to you in the political spectrum. ("Shallow ecology" was the severest opprobrium, analogous to the term "social democratic" in classical Marxist parlance.) As much attention was paid to the source of one's ideas as to their content and meaning. The Marxist would damn you as unscientific or idealist, the deep ecologist would dismiss you as Newtonian or anthropocentric. Like the Marxists, deep ecologists were always looking out for guilt by association; the polemics were ferociously personal.

Before leaving New Haven in the fall of 1987 I had written a critique of deep ecology. This was published, two years later, in *Environmental Ethics* under the title "Radical American Environmentalism and Wilderness Preservation: A Third World Critique." It generated a furious controversy whose ripples can still be heard.[35] The essay has been widely admired and just as widely condemned. It has been reprinted in at least thirty anthologies as the (usually lone) voice of opposition to the reigning orthodoxies of American environmentalism.

My essay offered four main arguments: that the anthropocentric/ biocentric distinction, so beloved of environmental philosophers and

---

[34] Warwick Fox, "Deep Ecology," *The Ecologist*, vol. 14, nos 5 and 6, 1984; Bill Devall and George Sessions, *Deep Ecology: Living as if Nature Mattered* (Salt Lake City: Peregrine Books, 1985).

[35] I still get mail from readers who have chanced upon the essay, accusing me of being anti-ecological as well as anti-American.

environmental activists, was of little help in understanding the dynamics of ecological degradation; that the most serious environmental problems worldwide were over-consumption and militarism, both of which deep ecology ignored; that deep ecology was in essence an elaboration of the American wilderness movement; and that in other cultures "radical" environmentalism expressed itself very differently. The last two charges gave most offence, for they challenged the claim of deep ecology to be a philosophy and program of truly universal significance.[36]

In retrospect I recognize that behind my attack on deep ecology lay a chauvinism of my own. In their celebration of American wilderness deep ecologists were echoing the wider climate of nationalism in the environmental movement. A particular influence on their work was Roderick Nash, a historian of the America First! tendency who saw the national park system as his country's great contribution to the culture of the world. His book *Wilderness and the American Mind* rested on superb historical scholarship somewhat distorted by triumphal nationalism. Nash wanted the "American invention of national parks" to be exported worldwide; he worried whether other countries were mature enough to receive them. But he did hope that "the less developed nations may eventually evolve economically and intellectually to the point where nature preservation is more than a business."[37]

This angered and irritated me, for I had spent five years studying what I thought to be rather evolved environmentalism in India. Where American environmentalists were hypocritical, driving thousands of miles in a polluting automobile to enjoy "unspoilt wilderness," men like Chandi Prasad Bhatt integrated their lives with their work. Deep ecology tended to ignore inequalities within human society, while the Gandhian Greens I knew worked among and for the poor.

[36] For a sampling of the debate, and of the different perspectives within it, see J. Baird Callicott and Michael P. Nelson, eds, *The Great New Wilderness Debate* (Athens: The University of Georgia Press, 1998).

[37] See Roderick Nash, *Wilderness and the American Mind*, 3rd edn (New Haven: Yale University Press, 1982); and idem, "The American Invention of National Parks," *American Quarterly*, vol. 22, no. 3, Fall 1970. In the best traditions of American scholarship and American democracy, the finest critique of "wilderness nationalism" was penned by one of Nash's students: see Alfred Runte, *National Parks: The American Experience*, 2nd edn (Lincoln: University of Nebraska Press, 1984).

My essay was frankly polemical, seeking to critique American environmentalism from a Third World perspective. But, as I came to see later, it was inflected by a chauvinism as real as that of Nash. I was arguing, in effect, that Indian environmentalism, *my* environmentalism, was superior to its American counterpart, more attentive to social inequality and more conscious of the long term. I even borrowed the rhetorical devices of my adversaries, offering a conspiracy theory of coincidence which went as follows: "Paradoxical as it may seem, it is no accident that Star Wars technology and deep ecology both find their fullest expression in that leading sector of Western civilization, California."[38]

VI

On my return to India in 1987 I joined the Centre for Ecological Sciences (CES) of the Indian Institute of Science in Bangalore. I was the only social scientist among the institute's nearly 400 faculty if one excluded the Chair of the CES, Madhav Gadgil, an ecologist by training but an anthropologist by temperament. (Later in this book I shall say more about Gadgil.) I was fortunate in being thrown so close to him on my return from America; for Gadgil knew that country and its environmental movement rather well. He listened to and read my critique of the deep ecologists and gently pointed out that they and I had polarized a very complex matter. They upheld a philosophy of Nature First!, to which I had counterposed my own slogan, People First! He rejected both positions, seeking in his own work to harmonize the interests of people and nature.

Gadgil tempered my chauvinism; so, in somewhat different ways, did the Spanish economist Juan Martinez-Alier. When I met Martinez-Alier he had just published *Ecological Economics*, a brilliant history of ideas showcasing scholars who analyzed the economy in terms of energy and material flows rather than money and prices.[39] I had not read

[38] Ramachandra Guha, "Radical American Environmentalism and Wilderness Preservation: A Third World Critique," *Environmental Ethics*, vol. 11, no. 1, 1989, p. 79.

[39] J. Martinez-Alier, *Ecological Economics: Energy, Environment, Society* (Oxford: Basil Blackwell, 1987).

the book, but my friend Paul Kurian had. Kurian had been a contemporary of my teacher Anjan Ghosh at JNU. In appearance he was everybody's idea of a JNU radical: a thin, intense man with a slight stoop, a shock of hair and a beard urgently in need of running repairs. He had an acute intelligence and a formidable knowledge of the Marxist scriptures. After taking a master's in economics at JNU he went off to work with the Solidarity movement in Poland and, later, with the Sandinistas in Nicaragua. Somewhere on his travels he had picked up a copy of *Ecological Economics*. The book so impressed him that he abandoned his Marxism and resolved to introduce its themes to the community of Indian economists, then largely ignorant of or dismissive about ecological issues. Kurian therefore prevailed upon his brother—who ran a NGO in Bangalore—to invite Martinez-Alier to India.

In August 1988 Kurian organized a conference in Bangalore around the themes of Martinez-Alier's book—namely, the links between energy, the environment, and society. I helped him put the meeting together and met its chief inspirer the day he landed in our town. Then I took Martinez-Alier on a day-long excursion to the great Hoysala temples of Halebid and Belur. Along the way he let it drop that he was, as he put it, a "lapsed Marxist." Well, so was I, and so of course was Kurian.[40]

With Martinez-Alier I was to forge a close and continuing collaboration. When I first met him, seventeen years ago, he still carried traces of his Marxist past. He was forced by Franco to study outside Spain and publish his first books in emigré editions in Paris. But over the years he changed his nationality—from Spanish to Catalan—and his name too.[41]

Martinez-Alier was my first introduction to the world of the European intellectual. If he is at all typical, then Americans, and Indians too,

[40] I write this with some feeling, for, by the time Martinez-Alier arrived in India, Paul Kurian had already come down with the depression that was to claim his life.

[41] He now spells his name "Joan," to the exasperation of bibliographers, and to the confusion of graduate students, who doubtless think that the author of *The Environmentalism of the Poor* (his latest book) is the wife or sister of the author of *Ecological Economics*. (Perhaps some of them even think that, like another celebrated economist—Deidre, once Donald, McCloskey—Juan has had a sex change.)

should feel decidedly inferior. For one thing, he speaks eight languages, and he can make jokes in at least six of them. He is a global citizen who has spent years in Latin America, living for extended periods of time in Cuba and Peru (he wrote a book comparing agriculture in the two countries), in Brazil, and most recently in Ecuador. By now he has made half-a-dozen trips to India, in the course of which he has visited parts of my country I scarcely knew of and certainly will never get to.[42] In disciplinary terms, too, Martinez-Alier is unclassifiable. His formal appointment is in a department of economics and economic history. But many know him principally as an anthropologist on account of his first book, a classic ethnographic study of the *hacienda* system.

That book features strongly in my favorite Martinez-Alier story. One day, I was walking with him toward his old college, St Antony's in Oxford. On the road we bumped into Jairus Banaji, a polymath Trotyskist who had come to Oxford after two decades of trade-union work in Mumbai to do a thesis on the olive oil economy of ancient Greece. When I introduced the two, Banaji more or less prostrated himself. "The author of *Landlords and Laborers in Southern Spain!*," he exclaimed: "That's the finest modern treatment of the dialectic between the formal and the real subsumption of labor. On my shelf, your book lies between [Marx's] *Capital* and [Lenin's] *The Development of Capitalism in Russia.*"

Martinez-Alier was not entirely displeased by the company his book was keeping. One of the heroes of *Ecological Economics* is the Ukranian thinker Podolinsky, who wrote to Marx about his idea that energy lay at the basis of economic activity—only to be dismissed with contempt by the prophet. Living in Europe Martinez-Alier found (as I had in India) that orthodox Marxism and Marxists were deeply hostile to ecological concerns, though there were other traditions of left-wing thought that were less insensitive. One of the little noticed tragedies of the Bolshevik revolution was that the victory of Marxism had consigned these other socialist traditions to oblivion. Now that the Berlin Wall had fallen, it was time to resurrect them.

Between 1990 and 1993 Martinez-Alier and I hosted a Social Science Research Council Working Group on the "environmentalism

---

[42] For the record, he has also been a Visiting Fellow at Stanford and Yale.

of the poor." Our members came from half a dozen countries and we held meetings in four of them. Independently, I was deepening my acquaintance with intellectual traditions other than those I grew up with. As it happened, on most of my trips outside India Martinez-Alier contrived to spend some time in the cities where I was. We met in Berlin and Berkeley, at Oxford and New York, and quite often in his native Barcelona.

My conversations with Martinez-Alier have been of fundamental importance to my work. I have found in him a congenial spirit who, like me, but more effortlessly, transgresses boundaries, both disciplinary and national. I found also a fellow radical disenchanted with the faith which, for most of the twentieth century, had professed to contain within itself all that was progressive and humane in modern social thought.

In 1988 I moved to a job in Delhi. Six years later I moved back to Bangalore, which has been my base ever since. In this time I have spent an average of two to three months a year abroad. I taught the odd term in American universities and was a Fellow of the Wissenschaftskolleg zu Berlin. The academic market being what it is, it is far easier for an Indian to travel to the West than to visit, for professional reasons, other countries of the South. Still, I have made three short trips to Africa, one to Latin America, and two apiece to Pakistan and Nepal. All through I have listened to and learnt from, and occasionally argued with, environmental scholars from cultures and traditions different from my own. These travels have enormously enriched my intellectual life and shaped, in imperceptible ways, the ideas in this book.

VII

The substantive chapters of *How Much Should a Person Consume?* move outward from the Indian experience to consider environmental ideas, institutions, trends, and thinkers in other parts of the world. Some chapters are largely or wholly focused on India and Indians; these would probably have been written differently had I never lived in Europe and the United States. By the same token, the chapter on Lewis Mumford would certainly have been written very differently by an American, if it had been written at all. Other chapters are consciously

comparative: they seek directly rather than implicitly to engage different environmental traditions in conversation and sometimes in contention.

This book is, I hope, catholic not merely in its geographical reach
but also in its intellectual influences and range of subjects. It is most
fundamentally the product of one historian's attempt to think through
the *environment*—to relate changes in social and economic life,
political institutions, popular mentalities, and scientific research to
the natural world in which humans are embedded. At a second level
it is also one man's attempt to think *through* the environment—to
assess without prejudice or sectarianism the many and differently oriented efforts toward forging a more peaceable and sustainable relationship between humans and the other species with which we must share
this earth.

The ecumenism of this book is reflected in the range of themes it
addresses. It seeks to understand how people think, what makes them
act in groups and sects, what means they use to act and think as they
do. As a work of social history it engages with ideas and interests as well
as institutions. As an analysis of a popular social movement it engages
with environmental philosophies and practices as well as policies.

That said, two caveats are in order. The first is that, as a work written
by a single hand, it is necessarily selective. This is not a comprehensive
comparative history of environmentalism, it is only one scholar's sense
of some of the important trends and debates within that very large history. Second, the older I get the more I am attracted to a methodological
credo which—with apologies to the last of Marx's "Theses on Feuer-
bach"—I want to state as follows: *Environmentalists may wish to change
the world, but environmental historians should seek merely to understand
and interpret it.*

When I first started out in the field I was perhaps more keen to put
my own research directly in the service of social and environmental
change. Since this book draws upon some twenty-five years of research
and reflection, there is probably a tension running right through it
between the more detached perspective of the scholar and the more engaged one of the citizen. In any case, my disavowal of an activist role
for the historian does not mean I subscribe to Rankean positivism, to
the notion that the historian's job is "merely to tell how it really was."

For Ranke the "strict presentation of the facts" was the "supreme law" of history. But the fact is that "facts" are open to multiple interpretation. The historian must be attentive to this polyvalence and must also be prepared to express his own choices and preferences. He is required both to tell a new story and tell it well. The first requirement rests on the uncovering of sources previously unseen or unused; the second on the capacity for evaluative judgment. The historian must be able to say that he finds one individual more attractive than another, or a particular event more significant than another.[43]

George Orwell once remarked that "a writer can never be a *loyal* member of a political party." Or of a social movement either. Or, indeed, of a particular faction within a social movement. This last is the seduction most prevalent in the field of environmental studies: very few scholars have not succumbed to it. Generations of American environmental historians have taken sides in the Muir-Pinchot debate. Writings on the Chipko movement have tended to see one wing as more real or more ecological than the other.

My view is that for a writer or scholar to take strongly partisan stances in an ideological debate of the past, or in favor of a popular movement in the present, is simply *unsustainable*. This is where Robi Chatterji's wise distinction comes to mind. If one is acting as an activist, it is perfectly fine to submerge one's self as well as one's critical

---

[43] I depart here from those (post-modernist and/or post-structuralist) scholars whose disenchantment with the possibility of an "objective" history has led them to abandon empirical research altogether. All sources are tainted, they say, and all writers ideological. True; but does that then mean that the task of the historian is only to point out how texts are contaminated? From Marc Bloch and Lucien Febvre onward, if not earlier, sensitive historians have learnt to look for (and accommodate) biases in writers and documents—biases with regard to provenance, context, ideology, and biography. Having done that, they go on with the business of digging deep and, having finished digging, construct a plausible narrative, understanding full well that this narrative might be overturned by subsequent research.

Doubts about "history" (in scare quotes, always), I also think, tend to be expressed by scholars in middle age, just as they are beginning to find original research somewhat laborious. How much easier it is to philosophize about "the Eurocentricism of history writing" and the "imperialism of the narrative mode," than to read barely legible manuscripts in dingy archives!

faculties in the Cause. But to do so in print and under one's individual signature is, for a writer or scholar, to put one's independence and integrity on the line.

That said, to be non-sectarian is by no means the same as to be non-political. Orwell also wrote that all he had ever written was in defence of "democratic socialism, as I understand it." But he never allowed himself to be captive to a party of the left, unlike so many travelers of his time who were happy to tailor their writings to the needs of the Communist Party of Great Britain or the British Labour Party. By the same token, most—perhaps all—environmental historians wish to see a world in which humans relate harmoniously with one another and with nature. They might be sympathetic to the broad goals of the environmental movement, but, I believe and argue in this book, they must never take sides on behalf of any particular sect, faction, group, or ideology within it.

CHAPTER 2

The Indian Road to Sustainability

T he British environmental movement has been described as "monumentally ahistorical," an indictment that applies with equal force to its Indian counterpart.[1] Thus, in an essay written to mark the fiftieth anniversary of India's independence from British rule, Anil Agarwal claimed that "when India began its planned development, *nobody* had heard of the word 'environment.' And the technologies adopted were intrinsically aggressive."[2]

The conventional wisdom holds that the Indian environmental movement began with the Chipko *andolan* (movement) in 1973. That wisdom was upheld by Agarwal, as also by numerous lesser environmentalists. As a social *movement*, Chipko was without precedent. But behind and before it lies the unacknowledged prehistory of environmental ideas.

This chapter distinguishes between two waves of Indian environmentalism: an early period of pioneering and prophecy, and a more recent phase when intellectual reflection has been allied to a popular social movement. The first wave of Indian environmentalism ran from the early twentieth century to the outbreak of the Second World War.

[1] Cf. Michael Rand Hoare, "When the Earth Moved," *Times Higher Educational Supplement*, February 1, 1991.

[2] Anil Agarwal, "Old Mindsets in a Changing Environment," *The Times of India*, August 19, 1997, emphasis added.

Active in its making were two distinct intellectual communities: thinkers close to the Indian national movement, and dissident scientists working within or on the fringes of the colonial administration.

After the attainment of political independence in August 1947 began an age of ecological innocence, when the urge to industrialize and catch up with the developed world relegated environmental concerns to the background. It was only from the early 1970s that these concerns re-emerged in the form of a vocal and articulate social movement. In this second wave of environmentalism, the groundswell of popular support has created the conditions for a sophisticated, yet also deeply contentious, public discourse on the conditions and prospects for sustainable development.

II

Let me now present the ideas of some forgotten pioneers of Indian environmentalism. The first of my exemplars is Patrick Geddes, who could be seen as an oxymoron—a Scottish internationalist. Born on October 2, 1854—the same day as Mahatma Gandhi, fifteen years before him—Geddes never took a degree but studied four years with Charles Darwin's bulldog T.H. Huxley. From 1880 he began a peripatetic career, teaching at universities in Scotland but also traveling widely across Europe and North America. Among the intellectual influences on Geddes we may single out three:

1. English craft socialists, such as John Ruskin and William Morris, from whom he learnt to view industrialism with a critical eye;
2. Continental historical geographers, notably Elise Reclus and Frederick Le Play, from whom he learnt to view culture and economy in their ecological context;
3. Russian anarchists, pre-eminently Prince Kropotkin, a reading of whose work reinforced Geddes's ecological focus while promoting a fear of centralization.

In his long and very productive career—he was active till his death in 1932—Geddes made important contributions to scientific debates on economics, sociology, zoology, botany, and geography. He even wrote a famous essay on art criticism. But his most enduring work was in the theory and practice of town planning. He was especially concerned with living conditions in the industrial city, and with the city's one-sided exploitation of the resources of the hinterland. As a professor of botany and activist city planner he inspired his students in Dundee and Edinburgh, primarily through the spoken word and force of example and, less evidently, through his writings.

Although respectful of tradition, Geddes was not a backward-looking reactionary. He was neither a nostalgic romantic nor a fervent modernizer. He spoke scathingly of the debris left by what he termed "carboniferous capitalism," while the polluting technologies of the nineteenth century he dismissed as "paleotechnic," based as they were on those non-renewable and "dirty" materials—coal and iron. Yet he looked forward to a time when clean and renewable energy sources, such as hydroelectricity, and long-lasting alloys would sustainably power economic development.

Geddes took a historical and ecological approach, studying the rise of the modern city and its impact on the natural environment. His ideas are summarized in *Cities in Evolution* (1915). This passage from the book neatly outlines his philosophy:

> Beauty, whether of Nature or art, has too long been without effective defense against the ever-advancing smoke-cloud and machine-blast and slum-progress of paleotechnic industry. Not but that her defenders have been of the very noblest, witness notably Carlyle, Ruskin, Morris, with their many disciples; yet they were too largely romantics—right in their treasuring of the world's heritage of the past, yet wrong in their reluctance, sometimes even passionate refusal, to admit the claims and needs of the present to live and labour in its turn, and according to its lights. So that they in too great measure but brought upon themselves that savage retort and war-cry of "Yah! Sentiment!" with which the would-be utilitarian has so often increased his recklessness towards Nature, and coarsened his callousness to art. The romantics have too often been as blind in their righteous anger as were the mechanical utilitarians in their strenuous labor, their dull contentment with it. Both have failed to see, beyond the rude present, the better future now dawning—in which the applied physical sciences are advancing beyond their clumsy and noisy first apprenticeship, with

its wasteful and dirty beginnings, towards a finer skill, a more subtle and more economic mastery of natural energies and in which these, moreover, are increasingly supplemented by a corresponding advance of the organic sciences, with their new valuations of life, organic as well as human.[3]

Geddes was a restless internationalist, seeking friends, converts, and associates in all parts of the globe.[4] His interest in India was first sparked by a chance encounter in Paris with the Irish spiritualist Margaret Noble. Noble had come to Calcutta in 1898, inspired by the Hindu reformer Swami Vivekananda. She had converted to Hinduism and adopted the name "Sister Nivedita." She and Geddes struck up a close friendship and, although she died suddenly in October 1906, her memory and the prospect of finding disciples in India attracted Geddes to this land: immediately after finishing *Cities in Evolution* he made plans for a visit to the subcontinent. He hoped to take his carefully-put-together exhibition on urban history around the cities of British India.

Geddes arrived in Madras in the autumn of 1914. The boxes of his "Cities and Town-Planning Exhibition" were being carried within another ship which, as luck would have it, was struck by a German destroyer—the First World War having just broken out. The vessel went down in the Indian Ocean and, with it, the work of half a lifetime. Geddes was now stranded in India with no exhibition to show.

Characteristically, he turned his mind instead on gathering new material, on studying the rise, decline, and transformation of the cities and towns of India. He was to stay nearly ten years in the subcontinent, first as a freelance town planner and then as the first Professor of Sociology and Civics of the University of Bombay. In his years in India he also wrote nearly fifty town plans, some commissioned by native princes, some written at the behest of colonial administrators. The towns he wrote about range from Dhaka in the east to Ahmedabad in the west, from Lahore in the north to Thanjavur in the south.

[3] Patrick Geddes, *Cities in Evolution: An Introduction to the Town Planning Movement and to the Study of Civics* (1915; rpnt London: Williams and Norgate, 1949), pp. 92–3.

[4] See, in this connection, Hellen Mellor, "Cities and Evolution: Patrick Geddes as an International Prophet of Town Planning before 1914," in Anthony Sutcliffe, ed., *The Rise of Modern Urban Planning* (London: Mansell, 1980).

Geddes's methodological contributions to the art of town planning were his concepts of the *diagnostic survey*—an intensive walking tour to acquaint oneself with the growth, development, and existing status of the city being planned; and *conservative surgery*—the practice of gentle improvements with minimal disruptions being caused to people and their habitat. In his work the ecological thrust is most marked. As he reflected in his Dhaka plan, the town planning movement—of which he was, by general acclaim, the leader—was itself "on this side a revolt of the peasant and the gardener, as on the other of the citizen, and these united by the geographer, from their domination by the engineer."[5] At a more philosophical level Geddes was an early harbinger of that "general revolution now in progress, the change from a mechanocentric view and treatment of nature and her processes to a more and more fully *biocentric* one."[6]

"Biocentric" is a term now much favored by environmentalists to describe their own worldview. But unlike the radical socialists of his day and the radical ecologists of ours, Geddes's interest lay not in dreaming of new communities but in studying and improving the habitats of existing cities. He was concerned not with Utopia, no place, but with Eutopia, the best place possible under the circumstances.[7] In his Indian town plans Geddes's practical ecological approach is manifest in the concrete recommendations for the setting aside of open space for recreation, tree planting, and protection especially, but not exclusively, around sacred sites, as well as for the provision of a sustainable and safe water supply. He commended the Indian tradition of narrow public thoroughfares allowing ample and leafy courtyards within houses. He criticized the modern tendency in favor of wide, dusty streets which he saw as an aid only to the automobile, an artifact he detested.[8] He strongly recommended the preservation and maintenance of tanks and reservoirs; simultaneously a protection against flooding after heavy rain, a beneficial influence on climate, and of

---

[5] Geddes, *Report on Town Planning: Dacca* (Calcutta: Bengal Secretariat Book Depot, 1917), p. 2.

[6] Ibid., p. 17, emphasis in the original.

[7] Cf. Donald Miller, *Lewis Mumford: A Life* (London: Weidenfeld and Nicolson, 1989), p. 156.

[8] Jacqueline Tyrwhitt, ed., *Patrick Geddes in India* (London: Lund Humphries, 1947), pp. 57–8.

course, the source of an assured supply of water. Geddes scoffed at the fear of sanitary engineers that these water bodies would constitute a malarial hazard, pointing out that they could easily be stocked "with sufficient fish and duck to keep down the Anopheles."[9] After a visit to the town of Thana, thirty miles north of Bombay, he recommended the protection of wells as a reserve to existing water supplies, remarking presciently that "any and every water system occasionally goes out of order, and is open to accidents and injuries of very many kinds; and in these old wells we inherit an ancient policy, of life insurance, of a very real kind, and one far too valuable to be abandoned"—words that should be pasted above the office desks of planners working today in Chennai, Hyderabad, and a dozen other cities of India.[10]

Geddes's inclusive, holistic, and deeply ecological approach is nicely expressed in the following:

> For us [i.e. town planners] the problem is not simply, as for municipalities and their engineers, today the removal of sewage, or tomorrow the supply of water, at one time the removal of congestion, or supply of communications; and at some other the problems of housing, or again of suburban extension. Our problem is to make the best of all these specialisms and their advocates . . . Our attitude differs from that of the specialist intent upon perfection in his own department, whatever be the outlays, whatever the delays to others accordingly; it is rather that of the housewife, the agriculturist or the steward, who has to make the best of a limited budget, and not sacrifice resources enough for general wellbeing to the elaboration of a single improvement.[11]

Geddes's approach to town planning was not only ecological but also participatory. In the greatest of his Indian plans—for the town of Indore—he has this to say:

> As the physician must make a diagnosis of the patient's case before prescribing treatment, so with the planner for the city. He looks closely into

[9] Ibid., pp. 78–83.

[10] Patrick Geddes, *Reports on Replanning of Six Towns in Bombay Presidency* (1915: rpnt Bombay: Government Central Press, 1965), p. 3.

[11] Idem, *Town Planning in Balrampur: A Report to the Honorable the Maharaj Bahadur* (Lucknow: Government Press, 1917), p. 3.

the city as it is, and enquires into how it has grown, and suffered. And as the physician associates the patient with his own cure, so must the planner appeal to the citizen. Hence the Indore reader should go round and look at the City for himself; and with its Plan for partial guide, he may check, and amplify, the diagnosis; and perhaps accelerate the treatment.[12]

Acutely aware of the resource-extractive characteristics of the modern city, Geddes sought to harmonize urban living with the countryside. Through tree planting and water conservation, one could work toward "that 'return to nature' which every adequate plan involves, with pure air and water, and cleanliness in surroundings again rural; so that, in Ruskin's phrase, the field gains upon the street, no longer merely the street upon the field."[13] He called often for a "return to the health of village life, with its beauty of surroundings and its contact with nature," but "upon a new spiral turning beyond the old one which, at the same time, frankly and fully incorporates the best advantages of town-life."[14] In the words of Lewis Mumford, his best-known disciple, "to the town-planner's art, Geddes brought the rural virtues; not merely respect for the land and for agricultural processes; but for the patience of the peasant, and the sense that orderly growth is more important than order at the expense of growth." And, one might add, more important than growth at the expense of order.[15]

A hallmark of Geddes's approach was his "esteem for every genuine material or spiritual value in the local heritage, his almost miserly reluctance to part with the least scrap of it." He found much to admire and retain in the Indian tradition of town planning. After a visit to "that wonderful city of religion," Benares, he wrote feelingly of the respect he found there for nature and life. In other letters to his family he marveled at the traditional architecture and planning of South Indian temple towns. These towns embodied the "spirit of hope, of impulsion, of growth, the temple of the elan vital, the spirit of evolution, of whom these Hindu gods, whom fools call idols, are as yet in many ways

---

[12] Idem, *Town Planning Towards City Development: A Report to the Durbar of Indore* (Indore: Holkar State Printing Press, 1918), vol. 1, p. xiii.

[13] Ibid., p. 23.

[14] Tyrwhitt, *Patrick Geddes in India*, p. 57.

[15] Lewis Mumford, "Introduction," in ibid., p. 11.

(I do not say in all ways) the most vital and vivid expressions yet reached by man."[16]

The work of Patrick Geddes waits to be properly discovered and reinterpreted by our generation. In their angry denunciations of the urban-industrial way of life, Indian environmentalists have, by and large, not yet come to terms with the fact that by 2020 or thereabouts India will have the largest urban population in the world. The consequences of such rapid and unregulated, urbanization are quite strikingly evident in terrible levels of air and water pollution, overcrowding, water scarcity, substandard housing and sanitation, and systems of transportation that are grossly inefficient from an energy conservation as well as environmental point of view. In engaging with these problems and trying to make our cities and towns habitable, Indian planners and environmentalists can derive far more from Geddes than they do.

III

In the West, his ideas were to live on in books written by his great American admirer Lewis Mumford. As discussed later (Chapter Six), Geddes's categories of social and ecological analysis were skilfully elaborated in Mumford's pioneering histories of the city and modern technology. But Geddes also acquired one important disciple in the East. This was Radhakamal Mukerjee, a long-time Professor of Sociology at Lucknow University whose work too deserves to be much better known among his countrymen today.

Born in 1889, Mukerjee had a brilliant record as a student in Calcutta University. He came from a family of intellect and achievement: his elder brother, Radhakumud Mukerjee, was a well-known and widely-published historian of ancient India. Radhakamal was a devotee of the poet Rabindranath Tagore and the physicist-biologist J.C. Bose. It was in their homes that he first met Geddes, in 1915, and began imbibing his socio-ecological approach to the study of humanity. The master saw in the disciple a worthy carrier of the tradition. In India, as in the West, there were two familiar responses to industrialism—the regretful and

---

[16] As quoted in Philip Mairet, *Pioneer of Sociology: The Life and Letters of Patrick Geddes* (London: Lund Humphries, 1957), pp. 119, 158, 164–7.

the triumphant. But Mukerjee, remarked Geddes approvingly, avoided both extremes by seeking to rebuild the old with the help of the new, thereby displaying "a cheering faith in the survival capacity of his old village as well as in the value of its villagers."[17]

This comes from Geddes's foreword to his pupil's book, *The Foundation of Indian Economics* (1916). These were early days for industrial development in India, and Mukerjee rather optimistically charted a path radically different from that followed in the West. Indian industrialization, he wrote—in rather ringing tones that seem to draw inspiration from Tagore—will

> tend to establish a solidarity between the villager and the city, the laborers and the employer, the specialist and the layman, the brain worker and the manual laborers . . . India will not allow the city to exploit the village, she will retain the vitality of life and culture of the village. She will not suck out the blood of one part of society to feed another part . . . but she will feel the pulsations of life deep and strong in her throbbing veins in every part of her social system.[18]

Over time Mukerjee developed a less fervent and more focused interest in the ecological infrastructure of social life. An essay entitled "An Ecological Approach to Sociology" that he published in the *American Journal of Sociology* in 1930 set out a framework for the discipline. These two excerpts outline both a new analytic approach for the scholar as well as a new morality for the species:

> There is a balance between the natural and the vegetable and the animal environment, including the human, in which nature delights. It is maintained by chains of actions and interactions, which link man with the rest of his living realm, reaching up and down and all around as his invisible biological and social destiny. Such a balance assumes great significance in old countries like India and China. Here we can discern, especially in the mature, densely-populated plains, every stage of the process by which the regional balance is kept stable and how it is upset both by natural fluctuations such as are caused by cycles of rainfall or changes of landscape and

[17] Patrick Geddes, "Introduction," in Radhakamal Mukerjee, *The Foundation of Indian Economics* (London: Longmans, Green and Co., 1916), pp. ix–xi.
[18] Ibid., pp. 448–9.

river, or by long continued human actions such as the destruction of forests, non-conservative agriculture, and artificial interference with natural drainage . . .

Human, animal and plant communities are subject to similar rules, though shifting ones, which maintain a balance and rhythm of growth for all. Each community cannot appropriate more than its due place in the general ordering of life, from which nothing can be obtained without influencing everything else. Working symbiotically, they represent interwoven threads of a complex web of life. No one thread can be isolated. None can be snapped or removed without the whole garment of the life of nature and human society being disfigured. The warp and the woof of the garment have become increasingly coherent as organic evolution has advanced. The inter-linkages of a fig tree, an earthworm, a rat and a bird are many, but the threads make much more intricate patterns as we reach the social economy of man. Though man often tears asunder the fabric through ignorance or selfishness, social progress no doubt consists in consciously weaving the forces of nature and society into finer and finer patterns of correlation and solidarity. It is the knowledge of and respect for the intricacy of the web of life that will guide man to his highest destiny.[19]

In a series of books and essays written over twenty years, Mukerjee explored the interconnections between human social groups and the biophysical world they shared with other species. There were, he argued, intriguing parallels between humans on the one hand and plants and animals on the other. Yet our species was singular in at least three respects: (i) as a tool maker, man alone was capable of a dynamic, interventionist relationship with nature. As the "superdominant of life's existing communities," humans had an awesome potential for ecological devastation and/or regeneration; (ii) humans had a history and traditions in a way that plants and animals did not; (iii) the human response to nature is characteristically collective rather than individual, and thus amenable to "synecology," the study of communities in their natural environment, rather than an individual-oriented "autoecology."

Mukerjee liked to speak of an emerging discipline called "social ecology," which would bring together the complementary skills of the

[19] Radhakamal Mukerjee, "An Ecological Approach to Sociology," *American Journal of Sociology*, vol. 32, no. 4, October 1930.

sociologist and the ecologist. Social ecology, he wrote, was a "vast and virgin field orienting social phenomena on the basis of the give and take between mind and region."[20] As with Geddes, for Mukerjee, too, theoretical reflection was merely the prelude to prescription and social action. In *all* regions of the world the natural environment set certain limits to human action, boundary conditions that humans must learn to respect. Thus, "the ecological process is constantly thwarted and modified by the [human] cultural process, but again and again reasserts itself."[21] And:

> synecology demands that men should work in harmony with the balanced relationships in nature, so as to accelerate and not put brakes on nature's continuous operations of recuperation and regeneration. Renewal and enrichment rather than exhaustion and depletion of the region should be man's synecological goal, if he wants to nourish his land–water culture in which civilization is rooted on a continuing basis for his species.[22]

These philosophical reflections were fleshed out by Mukerjee and his associates in studies of the region in which they lived, the Indo-Gangetic plain. The sociologist deplored man's continuing crimes against vegetation in northern India: "brand tillage in the hills and hill slopes, encroachment of arable land on forest and grove everywhere and in the valley close and persistent browsing and grazing by herds of co-dominant animals."[23] When he was a consultant to the princely state of Gwalior he found the peasants there crippled by soil erosion and poor yields. To overcome these problems he suggested programs of erosion control, afforestation, and rotational grazing.[24]

An outcome of these varied studies is the chart reproduced below. In it Mukerjee summarizes his view of the bad life and the good life. This is a veritable green charter for India, relevant in every detail fully

[20] Radhakamal Mukerjee, *Social Ecology* (London: Longmans, Green and Co., 1942), p. xv. The term "social ecology" was coined by the Chicago sociologists Robert Park and Ernest Burgess to capture the spatial distribution of population in a city; it was Mukerjee who first used it in a specifically ecological sense.

[21] Ibid., p. 112.

[22] Ibid., p. 129.

[23] Ibid., p. 131.

[24] Radhakamal Mukerjee, *Planning the Countryside*, 2nd edn (Bombay: Hind Kitabs, 1950).

seven decades after it was first drafted. It beautifully illustrates Mukerjee's dicta that humans have no option but "to some extent imitate Nature's extraordinarily slow methods," and that "applied human ecology is the only guarantee of a permanent civilization."[25] But even now we await the change in values for which Mukerjee hoped and strove, for that time when "ecological adjustment [will] be raised from an instinctive to an ethical plane."[26] Only then will man work toward an "alliance with the entire range of ecological forces," curb his "subtle and whole-sale, quick and far-reaching exploitative activities by importing new values—the thought for tomorrow, the sacrifice for inhabitants of the region yet unborn."[27]

Chart

Social Regression	Social Evolution
• Deforestation	• Protection and plantation of forests
• Mountain denudation and field erosion	• Tree-cropping in the hillsides
• Single and continual cropping	• Scientific pasturage and permanent agriculture
• Silting up of rivers and loss of natural drainage and flush irrigation	• Conservation of rain, river and sub-soil water supply
• Soil exhaustion	• Selection and use of micro-organisms in cropping
• Destruction of crops and herds by insects and animal pests	• Ecological control of plants and parasites
• Destruction of too large a number of animals and birds for food and materials	•Preservation of animals and birds from extinction
• Deficiency diseases of animals and humans, bacterial and protozoal infection, contamination of the region by wastes and sewage	• Conservation of the environment suitable for animal and human habitation

[25] Idem, *The Regional Balance of Man: An Ecological Theory of Population*, Sir William Meyer Foundation Lectures for 1935–6 (Madras: University of Madras, 1938), pp. 306, 304.

[26] Ibid., p. 36

[27] *Social Ecology*, pp. 336–7.

- Growth of jungle in human settlements and of weeds in streams
- Depopulation in the countryside and congestion in the big cities and manufacturing areas

- Economic balance between forest, meadowland, field and factory
- Regional planning of cities and industries

Source: Mukerjee, *The Regional Balance of Man*, p. 296.

IV

My final exemplar is the Gandhian economist J.C. Kumarappa. Born in 1892 in the southern part of the Tamil country, Kumarappa originally trained in accountancy in London. He had a flourishing practice as an auditor in Bombay, which he left to take a master's degree at Columbia University in New York. There he embarked on a study of public finance (under the supervision of E.R.A. Seligman), in the course of which he uncovered the colonial exploitation of the Indian economy.

Kumarappa returned home in 1929, now a nationalist, and soon came into contact with Mahatma Gandhi. His thesis on public finance was serialized in Gandhi's journal *Young India*, and Kumarappa abandoned his practice to join the Mahatma. He was put in charge of Gandhi's schemes of village reconstruction and, over the next decade, conducted important surveys of the agrarian economy while helping run two key Gandhian institutions, the All India Spinners Association and the All India Village Industries Association.

In a number of books written in the 1930s and 1940s Kumarappa attempted to formalize a Gandhian economics. Scattered through Kumarappa's writings—as in Gandhi's—we find observations with deep implications for the way we relate to the environment.[28] The following remark, for instance, could be seen as outlining a basic condition for ecological responsibility: "If we produce everything we want from within a limited area, we are in a position to supervise the methods of production; while if we draw our requirements from the ends of

[28] For an assessment of Gandhi's environmental thought, see Ramachandra Guha, *Mahatama Gandhi and the Environmental Movement* (Puné: Parisar Annual Lecture, 1993). Cf. also chapter 9 of the present book.

the earth it becomes impossible for us to guarantee the conditions of production in such places."[29]

Like his teacher, Kumarappa powerfully denounced industrial civilization. "There can be no industrialization without predation," he observes, whereas agriculture is, and ought to be, "the greatest among occupations" in which "man attempts to control nature and his own environment in such a way as to produce the best results." He expressed this contrast between agriculture and industry in terms of their impact on the natural world:

> In the case of an agricultural civilization, the system ordained by nature is not interfered with to any great extent. If there is a variation at all, it follows a natural mutation. The agriculturist only aids nature or intensifies in a short time what takes place in nature in a long period . . . Under the economic system of [industrial society] . . . we find that variations from nature are very violent in that a large supply of goods is produced irrespective of demand, and then a demand is artificially created for goods by means of clever advertisements.[30]

Like most Gandhians of his generation, Kumarappa was primarily interested not in theoretical reflection but in ameliorating the lot of the Indian peasant and artisan. A theme that runs through much of his work is the careful husbanding of natural resources within the rural economy. He viewed the substitution of chemical fertilizers with organic manure as an example of the Economy of Permanence yielding to the man-made Economy of Transience. He was strongly in favor of using nightsoil as manure, thereby simultaneously converting human waste into wealth and overcoming the prohibitions of caste. He was quick to observe that, in many villages where clean drinking water was available for upper castes, untouchables were not similarly privileged.[31]

Water and forests are perhaps the two resource sectors that have most exercised the Indian environmental movement in recent years.

[29] J.C. Kumarappa, *The Gandhian Economy and Other Essays* (Wardha: All India Village Industries Association, 1948), p. 10.

[30] Idem, *Why the Village Movement?* (Rajahmundry: Hindustan Publishing Corporation, 1938), pp. 27–8.

[31] See, for example, J.C. Kumarappa, Director, *A Survey of Matar Taluka, Kaira District* (Ahmedabad: Gujarat Vidyapith, 1931), pp. 36–8, 46–7, 117.

Here, Kumarappa was not slow to criticize the poor maintenance of irrigation tanks under British rule and urge the conservation of ground water, and thus reduce brackishness. In a pithy comment on actual and preferred models of forest management he says:

> The government will have to radically revise its policy of maintaining forests. Forest management should be guided, not by considerations of revenue but by the needs of the people . . . Forest planning must be based on the requirements of the villagers around. Forests should be divided into two main classes: (1) those supplying timber to be planned from the long range point of view, and (2) those supplying fuel and grasses, to be made available to the public either free of cost or at nominal rates. There are village industries such as palm gur, paper making, pottery, etc. which can flourish only if fuel and grass can be supplied to them at cheap rates.[32]

Equally farsighted are Kumarappa's remarks on biomass shortages in the rural economy. He was particularly concerned with scarcities of fodder, pointing out that cash crops like jute, tobacco, and sugarcane reduce food for both humans and their domestic animals. He also noted the widespread complaint of peasants that there was not enough pasture, thus taking the colonial government to task for its reluctance to allow grazing on wasteland without the payment of a fee. Nor were his horizons restricted to the cultivator. He asked that waste paper and grass from state forests—at the time auctioned to the highest bidder—be made over at modest rates to the handmade-paper sector. Kumarappa's preference for small industry was dictated in part by considerations of resource conservation. A large modern paper mill, he pointed out, relies upon freshly cut bamboo taken direct from the forest. By contrast, paper made by a cottage industry could draw upon discarded and rotten bamboo earlier used for mats, baskets, and roofing material.[33]

Kumarappa was virtually the only economist to question the centralized and resource-intensive path of development adopted in independent India. In 1937 he was appointed to the National Planning Committee (NPC) as a representative of the All India Village Industries Association. He resigned his seat shortly thereafter, when the

[32] J.C. Kumarappa, *The Economy of Permanence*, 2nd edn (Wardha: All India Village Industries Association, 1948), part II, p. 55.

[33] See, *inter alia*, idem, *A Survey of Matar Taluka*, p. 127; idem, *Gandhian Economy*, p. 6; idem, *Economy of Permanence*, part II, p. 34.

NPC refused to put the village at the center of planning. After independence, Kumarappa was deputed by the Sarva Seva Sangh to represent it in the Indian Planning Commission's advisory body, but he again failed to find a receptive audience for his views.[34]

In the mid-1930s Kumarappa had moved with the rest of Gandhi's entourage to Wardha in Central India. In between bouts in jail he continued his studies of the village economy and also worked closely with artisans, seeking to improve and adapt their technical skills to make them competitive in the modern world. After Independence and Gandhi's death, however, he fell foul of the self-appointed successor to the Mahatma's mantle, Acharya Vinoba Bhave. Bhave was a man of great spiritual achievement who lacked somewhat in common sense. In the early 1950s he initiated a movement for the voluntary transfer of land from the landed to the landless known as Bhoodan. In the very early days of the movement Kumarappa warned Bhave against the tendency to set targets—so many acres to be collected before March 31, etc.—advising him to instead work patiently at making the land already collected more productive. With decades of experience behind him the economist urged that the Bhoodan movement create committees of skilled and motivated volunteers who would work with peasants in the careful management of donated land. But Bhave hoped instead for an inner spiritual awakening among land grantees. In fact he even disbanded the committees that already existed, thus dooming the movement.[35]

Disenchanted with the turn the Gandhians had taken post-Gandhi, Kumarappa retreated to an ashram in T. Kallupatti, in the Madurai district of his native Tamil Nadu. Despairing of his former comrades he had, meanwhile, begun an interesting correspondence with S.K. Dey. An engineer trained in the United States, Dey was an able and energetic public official who had just been appointed Minister of Community Development in the Union Cabinet. "Community development" was half the price paid by the Government of India (the Khadi and Village Industries Commission being the other half), committed as it was

[34] Cf. M. Vinaik, *The Gandhian Crusader: A Biography of J.C. Kumarappa* (Gandhigram: Gandhigram Trust, 1987).

[35] See the correspondence between Bhave and Kumarappa in the Kumarappa Papers, Nehru Memorial Museum and Library (hereafter NMML), New Delhi.

to rapid industrialization, to settle its conscience for having allowed Gandhi, that certified rural romantic, to be named "Father of the Nation." Dey, who had made his mark rehabilitating refugees from West Punjab, was the rare politician willing to hear out men wiser than he. He invited criticism from Kumarappa, whom the minister admired as one of the "very few people left intact today with the baptismal fire still intact."[36]

The old Gandhian came out firing. At Dey's suggestion he undertook a survey of rural development work in twenty-seven villages of Madurai district, moving from place to place by bus and bullock-cart. Afterward, in the report Kumarappa wrote, his criticisms of the community development program were unforgiving. Most of its funds, he pointed out, were taken up in unproductive schemes like road building. Moreover, the "persons who have co-operated [with the government] belong to a small section of the public, though moneyed and influential." But the Harijans or lower castes "are notoriously neglected," the "poor are still standing apart suspiciously." "Generally speaking," he said, "the atmosphere around officials and gram sevaks [village workers] is not one of love for rural people and their life but one of their own employment and advancement."

The insensitivity of the public officials was compounded by their brief, handed down from above, which was completely at odds with the physical realities of Indian agriculture. In his report Kumarappa made a series of sharp criticisms, highlighting the ecological unwisdom of what passed for rural development.

On water conservation he said:

> The irrigation tanks are as a rule silted up and eroded . . . If these tanks are desilted four or five feet, much of the cry for water will cease and the farmers can get two or three crops a year where even getting one is a gamble today. Attention to these tanks will give us control over floods and reduce erosion. If properly advised and guided, I am sure, the villagers will gladly extend their co-operation in such schemes . . . This is a program that will quickly raise the production of food several-fold and thereby better village conditions in a very short time.

[36] See the correspondence between S.K. Dey and Kumarappa in the Kumarappa Papers, NMML.

On fertilizer overuse his view was:

> There are no facilities [in the agricultural demonstration centers] for soil and water analysis. In the absence of these no artificial or chemical manures should be used. Now such fertilizers are being supplied at favorable rates. They may prove ruinous in the end. At present the Government seems more anxious to dispose of their fertilizers than to observe the evil effects of their use in the course of years of indiscriminate use on all kinds of fields.

On forest protection he notes:

> Water supply depends on an efficient forest policy. The Government is overanxious on the revenue production of forests rather than there being a conserving ground for water. Every village should have its common lands properly taken care of.

On the protection of artisans, he argues:

> Welfare of villagers rests on the occupations open to those who are not fully employed on the land. [Village] industries provide the necessary complement to work on land. A few stray attempts are being made to help with the Ghani [oil-press], Khadi work, bee-keeping, etc. But these are not considered an essential feature of the development [work] and suffer from a lack of emphasis . . . All village industries will have to be resuscitated to put life into rural parts.[37]

Soil maintenance, water conservation, recycling, village forest rights, biomass budgets, protection of the artisan: this is an agenda of rural reconstruction that is still very much with us in India. By putting agriculture so firmly in its natural setting, Kumarappa began the task of building an ecological program on Gandhian lines. Environmentalists today, for the most part unaware of his work, are actually only taking up where he left off.[38]

---

[37] J.C. Kumarappa, "Report on Rural Development Work in Madurai District" (1956), unpublished copy in the Kumarappa Papers, NMML.

[38] At long last, and not a moment too soon, Kumarappa is being rediscovered by contemporary scholars. The American Gandhian Mark Lindley has just completed a careful analytic study of Kumarappa's economic ideas, to be published by Popular Prakashan, Mumbai. The Indian scientists Venu Govindu and Deepak Malghan are working on a definitive intellectual biography, work on which is also well advanced.

I have here highlighted the work of three pioneers; but there were others. A more comprehensive treatment would have to explore, for instance, the contributions to Indian environmental thought of Albert Howard, a prophet of ecological agriculture; and of Mira Behn (the Indian name taken by Gandhi's colleague Madeleine Slade), a far-seeing critic of colonial and commercial forestry. With Patrick Geddes, Radhakamal Mukerjee, and J.C. Kumarappa, these were thinkers ahead of their time who helped articulate a forward-looking "social ecology" for India.

V

There are periods in human history when concern for the careful hus-banding of resources acquires social visibility and political influence. At other periods the imperatives of intensive (and destructive) use of nature are paramount, as for example over the first two decades of Indian freedom when, in the surge toward rapid industrialization, development was promoted at all cost and the ideas of men such as Kumarappa and Mukerjee ignored. Although both men were alive and active in the 1950s they were, so to speak, voices in the wilderness. Their interest in ecological questions was not shared by the intelligent-sia at large, and certainly not by the political system.

For anti-colonial leaders like Jawaharlal Nehru imperialism had only been made possible by the economic and technological superior-ity of the colonial powers. Decolonization had now opened up the possibility of a previously "underdeveloped" India "developing" along the same lines as the West. Rapid industrialization, it was thought, would end poverty and unemployment and make for a strong and self-reliant society. Within this focus on production and productivity there was scarcely room for the promotion or propagation of environment-alist beliefs. The twenty years after the Second World War are known as the "development decades," but from our perspective they should be termed the "age of ecological innocence."[39]

[39] Scanning the proceedings of the Indian Science Congress for the decade of the 1950s, I found only one essay that could be seen even remotely "as eco-logical," this a warning about the health hazards that might be posed by the programs of planned industrialization. See J.K. Chaudhuri, "The Utilisation of Waste: The Need for a National Programme," Presidential Address to the

But worldviews change with every generation, perhaps every twenty-five years or so. A generation passed, and the consequences of the course the nation had taken in 1947 became more evident. The world-view began to shift and environmental concerns began slowly and subtly to figure once more in public discourse.

Then, in the first few months of 1973, the "ecological question" made a dramatic re-entry into national life. In the space of a mere few weeks three events occurred:

First, in April 1973 the Government of India announced the launching of "Project Tiger," an ambitious conservation program aimed at protecting the country's national animal. The population of the species had plummeted from an estimated 40,000 tigers at the turn of the century to less than 2000 in 1970. The reason for this decline was a combination of human population growth, expansion of cultivation at the expense of forests, and, especially, hunting for pleasure. Encouraged and helped along by international bodies like the World Wildlife Fund and the International Union for the Conservation of Nature, Indian conservationists prevailed upon the government to initiate systematic attempts to protect the tiger by banning hunting and setting aside large areas as national parks where human activities were to be strictly regulated. Project Tiger now has within its ambit some twenty sanctuaries spread all over India. It has also served as a model for schemes for the protection of other endangered species such as the elephant and the rhinoceros.[40]

Second, in its issue of March 31, 1973 the *Economic and Political Weekly* of Bombay, India's leading social science journal, published a long and impressively thorough paper by B.B. Vohra entitled "A Charter for the Land." The author, a high official in the Ministry of Agriculture, wrote here of the widespread deforestation, soil erosion, and waterlogging in the country. He called for a national policy to deal with these problems and for new departments to be created to monitor

---

Section of Chemistry, in *Proceedings of the 37th Indian Science Congress* (Poona: 1950), pp. 97–118.

[40] Mahesh Rangarajan, "Politics of Ecology: The Debate on Wildlife and People in India, 1970–1995," *Economic and Political Weekly* (hereafter *EPW*), Special Number (September 1996).

and manage environmentally appropriate land use. While the causes of degradation were many and varied, argued Vohra, only the state could effectively initiate remedial action. As he put it, the central government in New Delhi "has no option but to obtain a commanding position for itself in the field of land and soil management through financial and administrative means." This article was the first visible sign of official concern at the accumulating evidence of environmental deterioration, a modest forerunner of the creation of a National Committee for Environmental Protection and Control later that year, of a Department of Environment in 1980, and of a full-fledged Ministry of Environment and Forests five years later.[41]

Third, on March 27, 1973, in a remote Himalayan village named Mandal, high in the upper Gangetic valley, a group of peasants stopped a group of loggers from felling a stand of hornbeam trees. The trees stood on land owned by the state Forest Department. The peasants had been previously denied access to these very trees—which they sought to use to make farm implements. Now, the trees were to be felled by loggers acting on behalf of a sports-goods company in distant Allahabad. The company had been awarded a government contract to use the same trees to make badminton rackets. The peasants protested this shocking injustice by threatening to hug the trees. Behind their action lay the claims of justice and tradition, the legitimate subsistence requirements of local villagers against the commercial interest of outsiders. The Mandal episode sparked a series of similar protests through the 1970s, a dozen and more episodes whereby hill peasants likewise stopped loggers from felling trees for external markets. These protests collectively constitute the Chipko movement, which as we saw in Chapter One, is widely recognized as one of the most famous environmental initiatives of our times and the start of the environmental movement in India.[42]

These three events were apparently unconnected, but each was the harbinger of major changes in the environmental field. All were, and remain, significant for the ecological history of modern India, yet Chipko

[41] B.B. Vohra, "A Charter for the Land," *EPW*, March 31, 1973.

[42] Anupam Mishra and Satyendra Tripathi, *Chipko Movement* (New Delhi: Gandhi Peace Foundation, 1978).

alone captured a wider public and set alight the spark of consciousness that was to fuel a popular social movement. There were several reasons for this.

First, Chipko was authentically endogenous: not a product of international pressure but the creation of self-motivated peasants. Second, its historic and cultural associations were instantly recognizable: these were its presence in the valley of the Ganges, home to some of the holiest shrines in India, and its innovatively non-violent techniques of protest, which recalled the freedom movement and Mahatma Gandhi. Third, Chipko articulated a truly *social* ecology. Where Project Tiger focused on wildlife and B.B. Vohra on sustainable land management through state control, this movement of Himalayan peasants raised questions of equity and justice while not failing to highlight threats to ecological stability posed by commercial forestry. Finally, and most significantly, Chipko was representative of a spectrum of natural resource conflicts that erupted in different parts of India in the 1970s and 1980s. These included conflicts over access to forests, fish, and grazing resources; conflicts over the effects of industrial pollution and mining; and conflicts over the siting of large dams.

Chipko became famous owing to symbolic resonances unique to it, but its wider social representativeness must not be overlooked, for it is merely the best known of a series of nature-based conflicts in contemporary India. These conflicts are played out against a backdrop of visible ecological degradation, the drying up of springs, the decimation of forests, and the erosion of land. This has led, in turn, to acute resource shortages, and hence to the clash between competing claims: be they of peasants and paper mills over forest land or of country boat owners and trawlers over fish stocks. Where "traditional" class conflicts were waged in the cultivated field or in the factory, these newer struggles are waged over the gifts of nature, such as forests and water, gifts that are coveted by all but increasingly monopolized by some.

The language of class is apposite, for most of these conflicts have indeed opposed rich to poor: logging companies against hill villagers, dam builders against forest tribals, multinational corporations deploying trawlers against artisanal fisherfolk rowing country boats. Here one party (for example, loggers or trawlers) seeks to step up the pace of resource exploitation to service an expanding commercial–industrial economy, a process which often involves the partial or total dispossession of communities that earlier had control over the resource in question, and whose own patterns of utilization were both less resource-intensive and less destructive of the environment.

In most cases the theater of conflict has been a resource formally owned by the state: whether forest land or minerals or rivers or oceans. Typically, the agents of resource intensification are given preferential treatment by the state, through the grant of generously long leases over mineral or fish stocks, for example, or the provision of raw material at an enormously subsidized price. The injustice so compounded, local communities at the receiving end of this process have no recourse except direct action. Their techniques of resistance have often used traditional networks of organization—the village and the tribe; and traditional forms of protest—the *dharna* or sit-down strike, and the *bhook hartal* or hunger fast.

These conflicts take place over a variety of resources and at different spatial scales. In numerous individual hamlets the shrinking area of village commons is fought over between pastoralists searching for grass and laborers seeking to bring land under the plow. At the other extreme are conflicts that extend over several thousand square miles and involve two or more states: such as the building of the Sardar Sarovar Dam on the Narmada river in Central India, which aims to provide electricity and water to Gujarat while rendering homeless more than 100,000 peasants in upstream Madhya Pradesh.[43] Analysts of social conflict have, however, tended to focus on conflicts over caste and religion. Nature-based conflicts have been somewhat ignored although they

[43] On this most dramatic and contentious and still unresolved environmental controversy, see, *inter alia*, Amita Baviskar, *In the Belly of the River: Tribal Struggles over "Development" in the Narmada Valley* (New Delhi: Oxford University Press, 1995), and Jean Dreze, Meera Samson, and Satyajit Singh, eds, *The Dam and the Nation* (New Delhi: Oxford University Press, 1998). The problem of displacement in general is usefully discussed in Walter Fernandes and Eenakshi Ganguli-Thukral, eds, *Development and Rehabilitation* (New Delhi: Indian Social Institute 1988), and Eenakshi Ganguly-Thukral, ed., *Big Dams, Displaced People* (New Delhi: Sage Publications, 1992).

have an impact upon millions of people and have the potential of desta-
bilizing the political order. In the north-eastern states of India, for
example, seccessionist movements have originated in a sense of ecological deprivation—the feeling that the region's rich oil, timber, and
mineral resources are exploited by the central government and put to
productive use in other parts of the country.

When it began in the 1970s, the Indian environmental debate was
dominated by forest-related conflicts. In the 1980s and 1990s, however, movements such as the Narmada Bachao Andolan (Save the
Narmada movement) and the Kerala fisherfolk struggle brought the
question of appropriate uses of water and fish to centerstage.[44] At the
same time, protests arose over bauxite mining in Orissa and limestone
mining in the Himalaya, when extraction by outsiders led to the
degradation of village land and forests and, in some cases, to outright
dispossession. These struggles, taken collectively, punctured the claim
that a developing country like India could not afford to be environmentally prudent. They showed in fact that the converse was true:
environmental degradation had greater social costs in a poor country
and generated more intensive social conflicts.

A striking feature of environmental movements in modern India
has been the crucial role played by women. They have taken to the
streets to protest forest felling, unregulated mining, displacement, and
overfishing. They have also taken the lead in programs of environmental restoration; in the planting up of bare hillsides, in the conservation
of local sources of water supply, and in the promotion of energy-effi-
cient technologies.

Some writers have interpreted this "feminization" of the environmental movement in terms of culture. Hindu women, they suggest, are
intrinsically closer to nature than their Christian or pagan sisters.
Other scholars have—more plausibly in my view—argued that the
participation of women in environmental movements is better explained in terms of the division of labor within the farm household,

---

[44] On the fisherfolk struggle see John Kurien, "Ruining the Commons and
the Commoner: Overfishing and Fishworkers' Actions in South India," *The
Ecologist*, vol. 23, no. 1, 1993, as well as John Kurien and T. Thankappan Achari,
"Overfishing along Kerala Coast: Causes and Consequences," *EPW*, September
1–8, 1990.

which mandates that women and girls, and not men, forage for fuel, fodder, and water. Thus,

> the destruction of the environment clearly poses the biggest threat to marginal cultures and occupations like that of tribals, nomads, fisherfolk and artisans, which have always been heavily dependent on their immediate environment for their survival. But the maximum impact of the destruction of biomass sources is on women. Women in all rural cultures are affected, especially women from poor landless, marginal and small farming families. Seen from the point of view of these women, it can be argued that all development is ignorant of women's needs, and often anti-women, literally designed to increase their work burden.[45]

Women are more likely to perceive scarcity and shortage and are thus more keen to combat or overcome it. Their energetic participation in protest movements has been something of a surprise in this traditional, convention-bound society. Indeed, the most celebrated environmental activist in contemporary India is Medha Patkar, the woman who leads the Narmada Bachao Andolan. Patkar's predecessor in the Himalaya was Gaura Devi, a remarkable and still unsung heroine of the Chipko andolan. The story of this illiterate woman activist provides us in fact a deeper insight into the constituent elements of an "environmentalism of the poor."

VI

Gaura Devi was born in 1925 in the village of Latha, in the Garhwal Himalaya, high up in the upper Alakananda valley. The area around was lushly forested, the woods the source of crucial inputs for the traditional agro-pastoral economy of the hills. Latha lies just off the ancient trade route to Tibet and Gaura's community of Tholcha tribals was deeply involved in that trade. At the age of twelve she was married off to Meherban Singh who lived with his parents in the nearby village of

---

[45] Anil Agarwal, "Human–Nature Interactions in a Third World Country," World Conservation Lecture, 1986, reprinted in Ramachandra Guha, ed., *Social Ecology* (New Delhi: Oxford University Press, 1994), p. 362. Cf. also Bina Agarwal, "The Gender and Environment Debate: Lessons from India," *Feminist Studies*, vol. 18, no. 1, 1992.

Reni. Meherban was a farmer with a small holding; he also reared cattle and traded in wool. They were not prosperous but not terribly poor either. The combination of agriculture and animal husbandry, and the gains from trade, assured them an income somewhat in excess of a peasant family living in the plains.[46]

After ten years of marriage Meherban died, leaving Gaura Devi with a young son named Chandra Singh and Meherban's parents to look after. A hired hand came in to plow the fields while Gaura somehow kept the home fires burning. In time her son Chandra took up the work of farming, an activity that became more important when, in the late 1950s, India's tension with China led to the closing of the cross-border trade with Tibet. One consequence of this closure of trade, which Gaura Devi apparently well recognized, was that the forests around Reni became even more crucial to their lives.

Her son soon had children of his own and Gaura settled into the role of a matriarch. In 1972 she was chosen head of the Mahila Mandal, the women's self-help group in the village. The next year the Chipko movement began its activities, a little lower down the Alakananda valley. There were protests in the villages of Mandal and Rampur Phata, and these ripples soon reached Reni, for, in January 1974, 2500 *deodar* (cedar) trees were marked for felling in a forest above the village. The Chipko leaders Chandi Prasad Bhatt and Govind Singh Rawat came to Reni to speak about the importance of saving the trees. In early March there were several protest marches in the town of Joshimath, demanding that felling be stopped in the valley.

The trees of Reni, meanwhile, were auctioned off to a logging contractor in distant Dehradun. On March 16, 1974, a group of laborers from Himachal Pradesh reached the village with their felling implements. Cunningly, the local administration had fixed the same day for the payment of compensation for land taken away from the village for road construction, back in 1962. The money had not been handed over by the government for a decade; now it was finally going to be, the date carefully chosen to coincide with the planned felling of trees in Reni.

---

[46] This life-sketch of Gaura Devi is principally based on Shekhar Pathak, "Gaura Devi: Ek Ma ki Yaad" (Gaura Devi: Remembering a Mother), in *Uttara Mahila Patrika*, vol. 2, no. 1, 1991, supplemented by interviews with Chandi Prasad Bhatt, Gopeshwar, June 1982.

On the morning of the 26th the men of Reni left for the district town of Chamoli to collect the dues long owed them. Somewhere along the road they are likely to have passed the Himachali laborers going up the valley to their village. This crew got down before Reni and marched silently toward the forest. A little girl saw them and ran to her mother. Soon the news spread through the village. Housewives abandoned their work and gathered around the leader of their Mahila Mandal, Gaura Devi. Led by Gaura, a group of twenty women and children entered the forests. Here, the laborers were cooking their morning meal, preparatory to getting down to work. Meanwhile, officials of the Forest Department were with the contractor, drawing up the program for tree felling. Ten years later, in an interview with the historian Shekhar Pathak, Gaura recalled what she had told them:

> Brothers, these forests are like our maternal home [*maika*]. We get herbs, fuel, fruits and vegetables from them. Cutting the forests will result in floods. Our fields will be washed away. Please have your food and come with us to our village. When our men come back we will collectively take a decision.

The contractor and officials were unimpressed. Harsh words were uttered and, according to one version, a gun pulled out. But Gaura and her group were unyielding. Some women went down to obstruct further laborers who were coming up with their rations. A bridge leading to the forests was also barred. The contractor cursed and raged, but to no avail. Seeing the women standing firm, the laborers withdrew from the forest.

The next day, the 27th, Reni's men returned home. With them came the Chipko leaders Govind Singh Rawat and Chandi Prasad Bhatt. Over the next few weeks public meetings were held in the surrounding villages demanding a moratorium on forest felling. There were also well-attended demonstrations in the town of Joshimath. Bowing to the protests, the government set up an inspection committee under the botanist Virendra Kumar of Delhi University. The committee toured the area and recommended that forest felling be prohibited not just in Reni but in the entire catchment areas of six rivers in the region. With this decision "the silent, unknown Reni village became the talk of the region and Gaura Devi herself became the living symbol of the Chipko movement."

The single photograph of Gaura Devi that I have seen—there may be no other—shows a short, stocky woman in her fifties dressed in the traditional costume of upper Garhwal: a simple skirt and sweater, and a shawl draped around her shoulders. She is sporting a beaded necklace and a charmingly toothless grin. Gaura was a woman, a widow, and an illiterate. She was triply disadvantaged in conventional terms, and yet an authentic pioneer of Garhwali, Indian, even world environmentalism, the analog of Rosa Parks of the civil rights movement in the United States. For Gaura Devi was the leader of the first group of women to take part in Chipko, which was itself the first major environmental movement anywhere outside the Western world. As with Rosa Parks, who set the first stone of a landslide rolling, Gaura Devi's was the first move in what became a movement. Also, before the incident at Reni, Chipko had been an all-male affair; after it, women came to play an increasing role in the struggle to save the forest and in efforts to restore barren hillsides. Following Chipko other women, also often illiterate, played a key part in movements of artisanal fisherfolk to protect their resource base, in struggles against large dams, and in oppositions mounted against unregulated mining. Gaura Devi was called "Ma" by the inhabitants of her village, Reni, but in fact she effectively mothered a whole generation of environmental activists in India.

VII

How might we compare and contrast the Indian environmental movement with its better-studied American counterpart? Consider, first of all, the origins of the environmental impulse in the two contexts. Environmental movements in North America have, I think, been convincingly related to the emergence of a post-materialist or post-industrial society. The creation of a mass consumer society has not only enlarged opportunities for leisure but provided the means to put time off work to the most diverse uses. Nature is made accessible through the automobile, now no longer a monopoly of the elite but an artifact in almost everyone's possession. The car, more than anything else, has opened up the world of the wild, so refreshingly different from the world of the city and the factory. Thus, in a curious paradox, the car, the "most modern creation of industry," becomes the vehicle of anti-industrial impulses, taking one to distant adventures, to "homey little towns, enchanting fairytale forests, far from stale routine, functional ugliness or the dictates of the clock."[47] Herein lies the source of popular support for the protection of wilderness in the United States—namely, that nature is no longer restricted to the privileged few but available to all.

On the other hand the upsurge of environmental conflicts in India is related more directly to livelihood and survival. These conflicts are, in the main, protests against the encroachment on the natural resources of the community by the urban-industrial complex. There is here an *immediacy* to environmental protest somewhat absent in the American context, which might also explain why Indian groups have relied so heavily on direct action. In America environmentalism more typically uses the form of the social movement organization—such as the Sierra Club or the Friends of the Earth—with its own cadre, leadership, and source of funds properly audited. This organization then draws upon methods of redressal available in what is, all said and done, a more functional democracy: methods such as the court case, the lobbying of legislators and ministers, and the exposé on television or in the newspaper. Direct action in this context is the preserve only of fairly marginalized radical groups.

In both the United States and India, however, environmentalism has been in good measure a response to the failure of politicians to stem or stop the destruction of the wilderness, or the dispossession of peasants by large dams. In India, the environmental movement has in fact drawn upon the struggles of marginal populations—hill peasants, tribals, fisherfolk, dam oustees—neglected by the existing political parties. As a "new social movement," environmentalism in North America first emerged outside the party process. Some environmentalists thought of themselves as neither left nor right, and as representing a constituency that was anti-class or, more accurately, post-class.[48]

Origins and political styles notwithstanding, the two varieties of environmentalism differ most markedly, perhaps, in their ideologies. One originates as a clash over productive resources—a third kind of class conflict, so to speak, but one with deep ecological implications.

[47] Wolfgang Sachs, *For Love of the Automobile: Looking Back into the History of our Desires* (Berkeley: University of California Press, 1992), pp. 150–1.

[48] A point first made by the sociologist Stephen Cotgrove in *Catastrophe or Cornucopia?* (Chichester: Wiley, 1982).

Thus, in India issues of ecology are often linked with questions of human rights, ethnicity, and distributive justice. These movements, of peasants, tribals, and so on, are deeply conservative in the best sense of the word, refusing to exchange a world they know, and are in partial control over, for an uncertain and insecure future. They are a defense of the locality, or of the local community, against the nation.

In contrast, the wilderness movement in the North originates outside the production process. It is in this respect more a single-issue movement, calling for a focused change in attitudes toward the natural world rather than a wider change in systems of production or distribution. It is concerned less with relations within human society than with relations between humans and other species. Here, the claims of national sovereignty are challenged not from the vantage point of the locality but from the perspective of the biosphere. This is a movement whose self-perception is that of a vanguard moving from an "ethical present" in which we are concerned only with nation, region, and race to an "ethical future" where our moral development progresses from a concern with plants and animals to ecosystems and the planet.[49]

One must, of course, qualify this picture by acknowledging the diversity of ideologies and forms of action within these two trends. In the United States, for instance, anti-pollution struggles form a tradition of environmental action which has a different focus from the "wilderness crusade." Such is the movement for environmental justice, the struggles of low class, often black communities against the incinerators and toxic waste dumps that, by accident and frequently by design, come to be situated near them and far from affluent neighborhoods. One American commentator, Ruth Rosen, has nicely captured the contrast between the environmental justice movement and wilderness lovers. "At best," she writes, "the large, mainstream environmental groups focus on the health of the planet—the wilderness, forests, and oceans that cannot protect themselves. In contrast, the movement for environmental justice, led by the poor, is not concerned with overabundance, but with the environmental hazards and social and economic inequalities that ravage their communities."[50]

[49] Cf. Roderick Nash, *The Rights of Nature: A History of Environmental Ethics* (Madison: University of Wisconsin Press, 1989).

[50] Ruth Rosen, "Who Gets Polluted: The Movement for Environmental Justice," *Dissent*, Spring 1994, p. 229. Cf. also Andrew Szasz, *Ecopopulism: Toxic*

Likewise, the Northern wilderness crusade has representatives in the Third World who spearhead the constitution of national parks and sanctuaries, strictly protected from "human interference." Indian lovers of the wilderness have, by and large, shown little regard for the fate of the human communities which, after parkland is designated "protected," are abruptly displaced without compensation from territory that they have for generations lived on and come to regard as their own.[51]

These caveats notwithstanding, there remains on the whole a clear distinction, in terms of origins and forms of articulation, between how environmental action characteristically expresses itself in the North and in the South. Take for example these two episodes of direct action, one from California, the other from Central India.

In May 1979 a young American environmentalist, Mark Dubois, chained himself to a boulder in the Stanislaus river in California. The canyon where he lay formed part of the reservoir of the New Melones dam, whose construction Dubois and his organization, Friends of the River, had long but unsuccessfully opposed. In October of the previous year the Army Corps of Engineers had completed the dam and the following April it closed the floodgates. The level of the reservoir started rising and it appeared as if the campaign to "Save the Stanislaus" had failed. But then, in an act of rare heroism, Dubois went into the waters and chained himself to a rock. He chose a lonely hidden spot; only one friend knew of his location.[52]

Fourteen years later an uncannily similar strategy of protest was threatened against another dam, on another river, in another continent. In August 1993, with the onset of the monsoon, the vast reservoir of the Sardar Sarovar Dam on the Narmada river began filling up to capacity. It now seemed that the decade-long Narmada Bachao Andolan

---

Waste and the Movement for Environmental Justice (Minneapolis: University of Minnesota Press, 1994).

[51] This theme is treated more fully in chapter 5. Most recently, there have been signs of the emergence of a classically "bourgeois" environmentalism in India, initiated by the middle class in the cities and seeking the protection of urban parks as well as the shifting out of municipal limits of aesthetically defiling factories.

[52] Tim Palmer, *Stanislaus: The Struggle for a River* (Berkeley: University of California Press, 1982), chapter 8.

had irrevocably lost its fight. But then the leader of the movement, Medha Patkar, decided to drown herself in the swollen waters. She announced her decision to walk into the river on August 6th, with a group of colleagues, but at a place and time not to be disclosed. Fearing detention by the police Patkar disappeared into the countryside weeks before the appointed date.

I dare say Patkar had not heard of Dubois, but the parallels in their modes of protest are striking indeed. Both individuals were part of ongoing popular movements against large dams. It was only when the movement seemed to have failed that Patkar and Dubois decided to throw the last card in their pack, offering their lives to stop the dam. In both cases the political system was alert (or open) enough not to allow the environmentalists to make this supreme sacrifice. In Stanislaus, the Corps of Engineers stopped filling the reservoir and sent search parties by air and land to find and rescue Dubois. In the Narmada valley Patkar and her band were found and prevailed upon to withdraw their *samarpan dal* (martyrs squad), in return for which the Government of India promised a fresh, independent review of the Sardar Sarovar project.

While the strategies of direct action may have been superficially similar, their underlying motivations were not. Dubois and his colleagues were striving, above all, to save the Stanislaus canyon as one of the last remaining examples of the Californian wilderness. As Dubois wrote to the Colonel of the Corps of Engineers before entering the river:

> All the life of this canyon, its wealth of archaeological and historical roots to our past, and its unique geological grandeur are enough reasons to protect this canyon *just for itself*. But in addition, all the spiritual values with which this canyon has filled tens of thousands of folks should prohibit us from committing the unconscionable act of wiping this place off the face of the earth.[53]

By contrast, Patkar and her colleagues hoped not only to save the Narmada river but also, and more crucially, the tens of thousands of peasants to be displaced by the dam being built on it. When completed, the Sardar Sarovar project will submerge a total of 245 villages,

[53] Mark Dubois to Colonel Donald O'Shei, reproduced in Palmer, *Stanislaus*, pp. 163–4 (emphasis mine).

most of whose inhabitants are tribals and poor peasants.[54] True, the dam will also inundate old growth forests and historic sites, but it will most emphatically destroy the living culture of the human communities who live by the Narmada river. Thus it is that the struggle of Patkar and her associates becomes, as they put it (in a message written on the forty-second anniversary of Mahatma Gandhi's martydom), a move "towards our ultimate goal of [a] socially just and ecologically sustainable model of development."[55]

The Stanislaus/Narmada or Dubois/Patkar comparison illustrates a more fundamental difference between two types of environmentalism. The action by Dubois, heroic though it undoubtedly was, was quite in line with the dominant thrust of the environmental movement in the North, which is toward the protection of pristine, unspoilt nature—this being a reservoir of biological diversity and enormous aesthetic appeal which serves as an ideal (if temporary) haven from the workaday world. In protecting the wild, it asserts, we are both acknowledging an ethical responsibility toward other species and enriching the spiritual side of our own existence. By contrast, the action by Patkar was consistent with the dominant thrust of the environmental movement in India, which powerfully foregrounds questions of production and distribution within human society. The concern here is with "the use of the environment and who should benefit from it; not with environmental protection for its own sake."[56]

VIII

The environmental movement in India has contributed to a profound rethinking of the very idea of development. Intellectuals sympathetic to the movement have fashioned a critique of the industrial and urban bias of government policies, urging that it give way to a decentralized, socially aware, environmentally friendly and altogether more gentle form of development. Development as conventionally understood and practiced has been attacked on a philosophical plane, but critics

[54] Anon., *The Narmada Valley Project: A Critique* (New Delhi: Kalpavriksh, 1988).

[55] Circular letter from Medha Patkar and others, dated January 30, 1990, copy in the author's possession.

[56] Agarwal, "Human–Nature Interactions," in Guha, *Social Ecology*, p. 348.

have been forthcoming with nose-to-the ground, sector-specific solutions as well. In the realm of water management they have offered to large dams the alternative of small dams and/or the revival of traditional methods of irrigation such as tanks and wells. In the realm of forestry they have asked whether community control of natural forests is not a more just and sustainable option when compared to the handing over of public land on a platter to industrial plantations. In the realm of biodiversity they have critically contrasted top-down to bottom-up methods of national park management and urged that indigenous knowledge be integrated into conservation. In the realm of fisheries they have deplored the favors shown to trawlers at the expense of country boats, suggesting that a careful demarcation of ocean waters, by allowing indigenous methods sufficient play, might allow the renewal of rapidly depleting fish stocks.[57]

Since it began—in or about the year 1973—the environmental movement has passed through three broad phases. The first stage could be characterized as the "struggle to be heard." This lasted through most of the 1970s. Social action groups struggled to give greater visibility to the problems of deforestation, soil erosion, and water shortages—problems that affected millions of people in the countryside. However, for quite some time the political system in India met these protests with a resounding silence.

The second stage, corresponding broadly with the 1980s, saw the concerns of environmentalists being energetically taken up by the media, and less energetically by the political system and the state. The damage caused to human health and well being by industrial effluents,

---

[57] On water management see Nirmal Sengupta, "Irrigation: Traditional *versus* Modern," *EPW*, Special Number, August 1985; Anupam Mishra, *Rajasthan ké Rajat Bundé* (New Delhi: Gandhi Peace Foundation, 1994); and Jayanta Bandyopadhyaya, "Political Economy of Drought and Water Scarcity," *EPW*, December 12, 1987; on forest management see Mark Poffenberger and Betsy McGean, eds, *Village Voices, Forest Choices: Joint Forest Management in India* (New Delhi: Oxford University Press, 1994), and chapter 4 of the present book; on biodiversity, see Ashish Kothari, Saloni Suri, and Neena Singh, "Conservation in India: A New Direction," *EPW*, October 28, 1994; Madhav Gadgil and P.R.S. Rao, "A System of Positive Incentives to Conserve Biodiversity," *EPW*, August 6, 1994; and chapters 5 and 8 of the present book; on fisheries see the works of John Kurien cited in footnote 44 above.

as well as the serious scarcity of water and fuelwood in the countryside, were demonstrated by scientific studies and investigative reportage. Slowly, the Indian establishment responded to the evidence of the social costs of environmental abuse. Departments of environment were set up at central and state levels, while attempts were made to forge a forest policy more sensitive to nature and humans alike.[58]

However, in their desire to make the public and politicians more responsive to their agenda, environmentalists were often guilty of over-stating their case. They spoke in alarmist and even apocalyptic language, predicting death, disease, the collapse of national sovereignty as well as the extinction of Indian culture if their views did not immediately become state policy. This, as well as the radical transformation in global geopolitics wrought by the fall of the Berlin Wall, has in recent years generated a major anti-green backlash. This was the third phase, willed along by propagandists on the other side—by advocates of free-market capitalism who interpreted the collapse of the Soviet empire as constituting the End of History. It was now being said that there was a single successful economic model, the American one. The rest of the world, India and Indians included, needed to remake itself in the image of the American consumer. Only the environmentalists dared point out that there existed natural constraints to the globalization of consumer society. The average North American household uses more energy and materials than do, on average, fifty Indian households. Does the earth have the capacity to sustain the replication of the American model in all the countries of the globe?[59]

These questions were all brushed aside in the euphoria generated by the end of communism, a buoyancy reinforced in India by the promises held out by programs of economic liberalization. There is thus at present a tremendous backlash against environmentalists. They are frequently and routinely attacked as the major impediment to the successful Americanization of Indian society. Every summer, when the mercury touches 48° Celsius in North India, prominent columnists in

[58] Cf. Anil Agarwal, Kalpana Sharma, and Ravi Sharma, eds, *India: The State of the Environment 1982: A Citizens' Report* (New Delhi: Centre for Science and Environment, 1982); Jayanta Bandyopadhyaya, ed., *India's Environment: Crisis and Response* (Dehradun: Natraj Publishers, 1985).

[59] This question is more fully explored in chapter 9 of the present book.

New Delhi blame it on Medha Patkar: indeed the precise timing of printed attacks on this most famous of Indian environmentalists can almost be predicted from the weather reports. The attacks come typically in summer, when the airconditioners break down, or in the depths of winter, when the heaters do not get the required voltage.[60]

Holding Patkar responsible for the electricity crisis is to wish away the problems of theft, mismanagement, poor maintenance, and antiquated technology that lie behind the power shortages in India. It is also to ignore the fact that environmental campaigns have, for the first time, brought to centerstage the "victims of development," the poor peasants and tribals who have thus far had to unwillingly make way for the dams, steel mills, and highways that dispossess them while benefiting others. Indeed, old-style public-sector socialism and new-style market liberalization are akin in some crucial respects. Both have intensified social inequalities as well as devastated the natural environment.

So it is ironic that, today, the environmental movement is so much on the defensive. Whereas in the 1980s it looked as if their ideas might even translate into effective state policy, environmentalists are now the favorite scapegoats of politicians and industrialists as well as of a consumer-driven media.

In its countrywide implications the "environmental problem" is every bit as serious as the "Kashmir dispute" or the "fiscal crisis of the state." Yet it has been poorly recognized by the intelligentsia and insufficiently acted upon by the political class. However, as we move further into the twenty-first century, the future of India as a sovereign nation might come to centrally depend on how its people manage their natural bounty, on their success in distributing its fruits equitably, on the promptness with which they can take pre-emptive action against— or ameliorative action after—environmental degradation.

---

[60] A prominent columnist who often targets environmentalists in general is Swaminathan S. Aiyar of *The Times of India*; one who likes to target Medha Patkar in particular is Tavleen Singh, formerly of *India Today* and now of *The Indian Express*. See Tavleen Singh, "Luddite Sisters," "Beware the Eco-terrorist," and "The Light has Gone Out," in *India Today*, issues of November 17, 1997, June 22, 1998, and December 27, 1999, respectively.

CHAPTER 3

Three Environmental Utopias

The human world interests me more than the world of nature; maybe it is a heresy to say such a thing in America.—**Czeslaw Milosz**

D
iscussions on environmental ethics have reached their high-
water mark in the United States, whether measured in terms
of column inches of print space, enrolments in college courses,
or—the surest indicator—the intensity of the debate. With the setting
aside of wild areas being regarded as the best gauge of an ecological
conscience, the development of environmental ethics has been closely
linked to the growth of the American wilderness movement. Battles
over the creation, preservation, and extension of the national park
system form the backdrop against which the environmental community has examined and re-examined its ethical responsibilities toward
nature.

Three factors seem to have given a major impetus to modern debates on environmental ethics. The first, dealt with in Chapter One,
is the self-scrutiny of Christians following the indictment of their faith
by Lynn White Jr. Ever since White, theologians and laymen alike have
looked anxiously for signs of environmental responsibility within their
own tradition. Second, there is a guilt complex more specific to the
United States. In resisting the equation of a dollar sign with their culture, Americans have pointed increasingly to their remarkable system
of national parks. John Muir's life-work, wrote one of his early
followers, was to help Americans shake off the twin shackles of "phi-
listinism and commercialism," thereby advancing "with freedom

towards the love of beauty as a principle."[1] Some seventy years later a modern biographer of Muir argued that the wilderness movement was derived from a "deep stratum of the national experience which was surely as American as those of Joseph Coors and Union Carbide."[2]

The third crucial influence on the development of environmental ethics is rooted in nature rather than culture. As compared to tropical ecologies, temperate ecosystems are benign and hence more amenable to scientific exploitation for utilitarian ends. At the same time, for the ordinary city dweller the temperate forest is a good deal more welcoming than the tropical forest. The species diversity is far less—which means, among other things, that there are far fewer troublesome creatures such as leeches and cobras which, however attractive to the biologist, do not encourage a quiet walk in the woods. As Aldous Huxley pointed out long ago, the worship of nature came easily to those who lived "beneath a temperate sky and in the age of Henry Ford." In the tropics nature was fearsome, manifesting itself as "vast masses of swarming vegetation alien to the human spirit and hostile to it;" not, as in the North Atlantic world, a "chaste, mild deity" that could so easily be "enslaved to man."[3]

The relative simplicity of temperate ecosystems is complemented by their greater ability to recover from disturbance. There is no torrential monsoon beating down on land freshly cleared of forest and making it difficult for new growth to clothe it. In this respect the term temperate is wholly apt. Here, the even-tempered climate has allowed for and inspired radical programs of environmental modification. Thus, while some in the West have adored nature, others have just as easily controlled and dominated it. The ecology of the temperate zone has facilitated both the conquest and the worship of nature.

This triple heritage of Christianity, anti-philistinism, and benign ecology has given the debate on environmental ethics a distinctively

---

[1] Robert Underwood Johnson, "John Muir," tribute dated January 6, 1916, in *Academy Notes and Monographs* (New York: The American Academy of Arts and Letters, 1922), pp. 21–2.

[2] Frederick Turner, "So Necessarily Elite," in *Parks in the West and American Culture* (Sun Valley, ID: Institute of the American West, 1984).

[3] "Wordsworth in the Tropics," in Aldous Huxley, *Do What you Will* (1929; rpnt London: Chatto and Windus, 1956).

American stamp. Strongly rooted in US history, the debate as it stands is largely incomprehensible to environmentalists from other cultures.

A particular weakness of this debate has been its rather narrow focus on *individual* attitudes toward nature. There is little attempt to locate these attitudes in their cultural context, or indeed to examine their social, as distinct from ecological, consequences. This juxtaposition of singular man to singular nature gives rise to a series of binary oppositions, around which the history of environmental ideas is then written. Thus, Donald Worster's magisterial history of ecological ideas in the West is woven around the polar opposites of arcadian and imperial attitudes toward nature. Likewise, both Roderick Nash and Stephen Fox have tried to rewrite the history of American environmentalism as a struggle between "preservationists" who wish to preserve nature and wild species for their own sake, and "utilitarians" who, with the help of science and rational management, transform nature into useful commodities, working toward "the greatest good of the greatest number for the longest time." And for today's deep ecologists the only two admissible attitudes are "anthropocentric" (human centered) and "biocentric" (nature centered). The story of environmental ethics is thereby reduced to a Manichaean struggle between one set of good ideas (arcadian, preservationist, biocentric) and an opposing set of evil ones (imperial, utilitarian, anthropocentric).[4]

This chapter tries to see the American debate on environmental ethics from broader perspectives that may enrich it. To circumvent its idealist and individualist tenor I intend to recast the debate as one about social utopias. For, every theory of nature is embedded in a larger theory of society. As Raymond Williams warned us, "if we talk only of singular Man and singular Nature, we can compose a general history, but at the cost of excluding the real and altering social relations." Indeed, "the idea of nature contains an extraordinary amount of human history," and "what is often being argued. . . in the idea of nature

[4] Donald Worster, *Nature's Economy*; Roderick Nash, *Wilderness and the American Mind*; Stephen Fox, *The American Conservation Movement: John Muir and his Legacy* (Madison: University of Wisconsin Press, 1985); Devall and Sessions, *Deep Ecology*.

is the idea of man; the idea of man in society, indeed the ideas of kinds of societies."[5]

II

In the modern marketplace of ideas, environmentalism occupies the broad space between two sharply opposed views of the human predicament: the buoyantly optimistic vision of the economist and the profoundly pessimistic vision of the biologist. The neoclassical economist's mystical belief in the magic of the market as an instrument of human welfare contrasts with the population biologist's equally mystical belief in the human propensity for collective suicide through overbreeding. If the economist acknowledges no natural limits to growth, the biologist is obsessed only with such limits. What the two have in common is their skepticism of purposive action for the common good: in the one case it is not needed because of the mantra that the market takes care of all our problems; in the other case it is probably too late.

As compared to the dominant schools in economics and biology, environmentalists take a subtle view of the human prospect. They acknowledge that Spaceship Earth does set certain limits to economic expansion but argue that it is only at certain times and in certain places that environmental degradation is of sufficient magnitude to threaten the future of specific societies. However, like neoclassical economics and Malthusian biology, ecological consciousness must also be viewed as a distinctive response to the growth of industrial society. Here, I believe that, within the environmental movement, there are three generic responses to industrialization: the three environmental philosophies of our time are *agrarianism, wilderness thinking,* and *scientific industrialism.*

At one level, of course, these are simply three perspectives on the human–nature relationship. Scientific industrialism and wilderness thinking are the two old antagonists parading under new names: one advocating the conquest of nature, the other pleading for human submission to natural processes. And agrarianism is nothing but the

[5] "Ideas of Nature" (1972), in Raymond Williams, *Problems in Materialism and Culture* (London: Verso, 1984), pp. 70, 84.

search for a golden mean of stewardship and sustainable use.[6] However, each of these perspectives on nature also forms part of a larger philosophy of social reconstruction. They each rest on a distinct theory of history which outlines where society is coming from, where it seems to be heading, and in what direction it should go. I term these philosophies "utopian" for in each case their critique of the existing social order has as its point of reference an ideal society free of the blemishes of the one being attacked.

For agrarianism, the apogee of human history is represented by the grain-based civilizations of Europe and Asia. The agrarian views with disfavor both tribal society—where life was believed to be nasty, brutish, and short—and industrial society, where humans have succumbed to the pursuit of wealth. The ecological and social ideal here is peasant society, where technology is on the human scale and the bonds of community strong. The political program of agrarianism is therefore to resist the onslaught of commercialism and industrialism where they have not yet made inroads; and where they have, to resolutely turn one's back on modern society and go "back to the land."

As a social response to industrialization, agrarianism has usually invoked the traditions of a culture staring defeat in the face. In *Social Origins of Dictatorship and Democracy*, his great work on the making of the modern world, Barrington Moore Jr rather cynically remarked that the peasant rebellions of early modern Europe represented the "dying wail of a class over whom the wave of progress is about to roll."[7] Memories of these peasant movements were, however, kept alive by a galaxy of poets and writers whose moral, and indeed ecological, indictment of industrial capitalism has been brilliantly analyzed in the English case by Raymond Williams.[8] But even as the industrial economy of the North has transformed itself into a post-industrial one,

[6] Cf. Leo Marx, "American Literary Culture and the Fatalistic View of Technology," in idem, *The Pilot and the Passenger: Essays on Literature, Technology and Culture in the United States* (New York: Oxford University Press, 1988).

[7] Barrington Moore, Jr, *Social Origins of Dictatorship and Democracy: Lord and Peasant in the Making of the Modern World* (Harmondsworth: Penguin, 1966), p. 505.

[8] Raymond Williams, *The Country and the City* (New York: Oxford University Press, 1973). Cf. also Jonathan Bate, *Romantic Ecology: Wordsworth and the Environmental Tradition* (London: Routledge, 1991).

in other parts of the world agrarianism continues to exercise a compelling appeal.

Later I shall have more to say about the heritage of the best-known American agrarian, Thomas Jefferson, and that of the best known Indian agrarian, Mahatma Gandhi. For a succinct statement of the agrarian ideal, however, we need to turn to Gandhi's close contemporary, the poet and novelist Rabindranath Tagore, the first Asian to win the Nobel Prize for literature. In an arresting analogy—albeit one which modern feminists may find patriarchally irksome—Tagore observes that

> Villages are like women. In their keeping is the cradle of the race. They are nearer to nature than towns, and in closer touch with the fountain of life. They possess a natural power of healing. It is the function of the village, like that of women, to provide people with their elementary needs, with food and joy, with the simple poetry of life and with those ceremonies of beauty which the village spontaneously produces and in which she finds delight. But when constant strain is put upon her, when her resources are excessively exploited, she becomes dull and uncreative. From her time-honoured position of the wedded wife, she then descends to that of a maid-servant. The city, in its intense egotism and pride, remains unconscious of the hurt it inflicts on the very source of its life, health and joy.

In medieval civilization—or what Tagore calls the "natural state"—the "village and the town have harmonious interactions. From the one, flow food and health and fellow being. From the other, return gifts of wealth, knowledge and energy." This balance is rudely shattered by the growth of industrialization. Now, "greed has struck at the relationship of mutuality between town and village." For, "modern cities feed upon the social organism that runs through the village. They appropriate the life stuff of the community and slough off a huge amount of dead matter, while making a lurid counterfeit of prosperity." Indeed, cities today "represent energy and materials concentrated for the satisfaction of that bloated appetite which is the characteristic symptom of modern civilization."[9]

[9] "City and Village" (1928), in *Rabindranath Tagore on Rural Reconstruction* (New Delhi: Ministry of Community Development and Co-operation, 1962).

We come next to wilderness thinking, the environmental philosophy so firmly planted in American soil. There is widespread agreement within the wilderness movement on the need to fully protect and if possible expand the system of national parks; there is, however, no such consensus on a philosophy of social reconstruction based on the wilderness ethic. One school, among whose influential spokesmen is Roderick Nash, views nature appreciation as an indication of a culture's maturity. Here, wilderness is not counterposed to civilization but is in fact the surest indicator of the flowering of civilization. In this perspective automobiles and national parks, free-flowing rivers and power plants, universities and trails, can and must coexist.[10]

Of more interest to us is the radical strand in wilderness thinking, which we may call pre-agrarianism or, perhaps more accurately, *primitivism*. This believes that an original state of harmony with nature was rudely shattered by the white man. Here, BC may as well stand for "Before Columbus." The founder of the Wilderness Society, Robert Marshall, claimed that before Columbus the whole of North America was a wilderness where "over billions of acres the aboriginal wanderers still spun out their peripatetic careers, the wild animals still browsed in unmolested meadows and the forests still grew and moldered and grew again precisely as they had done for interminable centuries."[11] For the primitivist the victory of agriculture signals a precipitous fall in ecological wisdom. And, as the iron plough lacerates mother earth, human history spirals downward. Industrialism only further accentuates the separation of humans from nature, a partial brake on its excesses being provided, belatedly and ineffectively, by the movement to set aside areas of forest and wilderness as national parks.

The primitivist theory of history has inspired truly radical proposals—for example, the reduction of human population by 90 percent to allow the recovery of wilderness areas and species threatened with

[10] Cf. Roderick Nash, "The Exporting and Importing of Nature: Nature Appreciation as a Commodity, 1850–1950," in *Perspectives in American History, Volume XII* (Cambridge, Mass.: Charles Warren Center for Studies in American History, 1979).

[11] Robert Marshall, "The Problem of the Wilderness" (1930), in *Sierra Club Bulletin*, vol. 32, no. 5, 1947, p. 44.

extinction.[12] Pursuing the principle of "biocentric equality" which they hold dear, deep ecologists—perhaps constituting the leading edge of primitivism—turn their back on both agricultural and industrial society. Only hunting and gathering, they believe, can satisfy essential human needs without sacrificing the rights of non-human species. A return to pagan, pre-Christian origins is therefore a precondition for restoring harmony in nature. This return to origins would allow even white society to recover its humanity. To quote the Native American thinker Vine Deloria, Jr, "the white man must drop his dollar-chasing civilization and return to a simple, tribal, game-hunting, berry-hunting life if he is to survive. He must quickly adopt not only the contemporary [American] Indian worldview but the ancient Indian worldview to survive."[13]

The idea that hunter-gatherers were the first, and perhaps still the only *real*, environmentalists is pervasive among radical edges of the wilderness movement. It is upheld by many activists and implicitly present in the work of some scientists as well. Reviewing the biologist Jared Diamond's book *Collapse*, the Cambridge economist Partha Dasgupta sarcastically says: "reading Diamond you would think that our ancestors should all have remained hunter-gatherers in Africa, co-evolving with the native flora and fauna, and roaming the wilds in search of wild berries and the occasional piece of meat." The disdain is unmistakable, and redolent of the Oxbridge high table. But the fact is that even if Diamond does not quite think that way, many of his fellow greens in California do believe that not just our ancestors but our descendants should live in this fashion.[14]

The primitivist theory of history is in essence a theory of *de-development* or *un-development*, a steady fall from the natural high of hunter-gatherer society. For, the first humans were literally reared in the womb of nature. Exposed from birth to the sights, smells, and sounds of the natural world, hunter-gatherers were at one with their surroundings, feeling themselves to be the "guests rather than masters"

[12] Cf. Dave Forman, "A Modest Proposal for a Wilderness System," *Whole Earth Review*, no. 53, Winter 1986–7.

[13] Quoted in George Feaver, "Vine Deloria," *Encounter*, April 1975, p. 39.

[14] Dasgupta's review, published in the *London Review of Books*, is available at www.lrb.co.uk/v27/n10/print/dasg01_.html

of nature. This unity was disrupted by civilization which, in the words of the California ecologist Paul Shepard, "increased the separation between the individual and the natural world as it did the child from the mother . . ." Significantly, agriculture rather than industry is held to be the original culprit for fostering the dualism of humans and nature in which "wild things are enemies of the tame; the wild other is not the context but the opponent of 'my' domain."[15]

What distinguishes *scientific industrialism* is that, among the three environmental philosophies of history being considered here, it alone looks ahead. Here, human salvation lies in the future, not in return to an agrarian or pre-agrarian past. The task is to tame industrialism and temper its excesses, not turn our back on it. As a philosophy of *resource use* (a term abhorrent to agrarian and primitivist alike), scientific industrialism seeks to replace the anarchy of the market with a rational program of state control. Industrial capitalism may be ecologically wasteful but scientific expertise, when backed by legislation and an activist state, can assure the sustained yield of natural resources so crucial to human welfare.

Like agrarianism and wilderness thinking, scientific industrialism has a distinctive three-stage interpretation of human history. A fine statement comes from the pen of that pioneering American forester of the nineteenth century Bernhard Fernow. In an essay titled "Battle of the Forest" Fernow, giving an interesting twist to primitivist narratives, starts with the process of ecological succession. Thus, the process of glaciation is followed by the formation of the soil, the gradual emergence of plants and then trees, culminating at last in what we know as virgin forest. This painfully slow and by no means unidirectional process is the "unwritten history of the battle of the forest," a "product of long struggles extending over centuries, nay thousands of years."

But the hurdles of nature are nothing compared to the threats posed by humans. For, pre-industrial society in general, and most especially farmers and shepherds, take "sides against the forest." Through "willful or careless destruction" they have "wasted the work of nature through thousands of years by the foolish destruction of the forest

[15] Paul Shepard, *Nature and Madness* (San Francisco: Sierra Club Books, 1982), pp. 3–7, 28–39.

cover." They have "accomplished in many localities utter ruin . . . and turned them back into inhospitable deserts as they first were before the struggle of the forest had made them inhabitable."

Scientific forestry, next, inaugurates a more hopeful stage, but the habits of many lifetimes die hard. Fernow leaves us with a picture of the forester heroically battling the uneducated citizen, with the result very much in the balance: "The battle of the forest in this country is now being fought by man, the unintelligent and greedy carrying on a war of extermination, the intelligent and provident trying to defend the forest cover."[16]

Our three philosophies of environmental history do not usually speak directly to questions of gender. Still, one can between the lines distinguish three different kinds of emphases. The ideal role of women in agrarian society is vividly illustrated in the extract from Tagore. In her "time-honoured position of the wedded wife" she keeps the family and household going, while in the community at large women are the symbol of continuity, the vehicle by which traditions are passed on from one generation to another. From one point of view the role of women is here stable and well defined; from another it is severely circumscribed. Primitivists tend to believe the latter, holding that it is only in hunter-gatherer societies that we find a relative equality of the sexes. This is ascribed to the absence of private property in land, and to the fact that women, as the primary gatherers of food, play a far more important role in economic life. Respect for women in primitive society, it is further argued, goes hand in hand with the "feminine principle" in nature. Finally, scientific industrialists claim that modern science enormously expands opportunities for both men and women. Only in modern society are women not barred from professional careers, only in the cities are they free of the petty tyrannies and superstitions of the village.

Over a century and more the principles of these utopias have been articulated in print and, less often, action. Words and sometimes deeds are the forms in which they typically manifest themselves, words and deeds quoted and analyzed at different points through this book. I also offer below three visual representations that capture the core beliefs,

[16] Bernard Fernow, "The Battle of the Forest," *The National Geographic Magazine*, June 1894.

ENVIRONMENTAL PHILOSOPHIES: A GRAPHIC SUMMARY

AGRARIANISM

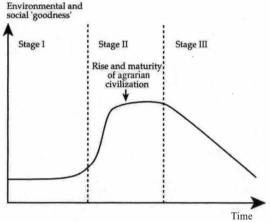

Agents of Evil   The Machine, materialistic philosophy
Key phrases   Technology 'on the human scale', back to the land
Policy   Go back to Stage II

PRIMITIVISM

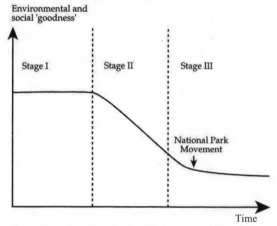

Agents of Evil   The plow that lacerates Mother Earth:
the white man
Key phrases   Pristine / primordial / virgin / unspoilt nature,
the equality of sexes and of all species
Policy   Go back to Stage I (eliminate 90% of the human
population if necessary?)

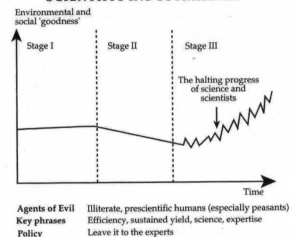

SCIENTIFIC INDUSTRIALISM

Agents of Evil	Illiterate, prescientific humans (especially peasants)
Key phrases	Efficiency, sustained yield, science, expertise
Policy	Leave it to the experts

suppositions, prejudices, and prescriptions of the great environmental philosophies of our time.

III

I have thus far sketched the broad outlines of three environmental utopias. I now examine their articulation in two different contexts, India and the United States. One is the most powerful country in the industrial world, now moving toward a post-industrial economy and post-material society; the other is a populous and largely agricultural country seeking desperately to industrialize as rapidly as possible.

What stands out in this comparison is that while the dominant environmental philosophy in India is agrarianism, in the United States it is wilderness thinking. The Indian movement bases itself on the traditions of an agrarian culture while invoking a more recent history of peasant movements against British colonialism led by Mahatma Gandhi. The rhetoric of this environmental movement is greatly influenced by Gandhi's anti-industrial philosophy, and its more vocal sections call for a return to the Mahatma's vision of a village-centered economic order.[17]

Of course, agrarianism is also a powerful current in American cultural history. Its most famous statement, Jefferson's *Notes on Virginia*

---

[17] These themes are explored in greater detail in chapters 2 and 9.

is, like Gandhi's pamphlet *Hind Swaraj* (Indian home rule), in the main a manifesto of social reconstruction based on the susbsistence farm. There are, however, two important ways in which American agrarianism differs from its Indian counterpart. While Gandhi invokes the spirit of community which he believes to be intrinsic to traditional peasant cultures, the yeoman farmer of Jefferson's imagination is a figure of sturdy independence. Private proprietorship of land is, in the Jeffersonian vision, a *sine qua non* of the individualist spirit, which is in turn the bedrock of democracy. And while Gandhian agrarianism is acutely aware of ecological limits, the American version is in fact premised on the ecological abundance of a sparsely settled continent.

Their occupation of a seemingly endless continent was, indeed, a source of great comfort to early American agrarians like Jefferson and Crèvecoeur. In Europe, limitations of space may have forced the working poor to accept the miseries of city life, but in the new continent "virgin land," the precondition for a society of yeoman farmers, "had been given to Americans in extreme, almost unbelievable abundance."[18] This optimism was shared by the writers and scholars who, following in Jefferson's footsteps, authored the inter-war manifesto called *I'll Take My Stand*. The most eloquent of these "Southern Agrarians," the poet John Crowe Ransom, claimed that the unemployment problem of the 1930s was a direct consequence of industrialization and the shift of population from country to city. Advocating the return of the unemployed to the land, Ransom observed: "So far as America is concerned, there always was land enough for [the farmer] to till; there was no such problem as overpopulation . . . the land is still with us, as patient and nearly as capable as ever."[19]

In our own time, there have been some interesting attempts to recast the Jeffersonian ideal along ecological lines, for example by Wendell Berry.[20] This is, however, a marginal strand in the American environmental movement, whose core is undoubtedly the wilderness ethic. In

[18] Cf. William Adams, "Natural Virtue: Symbol and Imagination in the Farm Crisis," *Georgia Review*, vol. 39, no. 4, 1985.

[19] J.C. Ransom, "Land! An Answer to the Unemployment Problem," *Harper's Magazine*, July 1932, p. 218.

[20] Among the many books by Wendell Berry defending the agrarian way of life, the most eloquent perhaps remains his early polemic, *The Unsettling of America* (San Francisco: Sierra Club Books, 1977).

fact wilderness lovers are in the main quite hostile to agriculture. Evidently, going back to nature does not imply going back to the land. Thus, the ecologist Ray Dasmann once confessed that he had for most of his career been interested only in "the extremes of land use, the city and the wilderness." The country in between—composed of farm, rangeland, pasture, and shrub jungle—had been to him "just space to be passed through as quickly as possible."[21]

What Dasmann ignored his compatriots have actively deplored: recall John Muir's characterization of sheep as "hoofed locusts," but in fact the prejudice against farming and farm animals is very widespread.[22] Coming from the cities, lovers of the wilderness condescend to the farmer and "take for granted the dependence of both city and country on the agricultural base."[23] Wilderness lovers, themselves urbane and cosmopolitan, look down on the farmer as uncouth. An editor of *Harper's Magazine* once remarked that "if a man perspires largely in a cornfield on a dusty day, and washes hastily in a horsetrough, and eats in shirt-sleeves that date their cleanliness three days back, and loves fat pork and cabbage neat, he will not prove the Arcadian companion at dinner."[24]

As for Muir, he saw the agriculturist not merely as a cultural philistine but as an ecological villain. He wrote once, of a farmer he knew, that the man had

> a call to plow, and woe to the daisy sod or ozalea thicket that falls under the savage redemption of his keen steel shares. Not content with the so-called subjugation of every terrestrial bog, rock, and moorland, he would fain discover some method of reclamation applicable to the oceans and sky, that in due calendar time they might be brought to bud and blossom as the rose . . . Wildness charms not my friend . . . and whatsoever may

[21] Ray Dasmann, "The Country In Between," *Sierra Club Wilderness Calendar*, 1982. I am grateful to my student Joel Seton for this reference.

[22] Muir used the term often in his writings and speeches, as in his "Address on the Sierra Forest Reservation," *Sierra Club Bulletin*, vol. 1, no. 7, 1896.

[23] Linda Graber, *Wilderness as Sacred Space* (Washington DC: Association of American Geographers, 1976), pp. 21–2.

[24] Donald Mitchell, quoted in Peter J. Schmitt, *Back to Nature: The Arcadian Myth in Urban America* (New York: Oxford University Press, 1969), pp. 6–7.

be the character of his heaven, his earth seems only a chaos of agricultural possibilities calling for grubbing-hoes and manners.[25]

Here again India provides an illuminating contrast. While it has an even greater diversity of ecological regimes than the United States, the movement for the protection of wild areas has not enjoyed much popular sanction. Support for the national park movement in India has come chiefly from international conservation organizations and from a class of big-game hunters turned preservationists—these include many former maharajas. Furthermore, the designation of parks and sanctuaries has been heavily biased toward the preservation of large mammals such as the tiger, the rhinoceros, and the elephant. The establishment of sanctuaries for their protection has led to the uprooting of villages situated within their boundaries, while the protected species themselves are often a serious threat to the lives and livelihood of human communities living adjacent to wilderness areas. The management of national parks is therefore a subject of quite some controversy, though it is fair to say that within the environmental movement the burden of opinion is ranged against wildlife management (as presently practiced) for its neglect of the interests of peasants and tribals.[26]

We have, therefore, a curious symmetry: the dominant environmental tradition in the United States, wilderness thinking, is hostile to agriculture, whereas the dominant tradition in India, agrarianism, is not favorably disposed to lovers of the wild.

What, then, of the third of our philosophies, scientific industrialism? This is an environmental tradition that is, in a sense, truly universal, transporting itself with ease across the world. In India and the United States, as indeed in China and Brazil, Germany and Indonesia, forestry experts and irrigation engineers uphold an identical vision of large-scale, centralized, and expert-controlled resource management.

Associated with the state and with state power, scientific industrialism has in fact come to be the common enemy of the environmental

---

[25] Quoted in Daniel B. Weber, "John Muir: The Function of Wilderness in an Industrial Society," unpublished PhD thesis, University of Minnesota (copy in Sterling Memorial Library, Yale University), pp. 159–60.

[26] This theme is picked up for more detailed treatment in chapter 5, below.

movement in India and the United States. In the latter, free-flowing rivers and natural forests are cherished by environmentalists for their beauty and ecological value but coveted by resource managers for the millions of board feet or kilowatt hours they may yield. This is the classic dilemma, preservationism *versus* utilitarianism, that has underwritten a good part of American environmental history and environmental conflict. In India, however, conflicts over water and forests more sharply foreground the question of alternative uses—subsistence *versus* commerce, local *versus* national, peasants *versus* industry. Thus, large dams and eucalyptus plantations, to cite just two examples of scientific conservation at work, are criticized both for their diversion of resources from the countryside to the city, and for the trail of environmental destruction they leave in their wake.

These conflicts are vividly represented in the symbols and slogans of the environmental movements in both countries. A focal point of the American movement has been the struggle between scientific industrialism and wilderness thinking, while in India scientific industrialism squares off against agrarianism. Not surprisingly, scientific conservationists loom large in the demonology of environmentalists everywhere. If the great icon of American environmentalism is Muir— a product of the "university of the wilderness"—its demon is indisputably Gifford Pinchot, founder of the United States Forest Service. Likewise, Indian environmentalists like to oppose Mahatma Gandhi, the prophet of a village-centered economic order, to Jawaharlal Nehru, the long-serving prime minister who initiated and guided programs of industrial development that have led both to environmental destruction and the impoverishment of many peasant and tribal communities.

All social movements need their symbols of good and evil, their icons and demons. These representations of Muir and Pinchot, Gandhi and Nehru, only indicate the ferocity of the debate between the three major environmental philosophies of our time. It is ironic that scattered through Muir's writings are warm references to Pinchot's programs for the takeover and rational management of American forests. After having read and heard a great deal about the Muir–Pinchot divide, I visited the Muir woods outside San Francisco, only to find a splendid redwood named the Gifford Pinchot Tree. And Nehru was, all said and done, the closest associate and political colleague of Gandhi over many decades—indeed, his chosen political heir, the man with whom the Mahatma left India "in safe hands."

IV

I have called these three environmental visions utopias, which they are in both senses of the word, in that they seek to fundamentally alter and reshape the world, and in that none can be realized in full. The claims of scientific industrialism notwithstanding, there are ecological limits to the global spread of the consumer society it creates; despite the deep ecologist's deepest yearnings, a return to our hunter-gatherer origins is quite out of the question; and over much of Asia and Africa the world of stable subsistence farming so beloved of the agrarians is rapidly giving way to a more thrusting, individualistic, and market-oriented way of life.

Perhaps the debate between these three visions has in fact run its course. I like to believe that we are on the threshold of a new phase in the development of environmental ethics, with a new synthesis coming to take the place of the three contending philosophies. This synthesis would take from primitivism the idea of *diversity*; from peasant cultures the ideal of *sustainability*; and from modern society in general, rather than scientific conservation in particular, the value of *equity*. Anthropologists and ecologists, working sometimes separately and at other times in tandem, have forced a retreat from the monocultural view of society and nature so typical of "high modernism," that which wished and indeed urged the remaking of the whole world in the image of Western Europe and North America. For this new appreciation of diversity, biological as well as cultural, we have also to thank wilderness thinking and activists working on behalf of indigenous people. Likewise, the ideal of sustainability has provided a powerful antidote to another core ideal of industrial society: that of economic growth without limits. This ideal has its roots in peasant cultures, which often used land and nature wisely, well, and with a view to the long term. Finally, while scientific industrialism may have ended up as a movement of experts, it was fired in the first instance by a passion for equality and democracy, the urge to bend science and nature so as to make the fruits

of economic growth accessible to all.[27] In the modern world and nowhere else challenges to principles of hierarchy have gained moral currency. In pre-modern times uprisings of slaves, peasants, women, and
workers had always to contend with a dominant ideology—whether
monarchism, absolutism, theocracy, or patriarchy—that legitimated,
justified, and enforced inequalities of race, sex, caste, class, and religion. Only from the French Revolution have social movements been
able to draw sustenance from the wide acceptance of equity as a value.

Diversity, sustainability, and equity: these are the building blocks of
an environmental ethic in the making. What might this philosophy
be called? I like the sound of "social ecology," the term used both by
the Lucknow sociologist Radhakamal Mukerjee and the veteran Vermont radical Murray Bookchin. For the scholar, this term allows a
coming together of the natural and social sciences, a union so crucial
for understanding the complexities of ecological processes and their
impact on human life. For the citizen it joins rather than separates the
most dominant species on earth with the other species and habitats
that we have to share the world with.

Social ecology, then, can serve both as an intellectual paradigm and
as a guide to civic or state action. And the term is inclusive in a way in
which its rivals are perhaps not. Thus, deep ecology not only privileges
wilderness protection over other forms of environmental work, it also
disparages these as shallow. In contrast the label "social" is capacious
enough to allow for multiple varieties of environmental thought and
action.

That, at any rate, is what the rest of this book attempts to demonstrate. Chapters Four and Five examine, within the domains of
the forest and the wild, the claims of competing environmental philosophies and suggest ways in which these claims can be harmonized

---

[27] As J. Leonard Bates once said, "in spite of its complexity, in spite of its
ambiguity, the [scientific] conservationist policy contained an inner vitality
that could not be obscured and destroyed. Here was an effort to implement
democracy for twentieth-century America, to stop the stealing and exploitation,
to inspire high standards of government, to preserve the beauty of mountain and
stream, to distribute equally the profits of the economy." J. Leonard Bates, "Ful-
filling American Democracy: The Conservation Movement, 1907 to 1921,"
The Mississippi Valley Historical Review, vol. 44, no. 1, 1957, pp. 36–7.

or resolved. Chapters Six through Eight profile three pioneering social ecologists—one American and two Indians—whose work and example is, I argue, of compelling importance and relevance.

The final chapter poses what is perhaps the most fundamental environmental question, the one contained in the title of this book, to answer which we shall have to summon the resources, traditions, insights, and moral force of all the utopias analyzed in the present chapter—and much else besides.

CHAPTER 4

Democracy in the Forest

Liberty and forest laws are incompatible.—**An English country vicar, *c*. 1720.**[1]

The history of state forestry has been a history of social conflict. In monarchies and in democracies, in metropolitan Europe as well as in colonial South Asia, the state management of forests has met with bitter and continuous opposition. As we saw in the last chapter, on one side have been professional foresters who believe that timber production can be ensured only through the exclusion of humans and their animals from wooded areas; on the other, and ranged against them, have been peasants, pastoralists, charcoal ironmakers, basket weavers and others for whom access to forests and forest resources has been crucial to economic survival. To the criticisms of these latter groups have now been added the criticisms of environmentalists, who charge foresters with simplifying complex ecosystems in the direction of commercially valuable but biologically impoverished monocultures.

The battle between these contending parties has been going on more than two hundred years. In continental Europe the eighteenth and nineteenth centuries were peppered with social protest movements against state management of forests. These protests inspired, among others, Marx's first political writings and a memorable novel

[1] Cited in E.P. Thompson, *Whigs and Hunters: The Origins of the Black Act* (Harmondsworth: Penguin, 1975).

by Balzac capturing peasant hostility to forest officials.[2] When the European model of strict state control was exported to the colonies, disaffected peasants and tribals responded with arson and violence. Movements over forest rights were a recurring phenomenon in regions ruled by the British, the Dutch, and the French. The conflicts persisted when post-colonial governments in countries such as India and Indonesia reproduced the imperial model of forest management.[3]

In recent decades, however, the global discourse on forestry has moved toward a more accommodationist perspective: foresters and peasant protesters seem at long last to be talking to, rather than talking past, each other. The rigid and uncompromising attitudes of the past have been replaced by a willingness to listen to and at least partially incorporate opposing points of view. Within the forestry profession itself, doubt has been cast on the contemporary relevance of custodial and policing approaches. The argument now goes that a system of natural resource management crafted in absolutist terms and colonial times needs to be seriously modified or even overthrown.[4] Social activists and community leaders have meanwhile moved from demanding total state withdrawal from forest areas to asking governments to more sympathetically consider the rights of forest-dependent communities.[5]

With this move from conflict to collaboration have come shifts in the language of forestry. Terms like "scientific forestry" and "rational land management," euphemisms for state control and commercial timber production, are being rapidly replaced by sweet-sounding phrases

[2] Karl Marx, "Debate on the Law on Theft of Wood" (1842), in Karl Marx and Frederick Engels, *Collected Works, Volume I* (Moscow: Progress Publishers, 1975); *The Peasantry: Volume XX of the Works of Honore de Balzac* (New York: E.R. Dumont, 1900).

[3] Cf. Nancy Peluso, *Rich Forests, Poor People: Resource Control and Resistance in Java* (Berkeley: University of California Press, 1992); Madhav Gadgil and Ramachandra Guha, *This Fissured Land: An Ecological History of India* (Berkeley: University of California Press, 1993).

[4] The work of the late Jack Westoby has contributed much in furthering the process of self-criticism among foresters. See his collection *The Purpose of Forests: Follies of Development* (Oxford: Basil Blackwell, 1987).

[5] Cf. Mark Poffenberger, ed., *Keepers of the Forest: Land Management Alternatives in Southeast Asia* (West Hartford, Conn.: Kumarian Press, 1990).

such as "community management," "participatory development," and "joint forest management." While these terms have come into vogue in the last two decades, this chapter suggests that they have in fact a very long genealogy. Drawing on the Indian experience, it argues that, from the very beginning of state forestry, there have been serious attempts at democratizing regimes of resource management. Dissidents within the bureaucracy as well as intellectual activists outside it tried hard to make the state respond more sensitively to the claims of local communities. As we shall see, ongoing programs of joint forest management can draw legitimacy and sustenance from a struggle that is at least a century old.

II

The crucial watershed in the history of Indian forestry is undoubtedly the building of the railway network. In a famous minute of 1853 the Governor General of India, Lord Dalhousie, wrote of how railway construction was both the means for creating a market for British goods and the outlet for British capital seeking profitable avenues for investment. Between 1853 and 1910 more than 80,000 kilometers of track were laid in the subcontinent.[6] The early years of railway expansion witnessed a savage assault on the forests of India. Great chunks of these were destroyed to meet the demand for railway sleepers, over 1,000,000 of which were required annually. The sal forests of Garhwal and Kumaon, for instance, were "felled in even to desolation." "And, thousands of trees were felled which were never removed, nor was their removal possible."[7]

This depredation brought home most forcefully the fact that India's forests were not inexhaustible. The British were at this time unquestionably world leaders in deforestation, having burnt or felled hundreds of thousands of acres of woodland in Australia, southern Africa,

---

[6] Amba Prasad, *Indian Railways* (Bombay: Asia Publishing House, 1960).

[7] G.I. Pearson, "Sub-Himalayan Forests of Kumaon and Garhwal," in *Selections from the Records of the Government of the North-west Provinces*, second series, vol. II (Allahabad: Government Press, 1869), pp. 132–3. For the devastation in other parts of India, see Hugh Cleghorn, *The Forests and Gardens of South India* (London: W.H. Allen, 1860); and G.P. Paul, *Felling Timber in the Himalaya* (Lahore: Punjab Printing Company, 1871).

north-eastern United States, Burma, and of course India.[8] Knowing little of methods of sustained-yield forestry, they called in the Germans, who did. Thus in 1864 was started the Indian Forest Department which, for the first twenty-five years of its existence, was serenely guided by three German Inspectors General of Forest: Dietrich Brandis, Wilhelm Schlich, and Bertold von Ribbentrop.[9]

For its effective functioning the new department required a progressive curtailment of the previously untrammeled rights of use exercised by rural communities all over South Asia. An act was hurriedly drafted to establish the claims of the state to the forest land it immediately required, subject to the provision that existing rights not be abridged. This act was "infinitely milder and less stringent than that which is in force in most European countries."[10] The search commenced for a more stringent piece of legislation. In 1869 the Government of India circulated to the provinces a new draft act which sought to strengthen the state's control over forest areas through the regulation and in some cases the extinction of customary rights.

The new legislation was based on the assumption that all land not actually under cultivation belonged to the state. However, it was not easy to wish away the access to forests exercised down the centuries by peasants and other rural groups. The colonial state now argued that such use, however widespread and enduring, had been exercised only at the mercy of the pre-colonial monarch. Unless it had been expressly recorded in writing, customary use was deemed to be a privilege, not a right. Ergo, since the British government was the successor to Indian rulers, ownership of forests and waste now vested in it. "The right of conquest is the strongest of all rights," emphatically remarked one forest official: "it is a right against which there is no appeal."[11]

---

[8] The classic account of the links between British colonial expansion and global deforestation remains R.G. Albion's *Forests and Sea Power* (Cambridge, Mass.: Harvard University Press, 1926).

[9] E.P. Stebbing, *The Forests of India*, 3 vols (London: John Lane, 1922–7).

[10] As described by Henry Maine, "Statement of Objects and Reasons," September 14, 1864, in A Proceedings, nos 1–6, October 1864, Legislative Department Records, National Archives of India, New Delhi.

[11] C.F. Amery, "On Forest Rights in India," in Brandis and Smythies, eds, *Report on the Proceedings of the Forest Conference Held at Simla, October 1875*, p. 27.

There were, however, dissenting voices within the colonial government. Sent the draft forest bill by the Government of India, the Madras Government in turn invited responses from its various officers. The views of one such, Narain Row, Deputy Collector of Nellore, are completely representative. The proposed legislation, he said, had no historical precedent, for "there were originally no Government forests in this country. Forests have always been of natural growth here; and so they have been enjoyed by the people."[12] Another Deputy Collector, Venkatachellum Puntulu of Bellary, argued that the burden of the new legislation would fall most heavily on the poor. While large landlords would find it relatively easy to deny the state any claim over their forest property, unlettered peasants would not be able to prove rights of ownership, even though forests had traditionally been used by them as common property. Criticizing the detailed rules prohibiting the collection of different kinds of forest produce, Puntulu penetratingly remarked that

> the provisions of this Bill infringe the rights of poor people who live by daily labour (cutting wood, catching fish and eggs of birds) and whose feelings cannot be known to those whose opinions will be required on this Bill and who cannot assert their claims, like [the] influential class, who can assert their claims in all ways open to them and spread agitation in the newspapers.[13]

After several such responses had come in, the Madras Board of Revenue told the Government of India that the claim of the state to uncultivated forests and wastes was virtually non-existent:

> There is scarcely a forest in the whole of the Presidency of Madras which is not within the limits of some village and there is not one in which so far as the Board can ascertain, the state asserted any rights of property unless royalties in teak, sandalwood, cardamoms and the like can be considered as such, until very recently. All of them, without exception are

[12] "Memorandum on the Forest Bill," dated Nellore, May 8, 1871, in Board of Revenue Proceedings, nos 5739–89, Tamil Nadu State Archives, Chennai. I am grateful to Dr R. Prabhakar for alerting me to this source.

[13] No. 186, dated June 27, 1871, from Deputy Collector to Acting Collector, Bellary, in ibid.

subject to tribal or communal rights which have existed from time immemorial and which are as difficult to define as they are necessary to the rural population . . . [In Madras] the forests are, and always have been common property, no restriction except that of taxes, like the Moturpha [tax on tools] and Pulari [grazing tax] was ever imposed on the people till the Forest Department was created, and such taxes no more indicate that the forest belongs to the state than the collection of assessment shows that the private holdings in Malabar, Canara and the Ryotwari districts belong to it.

The Madras Government advanced three basic reasons for rejecting the bill drafted by the Government of India:

First, because its principles, scope and purpose are inconsistent with the existing facts of forest property and its history.

Second, because, even if the Bill were consistent with facts, its provisions are too arbitrary, setting the laws of property at open defiance, and leaving the determination of forest rights to a Department which, in this Presidency at all events, has always shown itself eager to destroy all forest rights but those of Government.

Third, because a Forest Bill, which aims at the regulation of local usages ought to be framed, discussed and passed by the local legislature.[14]

The objections were disregarded and in 1878 the new bill—the very bill I discussed within Chapter One of this book—was passed into law. The act divided the forests of the subcontinent into three broad classes. State or reserved forests were to be carefully chosen and demarcated into large and compact areas that could lend themselves to commercial exploitation. The constitution of these reserves was to be preceded by a legal settlement which either extinguished customary rights of user, transferred them as "privileges" to be exercised elsewhere, or, in exceptional cases, allowed their limited exercise. In the second class, "protected" forests, rights, and privileges were recorded but not settled. However, all valuable tree species were to be declared as "reserved" by the state, while the Forest Department had the power to prohibit grazing and other ostensibly damaging practices.

[14] "Remarks by the Board of Revenue, Madras," dated August 5, 1871, in A Proceedings, nos 43–142, March 1878, Legislative Department, National Archives of India, New Delhi.

The 1878 Forest Act also provided for a third class of forests: village forests. But as these lands had first to be constituted as reserved forests, the procedure aroused suspicion among the villagers, and this provision remained a "dead letter."[15] Meanwhile, the area of forests under state control steadily expanded. In 1878 there were 14,000 square miles of government forest. By 1890 this had increased to 76,000 square miles, three-fourths of which were reserved forests. Ten years later there were 81,400 square miles of reserved forests and 8,300 of protected forests. Given increasing demand for wood products, the state sought to establish firmer control over forests, both by expanding the area taken over under the act and by converting protected forests to reserved forests.

The Indian Forest Act of 1878 was a comprehensive piece of legislation that came to serve as a model for other British colonies. Within India it allowed the state to expand the commercial exploitation of forests while putting curbs on local use for subsistence. This denial of village forest rights provoked countrywide protest: rebellions in Chotanagpur in 1893, in Bastar in 1910, in Gudem–Rampa in 1879–80 and again in 1922–3, in Midnapur in 1920, in Adilabad in 1940. Even where discontent did not manifest itself as open and collective rebellion, it was expressed through arson and other breaches of the forest law.

The participants in these protests were unlettered peasants and tribals, and we know far more of their deeds than their words. Nonetheless their voices do figure here and there in the archives of the state, sometimes mediated by the language of the officials reporting them. Thus in the 1880s, when the government of the Bombay Presidency was aggressively demarcating the rich teak forests of the Dang district preparatory to their constitution as state reserves, a Bhil tribal chief sent in a petition stating: "we do not wish to let the Dang jungle [be] demarcated, for thereby we shall lose our rights and we and our poor rayat [cultivators] shall always be under the control of the Forest Department and the Department will always oppress us."[16] Around the same time the colonial state was attempting to take over the deodar

---

[15] B. von Ribbentrop, *Forestry in British India* (Calcutta: Government Press, 1900), p. 121.

[16] Quoted in Ajay Skaria, *Hybrid Histories: Forests, Frontiers and Wildness in Western India* (Delhi: Oxford University Press, 1999), p. 216.

forests of the upper Jamuna valley. These trees had suddenly become marketworthy—for the fast expanding railway network. A peasant, left helpless, could only bitterly observe: "the forests have belonged to us from time immemorial, our ancestors planted them and have protected them; now that they have become of value, government steps in and robs us of them."[17] Consider, finally, these remarks of an administrator in the Bastar district of Central India, on the determination of his tribal subjects to continue practicing swidden cultivation in what was now "government" forest:

> On the road from Tetam to Katekalyan I found general dissatisfaction at the restriction of penda [swidden] cultivation. I was unable to convince them of its evils [*sic*]. Podiyami Bandi Peda of Tumakpal has to get his son married and for this purpose he wants to cultivate penda in the prohibited area. I told him he should not do it. He replied plainly that he would cultivate it and go to jail as he had to get his son married.[18]

Back in 1871 the Madras Government had predicted that the new forest act, if passed into law, would "place in antagonism to Government every class whose support is desired and essential to the object in view, from the Zamindar [landlord] to the Hill Toda or Korombar."

This was an astonishingly accurate prophecy. The story of the numerous popular movements against state forestry, so long neglected by historians, is now attracting an array of chroniclers.[19] The central aim of this chapter, however, is to complement the story of popular resistance by telling the story of the now forgotten intellectual critics of colonial forestry. These critics were of two kinds. On one side were

---

[17] File no. 2, Department I, Pre–Mutiny Records, Uttar Pradesh State Archives, Dehradun.

[18] Quoted in Nandini Sundar, *Subalterns and Sovereigns: An Anthropological History of Bastar* (New Delhi: Oxford University Press, 1997), p. 154.

[19] See, among other works, Ramachandra Guha and Madhav Gadgil, "State Forestry and Social Conflict in British India," *Past and Present*, no. 123, May 1989; David Baker, "A 'Serious Time:' Forest Satyagraha in the Central Provinces," *The Indian Economic and Social History Review*, vol. 21, no. 1, 1984; Atluri Murali, "Whose Trees? Forest Practices and Local Communities in Andhra, 1600–1922," in David Arnold and Ramachandra Guha, eds, *Nature, Culture, Imperialism: Essays on the Environmental History of South Asia* (New Delhi: Oxford University Press, 1995); Sundar, *Subalterns and Sovereigns*.

scholars and politicians with a deep knowledge of rural conditions; these were also sometimes part of popular movements. Their criticisms of state forestry drew richly upon the feelings and grievances of the people most affected by it. On the other side were the rare, but for that reason significant, dissidents within the colonial bureaucracy who opposed the centralizing thrust of state forest policy. The first set were outsiders as far as the apparatus of rule was concerned, but insiders with respect to popular opinion and popular consciousness. The second set were by virtue of race and status outsiders to Indian society but insiders with regard to the policy of the state and the functioning of government.

III

Our story begins in 1878 with contemporaneous objections to the new forest act by the Poona Sarvajanik Sabha (Poona Peoples' Forum), a vastly respected nationalist organization in West India. Despite its middle-class origins, this sabha had consistently fought for the rights of the cultivator, urging that the colonial government lower its burden of taxation on the peasantry. Now, in the context of the forest act debate, it pointed out that state usurpation grossly violated customary rights over forests, for both "private grantees and village and tribal communities" had "cherished and maintained these rights with the same tenacity with which private property in land is maintained elsewhere." The Sarvajanik Sabha did not, however, merely oppose the proposed act for its excessive emphasis on state control; it offered a more constructive and creative alternative, arguing that better maintenance of forest cover could more easily be brought about by

> taking the Indian villager into confidence of the Indian Government. If the villagers be rewarded and commended for conserving their patches of forest lands, or for making plantations on the same, instead of ejecting them from the forest land which they possess, or in which they are interested, emulation might be evoked between neighbouring villages. Thus more effective conservation and development of forests in India might be secured and when the villagers have their own patches of forest to attend to Government forests might not be molested. Thus the interests of the

villagers as well as the Government can be secured without causing any unnecessary irritation in the minds of the masses of the Indian population.[20]

The sabha was here advocating a far more democratic structure of forest management than that envisaged by the colonial government. Indeed, it was proposing the institution of a Vrikshamitra (Friends of the Trees) Award more than a century before the Indian Government's Ministry of Environment and Forests conceived and named such a scheme for rewarding individuals and communities that had successfully protected or replenished forest areas.

Three years after the 1878 act was passed, the impact of state forestry on rural communities was foregrounded by the social reformer Jotirau Phule, himself a gardener by caste and exceptionally alert to the problems of the agricultural classes.[21] This is how he described the impact of the Forest Department on the livelihood of farmers and pastoralists in the Deccan countryside:

> In the olden days small landholders who could not subsist on cultivation alone used to eat wild fruits like figs and jamun and sell the leaves and flowers of the flame of the forest and the mahua tree. They could also depend on the village ground to maintain one or two cows and two or four goats, thereby living happily in their own ancestral villages. However, the cunning European employees of our motherly government have used their foreign brains to erect a great superstructure called the forest department. With all the hills and undulating areas as also the fallow lands and grazing grounds brought under the control of the forest department, the livestock of the poor farmers does not even have place to breathe anywhere on the surface of the earth.[22]

[20] Memorial to the Government of India from the Poona Sarvajanik Sabha and the inhabitants of the city and camp of Poona, dated March 3, 1878, in A Proceedings, nos 43–142, March 1878, Legislative Department Records, National Archives of India, New Delhi.

[21] Cf. Dhananjay Keer, *Mahatma Jotirau Phooley: Father of our Social Revolution* (Bombay: Popular Prakashan, 1964).

[22] Jotirau Phule, "Shetkaryacha Asud" (The Whipcord of the Cultivator) (1881; rpnt in Dhananjay Keer and S.G. Malshe, eds, *The Collected Works of Mahatma Phule* (Pune: Maharashtra Sahitya and Sanskriti Mandal, 1969). This quotation is translated from the Marathi by Madhav Gadgil.

This dependence of the agriculturist on the produce of forests and other common lands was even more acute in the tribal regions of middle India, where communities of hunter-gatherers, swidden agriculturists, and charcoal ironmakers were likewise at the receiving end of the new forest laws. Such people found an eloquent spokesman in Verrier Elwin (1902–64), a brilliant Oxford scholar and renegade priest who became the foremost interpreter of adivasi (tribal) culture in India.[23] A pioneer of ecological anthropology, Elwin's many works vividly showcase the intimate relationship between forests and the life-world of the adivasi. All tribals, he argued, had a deep knowledge of wild plants and animals; some could even read the great volume of nature like an "open book." Swidden agriculturists, for whom forest and farm shaded imperceptibly into each other, had a special bond with the natural world. They liked to think of themselves as children of *Dharti Mata*, Mother Earth, fed and loved by her.

Elwin's ethnographies are peppered with references to the adivasi's love for the forest.[24] Tragically, forest and game laws introduced by the British had made them interlopers in their own land. Elwin quotes a Gond whose idea of heaven was "miles and miles of forest without any forest guards."[25] As the anthropologist put it in 1941:

> The reservation of forests was a very serious blow to the tribesman. He was forbidden to practice his traditional methods of cultivation. He was ordered to remain in one village and not to wander from place to place. When he had cattle he was kept in a state of continual anxiety for fear they should stray over the boundary and render him liable to heavy fines. If he was a Forest Villager he became liable at any moment to be called to work for the Forest Department. If he lived elsewhere he was forced to obtain a license for almost every kind of forest produce. At every turn the Forest Laws cut across his life, limiting, frustrating, destroying his self

[23] Elwin's life and work are the subject of my book, *Savaging the Civilized: Verrier Elwin, His Tribals, and India* (Chicago: University of Chicago Press, 1999).

[24] See, especially, Verrier Elwin, *The Baiga* (London: John Murray, 1939); idem, *The Agaria* (Bombay: Oxford University Press, 1942).

[25] Verrier Elwin, *Leaves from the Jungle: A Diary of Life in a Gond Village* (London: John Murray, 1936), p. 22.

confidence. During the year 1933–4 there were 27,000 forest offences registered in the Central Provinces and Berar and probably ten times as many unwhipped of justice. It is obvious that so great a number of offences would not occur unless the forest regulations ran counter to the fundamental needs of the tribesmen. A Forest Officer once said to me: "Our laws are of such a kind that every villager breaks one forest law every day of his life."[26]

Elwin's writings were addressed equally to the colonial state and Congress nationalists who, in the 1940s, were very much a government-in-waiting. The Congress, however, had not been specially sensitive to the rights of tribals. Elwin reminded them that "the aboriginals are the real swadeshi [indigenous] products of India, in whose presence everything is foreign. They are the ancient people with moral claims and rights thousands of years old. They were here first: they should come first in our regard."[27] He was deeply distressed when a Congress report on tribals mimicked the British authorities in asking for a ban on shifting cultivation: Elwin's ethnographies had shown that, contrary to modern prejudice, swidden as practiced by the Baiga, the Juang, and other tribes was an ecologically viable system of cultivation. When nationalists recommended the ban he wrote angrily that "the forests belong to the aboriginal. I should have thought that anyone who was a Nationalist would at least advocate swaraj [freedom] for the aboriginal!"[28]

The significance of the forest in tribal life is a running theme in Elwin's work. Noting that a majority of tribal rebellions had centered around land and forests, he pleaded for the greater involvement of tribals in forest management in free India. Even if adivasis had no longer any legal rights of ownership, they had considerable moral rights. And, because tribals were as much part of the national treasure as forests themselves, there should be an amicable adjustment between forest

[26] Verrier Elwin, *Loss of Nerve: A Comparative Study of the Contact of Peoples in the Aboriginal Areas of Bastar State and the Central Provinces of India* (Bombay: Wagle Press, 1941), p. 12.

[27] Idem, *The Aboriginals* (Bombay: Oxford University Press, 1943), p. 32.

[28] Verrier Elwin to A.V. Thakkar, July 7, 1941, in the P. Kodanda Rao Papers, NMML, New Delhi.

management and tribal needs. Even where commercial forest operations became necessary, Elwin believed that these should be undertaken by tribal co-operatives, not by powerful private contractors.[29]

After Indian independence in 1947, Elwin became the first foreigner to be granted citizenship of free India. In 1954 he was appointed Adviser on Tribal Affairs to the Government of India with special reference to the North East Frontier Agency (NEFA). He was also to serve on more than one high-level all-India committee on tribal policy. From his first official appointment until his premature death in 1964, Elwin repeatedly urged a reconsideration of forest policy such that it might, at last, come to more properly serve tribal needs. In this he had little success for forest management became, if anything, more commercially oriented in independent India.

From a great Englishman who devoted his life to the service of the Indian poor we move to a great Englishwoman who did likewise. This was Madeleine Slade, the daughter of an admiral who came from England to join Mahatma Gandhi at Sabarmati Ashram in 1926. Gandhi adopted her as his daughter and gave her the name Mira Behn. She was to play a prominent role in the anti-colonial struggle, being jailed several times.

In 1945 Mira Behn set up a *kisan* (peasant) ashram near the holy town of Hardwar, and two years later moved up the Ganges beyond Rishikesh where the river descends onto the plains. In 1952 she shifted her base again, to the Bhilangna valley in the inner Himalaya. Here she stayed till 1959 when ill health and, just possibly, dissatisfaction with the policies of independent India, made her migrate to Austria.[30]

The peasants of the central Himalaya are, of course, as dependent on forest produce as the tribals of the Indian heartland with whom Elwin long worked. Here, one unfortunate consequence of state forest

[29] Verrier Elwin, *A Philosophy for NEFA*, 2nd edn (Shillong: Government Press, 1959), pp. 62, 66–7; "Advances in Freedom," undated essay from the late 1950s, in the Elwin Papers, NMML, New Delhi.

[30] She moved to Austria rather than back to England because her first inspiration had been Beethoven, whose spirit she now sought to imbibe in the environs of Vienna, where the composer had lived. There is, as yet, no biography of Mira Behn. Her memoirs are entitled *A Spirit's Pilgrimage* (London: Longmans, 1960).

management was the gradual replacement of *banj* oak (*Quercus incana*), a tree much prized by villagers as a source of fuel, fodder, and leaf manure, by *chil* (or *chir*) pine (*Pinus roxburghii*), a species more commercially valuable as the source of timber and resin.[31] This was a transition with serious ecological implications, for the thick undergrowth characteristic of banj forests absorbed a high proportion of the rain waters during the fierce Himalayan monsoon. This water then slowly percolated downhill. Below the oak forests were thus found "beautiful sweet and cool springs," the main source of drinking water for hill villagers. By contrast, the floor of pine forests was covered by thin needles which reduced absorptive capacity. In hillsides dominated by pine, rain rushed down the slopes, carrying away soil, debris and rock, leading to floods.

Why were banj forests disappearing in the Himalaya? Mira Behn's explanation revealed a sharp awareness of the sociology of forest management in the hills. "It is not merely that the Forest Department spreads the Chil pine," she said,

> but largely because the Department does not seriously organize and control the lopping of the Banj trees for cattle fodder, and . . . is glad enough from the financial point of view to see the Banj dying out and the Chil pine taking its place. When the Banj trees grow weak and scraggy from overlopping, the Chil pine gets a footing in the forest, and once it grows up and starts casting its pine needles on the ground, all other trees die out . . .

Mira Behn continued:

> It is no good putting all the blame on the villagers . . . The villagers themselves realize fully the immense importance of these Banj forests, without which their cattle would starve to death, the springs would dry up, and flood waters from the upper mountain slopes would devastate their precious terraced fields in the valleys. Indeed all these misfortunes are already making their appearance on a wide scale. Yet each individual villager cannot resist lopping the Banj trees in the unprotected Government forests. "If I do not lop the trees someone else will, so why not lop them, and lop them as much as possible before the next comer."

[31] The following discussion, as well as all the quotes therein, is drawn from Mira Behn, "Something Wrong in the Himalayas" (1952), in *Khadi Gramudyog*, vol. 39, no. 2, 1992.

It appeared that this short-sighted behavior of the hill peasant was related to the loss of community control. With the takeover of forests by the state, peasant families no longer had a long-term stake in the maintenance of forest cover. This tendency was aggravated by the commercial orientation of the Forest Department. Could anything be done to restore banj to its rightful place in Himalayan economy and ecology? Mira Behn suggested that

> The problem is not without solution, for if trees are lopped methodically, they can still give a large quantity of fodder, and yet not become weak and scraggy. At the same time, if the intruding Chil pines are pushed back to their correct altitude (i.e. between 3000 and 5000 feet), and the Banj forests are resuscitated, the burden on the present trees will, year by year, decrease, and precious fodder for the cattle will actually become more plentiful. But all this means winning the trust and co-operation of the villagers, for the Forest Department, by itself, cannot save the situation. Nor can it easily win the villagers' trust, because the relations between the Department and the peasantry are very strained, practically amounting to open warfare in Chil pine areas. Therefore, in order to awaken confidence in the people, some non-official influence is necessary.
>
> With the aid of local constructive workers, it should become possible to organize village committees and village guards to function along with the Forest Department field staff which should be increased, and also given special training in a new outlook towards the peasantry. In this way it should be feasible to carry out a well-balanced long-term project for controlled lopping and gradual return of the Banj forests to their rightful place, by systematic removal of Chil pines above 5500 feet altitude to be followed by protection of the young Banj growth. The Banj forests are the very centres of nature's economic cycle on the southern slopes of the Himalayas. To destroy them is to cut out the heart and thus bring death to the whole structure.

Mira Behn sent reports of her findings, with photographs, to Prime Minister Jawaharlal Nehru. He passed them on to officials but nothing seems to have come of it: the Indian Forest Department of the 1950s could not be easily made to change its ways.

IV

The quotations provided in the previous section all have a strikingly contemporary ring. To those who know something of the people behind them, they are also perfectly in character. Phule, Elwin, and Mira Behn, as well as the leaders of the Poona Sarvajanik Sabha, all had a deep knowledge of agrarian life. Alert to inequities brought about by the new laws, they polemicized vigorously on behalf of the victims of state forest management.

I now turn to a prophet of community forestry who came from the unlikeliest of backgrounds. He was a forest officer; in fact he was no less than the first Inspector General of Forests (IGF) in India. In his nineteen years (1864–83) as IGF, Dietrich Brandis laid the foundations of state forestry in India. A man of great energy, he toured the subcontinent widely, writing authoritative reports on the direction forest management should take in the various provinces of British India.[32] In the realm of silviculture he formulated systems of valuation and forest working still widely used. As a former university don (he came to the service of the Raj from the University of Bonn), Brandis started a college for training subordinate staff, arranged for higher officials to be trained on the Continent, and helped set up the Forest Research Institute in Dehradun.

My concern here is not with the scientific and administrative aspects of Brandis's legacy.[33] It is rather with his sociology of forest management, his understanding of the social and political contexts within which state forestry had to operate in India. Here, Brandis's views must be immediately distinguished from those of almost all other forest officials, Indian or European, before or since. These officials counterpose "scientific" forestry under state auspices to the customary use of forests by rural communities—the latter they hold to be erratic, unsystematic, wasteful, and short-sighted. It is thus that forest officials justify their territorial control of over a fifth of India's land mass, claiming they alone possess the technical skills and administrative competence to manage woodland.

To be sure, Brandis shared this creedal faith in the scientific status of sustained-yield forestry. He certainly believed that the state had a central role to play in forest management. What he did not share was

[32] A fascinating fictional portrait of Brandis is contained in Rudyard Kipling's short story "In the Rukh," in Kipling, *Many Inventions* (London: Macmillan, 1905).

[33] For which see Herbert Hessmer, *Leben und Werk von Dietrich Brandis (1824–1907)* (Dusseldorf: Westdeutscher Verlag, 1975).

his colleagues' wholesale skepticism of the knowledge base of rural communities. For instance, Brandis wrote appreciatively of the widespread network of sacred groves in the subcontinent. These he termed, on different occasions, the "traditional system of forest preservation" and examples of "indigenous Indian forestry." In his tours he found sacred woodlands "most carefully protected" in many districts, from the *devara kadus* of Coorg in the south to the deodar temple groves in the Himalaya. At the other end of the social spectrum Brandis also wrote appreciatively of forest reserves managed by Indian chiefs. He was particularly impressed by the Rajput princes of Rajasthan, whose hunting preserves provided game for the nobility as well as a permanent supply of fodder and small timber for the peasantry. The British stereotype of the Indian maharaja was a feckless and dissolute ruler; but, as Brandis pointed out, by strenuously preserving brushwood in an arid climate the Rajputs had "set a good example, which the forest officers of the British government would do well to emulate."[34]

In Brandis's larger vision for Indian forestry a network of state reserves would run parallel to a network of village forests. The Forest Department would take over commercially valuable and strategically important forests while simultaneously encouraging peasants to manage areas left out of these reserves. Through a series of reports and memoranda written over a decade the IGF tried to persuade the colonial government that a strong system of village forests was vital to the long-term success of state forestry.

The first such report was written in 1868 and pertained to the southern province of Mysore.[35] It is a closely argued document suggesting the creation of village forests throughout Mysore, managed on a rotational cropping system, with freshly cut areas closed to fire and grazing. Ideally, each hamlet would have its own forest, but in many cases it might become necessary to constitute a block to be used by a group of villages. Such forests would provide the following items free of charge to villagers: firewood for home consumption and for sale by

[34] D. Brandis, *Indian Forestry* (Woking: Oriental Institute, 1897), pp. 12–14; idem, *The Distribution of Forests in India* (Edinburgh: Macfarlane and Erskine, 1873), pp. 24–5.

[35] Mysore was at the time under direct British rule; only in 1881 was it reconstituted as a "princely state," under the rulership of the Wodeyar dynasty.

"poor people with headloads;" wood for agricultural implements and the making and repairing of carts; wood, bamboo, and grass for thatching, flooring, and fencing; leaves and branches for manure; and grazing except in areas closed for forest regeneration. On payment of a small fee wood would be made available for the construction of village homes and use by local artisans.

In Brandis's scheme these forests would be put under a parallel administrative system, with a Village Forester for each unit, a Forest Ranger for all village forests in each *taluk* (county), and a Head Forest Ranger for the district as a whole—this man reporting to an Assistant Conservator of Forests. He anticipated that the system would be self-supporting, with surplus used for local improvements. In this manner, peasants would come to feel an interest "in the maintenance and improvement of their forests." Brandis also hoped that Forest Department control over village forests would give way in due course, with the "leading men" of each village assuming responsibility for management.[36]

Forwarding his report to the Government of India, Brandis noted that it was "the first of a series of measures" which he proposed "to suggest in various Provinces for the better utilization and for the improvement of the extensive wastelands which will not be included in the State Forests;" that is, as a prelude to recommending a countrywide system of community forests.[37] Unhappily, British officials of the Raj lacked Brandis's understanding of the biomass economy of rural India, of the vital dependence of agrarian life on the produce of forests. They also lacked his faith in local knowledge and initiative. Opposition to Brandis claimed that his scheme would lead to a loss of state revenues while undermining the powers of district officials. Also invoked was an early version of the "Tragedy of the Commons" argument. For one official, "the village communities of Mysore, without cohesion and often split up into factions by caste, could not be entrusted with the powers, or competent to perform the functions assigned to them in [Dr Brandis's] scheme." Another commented that the scheme would

[36] D. Brandis, "On the Formation of Village Forests in Mysore," report of May 1868, Forest Proceedings, nos 63–6, June 1870, National Archives of India, New Delhi.

[37] Brandis to Secretary, Public Works Department, January 9, 1869, in ibid.

fail "as each man, when the least removed from supervision, would cut whatever he might require for himself without any regard to the interests of his neighbours..."[38] The Government of India's final negative verdict rested on a classic piece of colonial stereotyping. "The prejudices and rivalries of Natives," it said, "might be excited if men of different classes and castes shared in the same forests."[39]

This judgment was not lightly accepted by Brandis. In a defiant note he reviewed the case afresh and made another forceful plea in favor of village forests. He drew pointed attention to the flourishing system of community forests on the Continent, where scientific foresters exercised technical supervision over woodland managed for the exclusive benefit of villages and small towns. In Europe, he said:

> Such Communal Forests are a source of wealth to many towns and villages in Italy, France and Germany; property of this nature maintains a healthy spirit of independence among agricultural communities; it enables them to build roads, churches, school-houses, and to do much for promoting the welfare of the inhabitants; the advantages of encouraging the growth, and insisting on the good management of landed communal property, are manifold, and would be found as important in many parts of India as they have been found in Europe.[40]

Following his failure in Mysore, Brandis resurrected his proposals in the debate leading up to the 1878 Forest Act. He now urged the administration "to demarcate as state forests as large and compact areas of valuable forests as can be obtained free of forest rights of persons," while leaving the residual area, smaller in extent but more conveniently located for their supply, under the control of village communities. He hoped ultimately for the creation of three great classes of forest property based on the European experience: state forests, forests of villages

[38] L. Ricketts, Officiating Deputy Superintendent, Mysore, to Officiating Superintendent, Ashtagram Division, February 15, 1869; I.G. Cumming, Deputy Superintendent, Shimoga, to Superintendent, Nagar Division, February 22, 1869, both in ibid.

[39] Chief Commissioner of Mysore to Secretary, Public Works Department, Government of India, May 6, 1869; Resolution No. 172 in the Foreign Department, June 24, 1870, both in ibid.

[40] Note on "Village Forests, Mysore," by D. Brandis, May 28, 1870, in ibid.

and other communities, and private forests. State ownership had to be restricted, he argued, on account of the "small number of experienced and really useful officers" in the colonial forestry service, and out of deference to the wishes of the local population. For, "the trouble of effecting the forest rights and privileges on limited well-defined areas is temporary and will soon pass away, whereas the annoyance to the inhabitants by the maintenance of restrictions over the whole area of large forest tracts will be permanent, and will increase with the growth of population."[41]

This is an uncanny anticipation of the widespread popular opposition that has been such a marked feature of the subsequent history of Indian forestry. Brandis was overruled by more powerful civil servants within the colonial bureaucracy, and the 1878 Forest Act was based firmly on the principle of state monopoly.[42] But the German forester was a remarkably persistent man. As he remarked shortly after relinquishing the post of Inspector General of Forests, systematic forestry in India "was like a plant of foreign origin, and the aim must be to naturalize it." On the social side this process of indigenization could be accomplished by encouraging native chiefs, large proprietors, and especially village communities to develop and protect forests for their own use. In the last instance the initiative lay with the government, which, insisted Brandis, stood to gain enormously from a successful system of communal forests. "Not only will these forests yield a permanent supply of wood and fodder to the people without any material expense to the State," he wrote, "but if well managed, they will contribute much towards the healthy development of municipal institutions and of local self-government."[43]

[41] See especially, D. Brandis, "Explanatory Memorandum on the Draft Forest Bill," August 3, 1869, in Forests, B Proceedings, nos 37–47, December 1875, National Archives of India, New Delhi; D. Brandis, *Memorandum on the Forest Legislation Proposed for British India (Other than the Presidencies of Madras and Bombay)* (Simla: Government Press, 1875).

[42] For which see my essay, "An Early Environmental Debate: The Making of the 1878 Forest Act," *Indian Economic and Social History Review*, vol. 27, no. 1, 1990.

[43] D. Brandis, "The Progress of Forestry in India," *Indian Forester*, vol. 10, no. 11, November 1884, pp. 508–10.

In 1897, well into his retirement in Germany, Brandis returned to the subject of community forests. Long after he had severed all formal contacts with British India, he continued to be deeply concerned that Indian forestry should cease to have "the character of an exotic plant, or a foreign artificially fostered institution." This concern was consistent with his larger democratic vision for forestry in the subcontinent. He suggested that "native" forest officers, once they distinguished themselves in service, be sent to study the forestry system operating in Germany. Brandis had in mind their social as well as silvicultural education. Indian foresters, if sent to Germany, "will find that the villages, which own well-managed communal forests, are prosperous, although now and then they complain of the restrictions which a good system of management unavoidably imposes. What Indian Forest Officers will learn in this respect in Germany will be really useful to them in India."[44]

Perhaps by now Brandis despaired of *British* officials in India taking seriously his proposals for the constitution of village forests. Hence this indirect approach, whereby Indian forest officers trained on the Continent might be able to better see the benefits of community forests. In the event Indian officials, whether trained in Germany or not, have for the most part been hostile to any suggestion that local communities be encouraged to manage forest areas for their own use. It is, indeed, this territorial monopoly and indifference to the demands of rural communities that has made the Forest Department the object of such relentless criticism in recent years.

The Indian Forest Department has been the subject of sharp attack for its authoritarian style of functioning; and yet, in an interesting paradox, the founder of the department had himself anticipated that a narrow reliance on state control and punitive methods of management would lead to popular disaffection. While terms like "social forestry," "community forestry," and "joint forest management" have only now come into currency, the principles they embody would have been readily recognized, and indeed warmly commended, by the first head of the Forest Department in India.

---

[44] Idem, "Indian Forestry: The Extended Employment of Natives," *The Imperial and Asiatic Quarterly Review*, April 1897, esp. pp. 255–6.

V

For all their insight, knowledge, and passion, these precocious advocates of community forestry did not have much impact on state policy. Control and commercialization remained the dominant motifs of state forest policy. The chapter on village forests in the 1878 Act remained a dead letter. Government forest policy, in the colonial as well as post-colonial periods, continued to seriously ignore village needs, demands, and interests. The principle of state monopoly remained paramount, with one very partial exception, to which we now turn.

The Kumaon and Garhwal hills of present-day Uttar Pradesh contain the best stands of softwood in the subcontinent. These coniferous species have been highly prized since the early days of colonial forest management. Between 1869 and 1885, for example, some 6.5 million railway sleepers made from deodar were exported from the valley of the Yamuna in the princely state of Tehri Garhwal.[45] Adjoining Tehri Garhwal to the east was the British-administered Kumaon division, with its rich stands of chir pine. Here forestry operations concentrated simultaneously on expanding the area under chir (at the expense of oak) and exploiting the tree both for timber and resin. Between 1910 and 1920, for example, the number of trees tapped for resin increased from 260,000 to 2,135,000.[46] The pine trees of the central Himalaya were the only source, within the British empire, of oleo-resin, an extract with a wide range of commercial and industrial applications. Likewise, the timber of deodar and chir, as well as fir and spruce, constituted a strategically valuable resource for the colonial state, exploited with profit to service the military campaigns of the two world wars.

As we noted, in the Himalaya as elsewhere, commercial forestry under state auspices was made possible only through a denial of customary rights of ownership and use. In these hills, forests and grassland were a crucial resource for the agro-pastoral production system. In fact the fragmentary evidence available to historians suggests the existence of a fairly widespread system of common property resource management, evident from grass reserves walled in and well looked after, oak

[45] See N. Hearle, *Working Plan for the Tehri Garhwal Leased Forest* (Allahabad: Government Press, 1888).

[46] Stebbing, *Forests of India*, vol. III, p. 660.

forests managed by the village community, and sacred groves lovingly protected. Not surprisingly, the government's attempts to seize vast areas under local control and reconstitute them as "reserved forests" evoked opposition. In the early years of state forest management a petition from a discontented hillman evocatively recalled a golden age when the villagers had full control over their wooded habitat:

> In days gone by every necessities [*sic*] of life were in abundance to villagers than to others [and] there were no such government laws and regulations prohibiting the free use of unsurveyed land and forest by them as they have now. The time itself has now become very hard and it has been made still harder by the imposition of different laws, regulations, and taxes on them and by increasing the land revenue. Now the village life has been shadowed by all the miseries and inconveniences of the present day laws and regulations. They are not allowed to fell down a tree to get fuels from it for their daily use and they cannot cut leaves of trees beyond certain portion of them for fodder to their animals. But the touring officials still view the present situation with an eye of the past and press them to supply good grass for themselves and their [retinue] without thinking of making any payment for these things to them who after spending their time, money and labor, can hardly procure them for their own use. In short all the privileges of village life, as they were twenty years ago, are nowhere to be found now, still the officials hanker after the system of yore when there were everything in abundance and within the reach of villagers.[47]

When such verbal protests went unheeded, the sentiments underlying them became manifest in sustained resistance. In fact, this region probably witnessed more serious social conflict than any other forested region of India. There were major peasant movements against state forestry in 1904, 1906, 1916, 1921, 1930, and 1942.[48] These recurrent conflicts, remarked one sensitive official, were a consequence of "the struggle for existence between the villagers and the Forest Department; the former to live, the latter to show a surplus and what the department looks on as efficient forest management."[49]

[47] Petition to Sir James Meston, Lieutenant-Governor, United Provinces, from Pandit Madan Narayan Bist (village Ulaingad, Almora District), May 17, 1913, in File 398 of 1913, General Administration Department, Uttar Pradesh State Archives, Lucknow (grammar and punctuation as in the original).

[48] These protests are narrated in Guha, *The Unquiet Woods.*

[49] Percy Wyndham, Commissioner, Kumaun Division, to H.S. Crosthwaite,

The most significant forest protests in Kumaon and Garhwal took place in 1921. This took the shape of labor strikes which crippled the administration, followed by the widespread burning of pine forests. A total of 395 recorded fires burnt an estimated 2,46,000 acres of forest. Hundreds of thousands of resin channels were destroyed. Constituting a direct challenge to the state to relax its control over forest areas, these protests enjoyed enormous popular support, making it virtually impossible for the administration to detect the people responsible for the fires. The fires were generally directed at areas where the state was at its most vulnerable: for example, compact blocks of chir forest worked for timber and/or resin. Significantly, there is no evidence that the large areas of broad-leaf forest, also controlled by the state, were at all affected. Thus, arson was not random but carefully discriminating: it spared species more useful to the village economy.[50]

In the vanguard of the 1921 movement were soldiers who had fought for the British in the First World War. Kumaon and Garhwal had long supplied hardy and exceptionally brave soldiers for the British army. In fact, three of the five Victoria Crosses awarded to Indians in the 1914–18 war went to this region. These former men in uniform saw the forest regulations as a bitter betrayal of their interests by the white overlord for whom they had so recently risked their lives. Their protests alarmed the colonial state, for, apart from being a reservoir of able-bodied men whom it hoped to continue recruiting for future wars, the Kumaon hills bordered both Nepal and Tibet, regions not under direct British suzerainty but in which it had strong trading and political interests.

In the wake of these popular protests, a magisterial critique of government forest policy was published by Govind Ballabh Pant. Pant was a rising lawyer from a peasant household in Almora who went on to become one of the foremost Indian nationalists, taking office after independence successively as Chief Minister of Uttar Pradesh and Home Minister of the Government of India. His 1922 booklet *The Forest Problem in Kumaun* described the "burial of the immemorial and indefeasible rights of the people of Kumaun," burial, that is,

Secretary to Government, United Provinces, February 21, 1921, in Forest Department File 109 of 1921, Uttar Pradesh State Archives, Lucknow.

[50] For details, see Guha, *The Unquiet Woods*, chapter 5.

"between the property-grabbing zeal of the revenue officers and the exhortations of experts of the forest department . . ." As he put it, with legal precision: "the policy of the Forest Department can be summed up in two words, namely, encroachment and exploitation." Several decades of a single-minded commercial forestry had led to a manifest deterioration of the agrarian economy. "Symptoms of decay are unmistakably visible in many a village," wrote Pant.

> Buildings are tottering, houses are deserted, population has dwindled and assessed land has gone out of cultivation since the policy of [forest] reservation was initiated . . . Cattle have become weakened and emaciated and dairy produce is growing scarce every day: while in former times one could get any amount of milk and other varieties for the mere asking, now occasions are not rare when one cannot obtain it in the villages, for any price for the simple reason that it is not produced there at all.[51]

Pant's analysis was rooted in a deep knowledge of the local context. He took it upon himself to combat the charge, commonly levied against the hill peasant, "of reckless devastation," a charge "sedulously propagated by prejudiced or ignorant persons." In his opinion:

> The spacious wooded areas extending over the mountain ranges and hill sides bear testimony to the care bestowed by the successive generations of the Kumaonies. All of them are not of spontaneous growth and specially the finer varieties bespeak his labour and instinct for the plantation and preservation of the forest. A natural system of conservancy was in vogue, almost every hill top is dedicated to some local deity and the trees on or about the spot are regarded with great respect so that nobody dare touch them. There is also a general impression among the people that everyone cutting a tree should plant another in its place . . . Grass and fodder reserves are maintained, and even *nap* [cultivable] lands are covered with trees, wherever, though in few cases could such land be spared from the paramount demand of cultivation. Special care is also taken by the villagers to plant and preserve trees on the edges of their fields . . .[52]

From this analysis the solution logically offered was to give back to the peasants the forest land that they traditionally regarded as being within

[51] G.B. Pant, *The Forest Problem in Kumaun* (1922; rpnt NainiTal: Gyanodaya Prakashan, 1983), pp. 39, 84, 70–1, 72.

[52] Ibid., pp. 75–6.

their village boundaries. "If the village areas are restored to the villagers, the causes of conflict and antagonism between the forest policy and the villagers will disappear, and a harmony and identity of interests will take the place of the distrust, and the villager will begin to protect the forests even if such protection involves some sacrifice or physical discomfort." Pant envisaged that these areas would be under the control of village *panchayats* (councils), under whose direction the "natural system of conservancy" would once again come to the fore. As he shrewdly observed, "some restrictions will be there, *but these will proceed from within, and will not be imposed from without.*"[53]

After the 1921 protests, a Kumaon Forest Grievances Committee was set up by the Government of the United Provinces. This committee toured the hills, examining some 5000 witnesses. Peasant activists submitted dozens of petitions to the committee on behalf of individual villages. These identified blocks of forest near every village where peasants would have exclusive rights of fuel and fodder collection, timber for building, wood for plows, bamboos for basket-making, and so on. It was being proposed that villagers should have full rights over these forests which they would manage through their own panchayat.[54]

Based on the evidence it collected the committee concluded that "any attempt to strictly enforce these [forest] rules would lead to riots and bloodshed." It divided the existing reserved forests into two categories: Class I, which were to be managed not by forest officials but by the civil administration—which was in theory more sympathetic to rural needs; and Class II, constituting commercially valuable wooded areas which were to remain with the Forest Department. It also recommended that the government consider the constitution of village forests as per the demands of the people of Garhwal and Kumaon.[55]

Bureaucracies move at their own pace, and it was only in 1930 that rules were passed allowing for the formation of *van panchayats* (village

---

[53] Ibid., pp. 87–8, emphasis added.

[54] "Garhwal Janta ki Janglaat Sambandi Maang" (The Forest–Related Demands of the People of Garhwal), *Garhwali* (Hindi weekly published from Dehradun), June 18, 1921.

[55] Report of the Kumaon Forest Grievances Committee, in A Proceedings, nos 19–24, June 1922, in File 522 of 1922, Department of Revenue and Agriculture (Forests), National Archives of India, New Delhi.

forests), in the hill districts of the United Provinces. These allowed for a forest patch to be handed over to a village if it lay within its settlement boundaries, and if more than a third of its residents had applied for permission to the Deputy Commissioner (DC). Once the DC gave the go-ahead, then the villagers elected, by voice vote, a council (*panch*) of five to nine members. This council in turn elected a head (*sarpanch*) among themselves. The van panchayat was empowered to close the forest for grazing, regulate the cutting of branches and the collection of fuel, and organize the distribution of forest produce. It could appoint a watchman whose salary would be paid by villagers' contributions to the panchayat. The panchayat could levy fines, although if the offender did not pay it had then to go to the civil courts for redressal. The felling of trees, however, required the prior permission of the Forest Department. The department also claimed 40 percent of the revenue from any commercial exploitation. Of the rest, 20 percent would go to the *zilla parishad* (district council), with the balance 40 percent kept with the DC on behalf of the van panchayat. With that official's written consent, the villagers could use the funds for roads, schools, and other local "improvements."

There are now in excess of 4000 van panchayats in Kumaon and Garhwal covering an area of a little less than 500,000 hectares. An official report of 1960 remarked that many of these village forest councils had done "exemplary work in connection with forest protection and development."[56] An independent survey conducted thirty years later found that panchayat forests are often in a better condition than reserved forests. Of 21 van panchayats surveyed in 3 districts, the forest stock in 13 panchayats was of good condition, in 4 of medium condition, in 3 of poor condition. The researcher supervising the survey concluded that

> Van panchayats have, by and large, maintained oak forests very well, especially in contrast to the dismal condition of the reserves (except for those reserves distant from habitations). The position in respect of chir forests is not so clear, but these seem to have done about as badly under van panchayat control as in the reserves. Various studies suggest that, overall,

[56] *Report of the Kumaun Forests Fact Finding Committee* (Lucknow: Government of Uttar Pradesh, 1960), p. 37.

panchayat forests seem to be in as good or better condition than the reserves.[57]

The van panchayat system constitutes the only network of village forests mandated by law in the whole of India.[58] The concession was made by a colonial state worried about losing control in a sensitive and strategically important border region, and the model was not to be replicated elsewhere. After independence, the van panchayat regime was not extended to the adjoining region of Tehri Garhwal, where Mira Behn worked in the 1950s, and where it could very well have contributed to renewing oak forests. Within Kumaon, too, there has been great resentment over curbs placed on the autonomous functioning of van panchayats.[59] Though technically under the control of villagers, the Forest Department can veto schemes for improvement, while of the revenue generated 40 percent is swallowed by the state exchequer; 40 percent of the rest is by law granted to the village, but this money too first finds its way into a "consolidated fund" controlled by the DC, to which individual panchayats have then to apply. There are signs of a movement to do away with these constricting rules, to make the management of panchayats come fully under the control of villagers. A chronicler of this discontent, himself quite aware of the long history of forest-related protests in Kumaon and Garhwal, writes that "those

[57] E. Somanathan, "Deforestation, Incentives and Property Rights in Central Himalaya," *EPW*, January 26, 1991. These conclusions are reinforced by my own field visits to Kumaon and Garhwal in 1981, 1983, and 1990.

[58] This statement needs to be slightly qualified. Madhu Sarin (personal communication) informs me that in 1985 the Government of Orissa enacted rules allowing for the constitution of village forests. However, the extent of these forests and their status is unclear. Again, immediately after the First World War, panchayat forests were initiated in the Madras Presidency. These functioned desultorily for several decades and were finally wound up. Cf. Franklin Pressler, "Panchayat Forests in Madras, 1913–52," paper presented to the Second Conference of the American Society of Environmental Historians, Duke University, May 1987.

[59] S.L. Shah, *Functioning of Van Panchayats in Eight Hill Districts of Uttar Pradesh: An Analysis of Present Malaise and Lessons for Future in the Context of the Proposed Van Panchayat Niyamwali* (mimeo, Almora: the author, 1989); Vishwa Ballabh and Katar Singh, *Van Panchayats in Uttar Pradesh Hills: A Critical Analysis* (Anand: Institute of Rural Management, 1988).

who know the history of forest struggles say that . . . the van panchayat movement will be the biggest such movement in the hills."[60]

VI

This chapter has traced the long debate on community forestry in India. It has shown that, from the very inception of state forestry, there have been critics who argued for a democratization of resource control, for a correction of the commercial bias promoted by successive governments, for a proper participation in management and decision-making by local user groups. Arguments first offered in the 1870s and reiterated in subsequent decades were revived, or should one say reinvented, in the 1970s by the now famous Chipko movement. It is no accident that Chipko originated in Garhwal and Kumaon, the part of India which has seen some of the most serious conflicts between state and peasantry over forest resources.

The 1970s were also marked by a series of forest movements in different parts of India. These took place in the Himalaya, in the Western Ghats, and, above all, in the vast tribal belt extending across the heart of the Peninsula. In the Chotanagpur plateau, forest protests formed an integral part of the larger movement for a separate tribal homeland of Jharkhand, to be carved out of the huge, unwieldy, and predominantly non-tribal state of Bihar. In one much celebrated case tribals demolished a plantation of teak (a highly prized furniture wood) that was coming up on land previously under the sal tree (*Shorea robusta*), a species of far greater benefit to the local economy. Their slogan, "Sal means Jharkhand, sagwan [teak] means Bihar," was a one-sentence critique of the narrow commercial orientation of state forestry.[61]

Over the past three decades now there has been an ongoing, nationwide debate on forest policy in India, a debate fueled by the continuing social tension in forest areas and the evidence of massive deforestation provided by satellite imagery. This debate has passed through three

[60] Jai Prakash Pawar, "Chipko ki Parampara mein ab Van Panchayatain Janta ko Andolit kar Rahi Hain" (The Tradition of Chipko is Making the People Prepare for an Upsurge on the Question of Van Panchayats), *Naini Tal Samachar*, September 1, 1994 (my translation).

[61] Cf. Peoples Union for Democratic Rights, *Undeclared Civil War*.

distinct if chronologically overlapping phases. The first might be designated the "politics of blame." Here, activists speaking on behalf of disadvantaged groups have held forest officials responsible for environmental degradation and popular discontent. The officials, in turn, have insisted that growing human and cattle populations are the prime reason why fully half of the 23 percent of India legally designated as "forest" is without tree cover.

The forestry debate of the 1970s and 1980s drew at times on the heritage of earlier movements and critiques. The peasants of Garhwal and Kumaon, as I found out while doing fieldwork there, were acutely conscious of how Chipko had drawn on a long and honorable history of peasant resistance to state forestry. Tribal activists in Madhya Pradesh and Bihar, meanwhile, were not unfamiliar with the work and message of Elwin. And in the villages of the Deccan social workers liked to offer the very words by Phule, reproduced earlier in this chapter, as proof that proper access to forests and pasture was vital to survival, and that it was the "great superstructure" of the Forest Department which continued to deny herders and farmers this access.[62]

As tempers cooled and the polemic exhausted itself, there came a second phase which we might call the "politics of negotiation." In villages and state capitals, forest officers and their critics found themselves at the same table, talking and beginning to appreciate, if not fully understand, the other's point of view. Concessions were made by each side, protests suspended by one and leases of forest produce to industry cancelled by the other. One product of the growing dialog between activists and bureaucrats was the approval by India's parliament in 1988 of a new National Forest Policy. Where the ruling Forest Policy of 1952 had stressed state control and industrial exploitation, the new document instead emphasized the imperatives of ecological stability and peoples' needs.

Then, slowly and hesitatingly, began the third phase which we can term "the politics of collaboration." In the state of West Bengal, for example, the Forest Department initiated remedial action on its own, abandoning its traditional custodial approach by inviting peasants to co-operate with it. Thousands of village forest protection committees

[62] Anon., *Whither Common Lands?* (Dharwad: Samaj Parivartan Samudaya, 1988).

(VFPCs) were constituted, each of which agreed to protect nearby forests in collaboration with the state. These VFPCs signed individual agreements with the Forest Department, pledging to protect forests from outsiders and smugglers, not to graze their cattle in areas undergoing reproduction, and not to lop tree branches. In exchange they were allowed to enter the forests on foot to take away firewood and collect non-timber forest produce such as honey, fruit, and rope-making material. Each village was also granted 25 percent of the final timber harvest undertaken by the Forest Department—this an unprecedented concession because over the past century all such monies had been credited directly into the state treasury.

In this manner, previously authoritarian government officials joined with previously suspicious villagers to jointly manage forests. As time went by, the scheme was refined to make the division of rights and responsibilities more precise. The incentive for village participants was also increased by making their share 40 percent of the timber harvest. In some parts of Bengal the new programs have been spectacularly successful. Badly degraded sal forests have been regenerated so successfully in fact that they now attract migratory elephants in search of food. A steady stream of benefits has ensued to the local economy and the conflict between state and peasant has come down to very manageable levels.[63]

The success of Joint Forest Management (JFM) in West Bengal has encouraged scholars, activists, and sympathetic civil servants to demand its replication in other parts of India. Outside its original home, however, the progress of JFM has been slow. Administrative styles and cultures of governance vary widely among the states and regions of India. So do individual orientations, with some forest officials still loath to relinquish control; while others have been inspired to start village protection committees on their own.

A mapping of the forestry debate in contemporary India would therefore show significant regional variation. In some states it is still

[63] Cf. K.C. Malhotra and M. Poffenberger, *Forest Regeneration through Community Protecton: The West Bengal Experience* (Calcutta: Indian Statistical Institute, 1989); S. Palit, "Structural Changes in Forest Departments," paper presented at the workshop organized by the World Wildlife Fund (WWF)–India, Hyderabad, March 14–15, 1997.

stuck in the politics of blame; in others, it has moved tentatively on to the politics of negotiation. In West Bengal and parts of Andhra Pradesh, Madhya Pradesh, and Himachal Pradesh it has gone further, embracing the politics of collaboration through the creation of JFM regimes. In this last scenario, too, there is abundant room for improvement. For the JFM model promoted by the Government of India reflects and sometimes reinforces inequities within rural society. Gender and caste are two axes of discrimination, with women and low-caste members of the village community not having adequate representation or voice in the decision-making process (this is also true, to a great extent, of van panchayats in Kumaon.) Likewise, pastoral groups and artisans who have legitimate claims on forest resources are sometimes given short shrift. Moreover, forest officials still claim a monopoly of "scientific expertise," refusing to entertain villagers' own ideas on species choice, spacing, and harvesting techniques.[64]

One serious problem with the JFM model, as currently promoted by the state and donor agencies, is that it allows for the constitution of village forest committees only on forest land with less than 40 percent crown cover. This is a deeply constricting rule which exclusively reserves to the state rights over the best wooded lands of India. Thus, forests situated close to hamlets cannot come under JFM regimes if they have more than 40 percent tree cover. Again, the regulations, strictly interpreted, would mean that if local communities were to effectively protect and replenish degraded lands, such that the crown cover exceed that magic figure of 40 percent, the state could step in and

[64] There is a growing literature on these issues. Among the studies I have found especially useful are: Madhu Sarin, *et al.*, *Who is Gaining? Who is Losing? Gender and Equity Concerns in Joint Forest Management* (New Delhi: Society for Promotion of Wastelands Development, 1998); Bhaskar Vira, "Institutional Changes in India's Forest Sector, 1976–1994—Reflections on Policy," Research Paper Number 5, Oxford Centre for the Environment, Ethics and Society, November 1995; Sushil Saigal, *Beyond Experimentation: Emerging Issues in the Institutionalization of Joint Forest Management in India* (New Delhi: Society for Promotion of Wastelands Development, 1997); K. Sivaramakrishnan, "Comanaged Forests in West Bengal: Historical Perspectives on Community and Control," *Journal of Sustainable Forestry*, vol. 7, nos 3/4, 1998; Nandini Sundar, "Unpacking the 'Joint' in Joint Forest Management," *Development and Change*, vol. 31, no. 2, 2000.

remove the area from JFM—a bizarre outcome indeed. Nor have changes in policy and orientation been accompanied by concomitant changes in legislation. The present regime is not flexible enough to allow spontaneous community-initiated forest regimes to exist along with more orthodox JFM regimes. In some parts of India the Forest Department is casting a covetous eye on areas well protected by village communities. Thus, in the Uttar Pradesh hills the old established panchayat forests managed by villagers are sought to be brought under the JFM system only so that bureaucrats have a greater say in their management. A new, carefully-thought-out Indian Forest Act is required which allows both for areas to be managed under state-village partnerships as well as by self-generated, autonomous community regimes.

One can thus envision a fourth, possibly final, phase for the Indian forestry debate, the "politics of partnership." For collaboration, even where it does exist, takes place on terms set down by the state, through officials of the Forest Department. We need to move to a more inclusively democratic structure where the state listens to and learns from the community, and where the community recognizes and deals fairly with the inequities within its own ranks.

Although their path has been anything but smooth, contemporary advocates of decentralized forestry have had somewhat greater success than their precursors. One reason for this is the altered political context. While Brandis, Pant & Co. worked under an authoritarian colonial regime, the partisans of Chipko and similar movements operated in a democratic political system. The revival of forest protest in the 1970s also coincided with the international environmental debate which foregrounded the use and abuse of forests worldwide. The work of Indian scholars had, meanwhile, demonstrated with authority that the century-old history of state forestry in India had to be reckoned a failure from both an ecological as well as a social point of view. Finally, the problems with government-directed development programs in much of the developing world had led to an increasing interest in non-governmental forms of management and control.

These calls for forest reform from the outside, so to say, were complemented by pressures for change from within. Starting in West Bengal, the governors themselves, that is, forest officials in charge of their vast landed estate, realized that old methods of control and exclusion were merely fueling social conflict. An overworked and underfunded bureaucracy then slowly started to involve communities in forest working. What began as a strategic imperative became, at least for some forest officers, a sincere change of heart. Once critics from without were being echoed by dissidents from within, the process of reform accelerated. This is indeed the signal lesson of Indian forest history: namely, that meaningful policy change comes about only when the sustained pressure by social movements and their intellectual sympathizers resonates with the feelings of powerful officials within the state bureaucracy. One or the other, by itself, will not do. When, in the 1870s, Brandis was active, he was handicapped both by being a lone dissident voice within the Forest Department and by the fact that there had not yet emerged an effective critique from outside. When, in the 1940s and 1950s, Elwin and Mira Behn articulated the feelings and aspirations of peasants and tribals, the forest bureaucracy was, collectively and to the last man, deaf to their arguments and entreaties. Forest policy remained unbending and unchanging, with the exception only of the Kumaon hills. There, as we have seen, popular protests and external critics were partially successful not because of honest rethinking by the state but because of its concern that this sensitive border region must not be tempted into outright rebellion. Elsewhere, because this political imperative did not exist, the colonial regime refused to heed the widespread criticism of its exploitative forest system.

In more recent times, however, the radical critics have been aided by the auto-critique of influential sections of the forest establishment. This confluence of external pressure and internal rethinking explains why and how contemporary proponents of community forestry have, unlike their predecessors, been able to see their ideas and polemic translated into official policy and (though less assuredly) into official practice. Nonetheless, there are striking parallels between the ideas underlying the application of JFM today and the prescience of brave but for the most part unheard critics of state forestry discussed earlier in this chapter. With respect to the role of forest-dependent communities, for example, there is a shared faith in indigenous knowledge, in the management capacity and robustness of local institutions, and above all a sharp focus on local access to the usufruct of forests. Again, with respect to the role of the state, there is a common recognition of the essentially advisory role of the Forest Department, of its need to collaborate with rather than strictly regulate customary use, and of the justice of sharing revenues from forest-working with villagers. Then as now, critics have called strongly for attitude change among state officials, for retraining and retooling in keeping with the democratic spirit of the age. Finally, both past and present proponents of decentralization seem to converge in their larger vision of forest policy in India, a vision which, in my understanding, consists of three cardinal principles: (i) that benefit sharing (between state and community) and local control are the key incentives to ensuring sustainable management; (ii) that community-controlled forests must work as a complement to a network of more strictly protected areas, further from habitations that continue under more direct state control; (iii) that the restricting of state control to these latter areas is vital on grounds of equity (respect for local rights and demands), efficiency (as the most feasible course, with the state not biting off more than it can chew), and stability (as the most likely way to reduce conflict).

There is little question that ongoing attempts at reversing or mitigating state monopoly over forest ownership and management constitute a significant departure from past trends. In a deeper sense, however, contemporary attempts at fostering participatory systems of forest management hark back to a much older tradition. In the late twentieth century, as in the late nineteenth century, there arose a movement for the democratization of forest management, for a system founded not on mutual antagonism but on genuine partnership between state and citizen. The first Inspector General's vision for Indian forestry was abruptly cast aside by his contemporaries, but it may yet come to prevail.

Were that to happen, it would vindicate the work of, among others, Dietrich Brandis, Jotirau Phule, Verrier Elwin, Mira Behn, Govind Ballabh Pant, and the Poona Sarvajanik Sabha.

CHAPTER 5

Authoritarianism in
the Wild

Where will be taxonomists and evolutionists when cows and corns dominate the earth?—**Hugh Iltis (1967)**

If biologists want a tropics in which to biologize, they are going to have to buy it with care, energy, effort, strategy, tactics, time and cash.—**Daniel Janzen (1986)**

Conservation and biology are interdependent and inseparable because biology is at the heart of *all* phases of conservation and is the *ultimate arbiter* of its success and failure.—**David Ehrenfelds (1987)**

Any grandiose plan for the conservation of wild life without adequate provision for human interests is doomed to fail. Conservation in developing countries often has to be a compromise between scientific idealism and practical reality.—**Raman Sukumar (1985)**

When India became independent in 1947 it had less than half a dozen wildlife reserves; it now has in excess of 400 parks and sanctuaries covering 4.3 percent of the country (there have been proposals to double the area). Wildlife conservation controls big territory and is now big business too. Nor is India exceptional in this regard. In response to a growing global market for nature tourism, and egged on by strong domestic pressures, other Asian and African nations have undertaken ambitious programs to conserve and demarcate habitats and species that need to be "protected for posterity."

One might, at a pinch, identify five major groups that together fuel the movement for wildlife conservation in the developing world. The first are the city dwellers and foreign tourists who merely season their lives, a week at a time, with the wild. Their motive is straightforward: pleasure and fun. The second group consists of ruling elites who view the protection of particular species, for example the tiger in India, as central to the retention or enhancement of national prestige. Spurring on this process are international conservation organizations such as the International Union for the Conservation of Nature and Natural Resources (IUCN) and the World Wildlife Fund (WWF—now renamed the Worldwide Fund for Nature), who work with a sense of mission at educating people and politicians about the virtues of biological conservation. A fourth group consists of functionaries of the state forest or wildlife service, mandated by law to be in physical control of the parks. While some officials are genuinely inspired by a love of nature, the majority—at least in India—are motivated merely by the power and spin-off benefits (overseas trips, for example) that come with the job. The final group are biologists who believe in wilderness and species preservation for the sake of science.

These five groups are united in their hostility to farmers, herders, swiddeners, and hunters who have lived in the wild from well before it became a park or sanctuary. Conservationists see these communities as causing a destructive effect on the environment, their forms of livelihood aiding the disappearance of species and contributing to soil erosion, habitat simplification, and worse. Often their feelings are expressed in strongly pejorative language. Touring Africa in 1957, one prominent member of the Sierra Club sharply attacked the Masai for grazing cattle in African sanctuaries. He held the Masai as illustrating the larger trend in which "increasing population and increasing land use," rather than industrial exploitation, constituted the main threat to the world's wilderness. The Masai and "their herds of economically worthless cattle," he said, "have already overgrazed and laid waste to much of the 23,000 square miles of Tanganyika they control, and as they move into the Serengeti, they bring the desert with them, and the wilderness and wildlife must bow before their herds."[1]

[1] Lee Merriam Talbot, "Wilderness Overseas," *Sierra Club Bulletin*, vol. 42, no. 6, 1957.

Thirty years later the WWF initiated a campaign to save the Madagascar rainforest, the home of the Ring Tailed Lemur, the Madagascar Serpent Eagle, and other endangered species. Their fund-raising posters had spectacular sketches of the lemur and the eagle and of the half-ton Elephant Bird which once lived on the island but is now extinct. Man "is a relative newcomer to Madasgascar," noted the accompanying text, "but even with the most basic of tools—axes and fire—he has brought devastation to the habitats and resources he depends on." The posters also had a picture of a muddy river with the caption: "Slash-and-burn agriculture has brought devastation to the forest, and in its wake, erosion of the topsoil."[2]

The WWF posters succinctly sum up the conservationist position with regard to tropical rainforests. This view is that the enemy of the wild is the hunter and farmer living in the forest who is too short-sighted for his and our good. This belief, or prejudice, has informed numerous projects spread across the globe, advocating nature parks that throw out the original human inhabitants of these areas, with scant regard for their past or future. All this is done in the name of the global heritage of biological diversity. Cynics might fairly conclude, however, that tribals in the Madagascar and Amazon forest are expected to move out so that men in London and New York have the comfort of knowing that the lemur and toucan have been saved for posterity. Evidence of all this conservation is then provided them by the wildlife documentary that they watch on their home theatre screens.

II

Let me now focus on the motives and motivations of one of the groups outlined above: conservation biologists. Biologists have, of course, been in the vanguard of the environmental movement. The author of *Silent Spring*, the book that sparked modern environmentalism, was the biologist Rachel Carson, as were numerous scholars and writers who contributed to shaping the environmental debate of the 1960s and 1970s. Think, for example, of the influence once enjoyed by

[2] These quotations are from a WWF poster on display at the School of Forestry and Environmental Studies, Yale University, in the summer of 1989.

Garret Hardin, Paul Ehrlich, and Ray Dasmann in the United States: of C.J. Brejér in the Netherlands; of F. Fraser Darling and Julian Huxley in the United Kingdom; and of Björn Gillberg and Hans Palmstierna in Sweden. These examples could be multiplied.

As a science, biology differs in three major respects from physics and chemistry. First, biologists are taught to look for interdependence in nature, viewing individual life forms not in isolation but in relation to one another. Second, ever since Darwin biologists have been oriented toward longer time frames, thinking in eons and generations rather than months and years. Third, biologists have a direct professional interest in species other than their own. As ornithologists, botanists, and zoologists they are willy nilly more alert to the interests of bird, plant, and animal life. It must be said at once that this interest in other species sometimes blinds them to the legitimate interests of less fortunate members of their own species.

The impatience with other humans is especially marked among conservation biologists, for whom farmers and forest dwellers have come to represent a messy obstacle to the unimpeded progress of scientific research. A "seeming goal of humanity," writes Daniel Janzen in the *Annual Review of Ecology and Systematics,*

> is to convert the world to a pasture designed to produce and sustain humans as draught animals. The challenge, in which the tropical ecologist is a general, knight, foot soldier, and technical specialist, is to prevent humanity from reaching this goal. *The true battle, is, however, to reprogram humanity to a different goal.* The battle is being fought by many more kinds of professionals than just ecologists; however, it is a battle over the control of interactions, and by definition, the person competent at recognizing, understanding, and manipulating interactions is an ecologist.[3]

While the article's military metaphors and its publication in a prestigious scientific journal are noteworthy, Janzen is only reiterating a well-worn theme. Long before him, a similar claim was made by a botanist from the University of Wisconsin:

> If there is *anybody* who should provide *leadership in the preservation movement* it is the systematic or environmental *biologist . . .* We are not only citizens and humans, each with individual desires. We are not only trained

[3] Daniel Janzen, "The Future of Tropical Ecology," *Annual Review of Ecology and Systematics,* vol. 17, 1986, p. 307, emphasis added.

taxonomists and ecologists, each perhaps wishing to preserve the particular organisms with which we work. But we, the taxonomists and ecologists, are the *only ones in any position to know* the kinds, the abundance and the geography of life. This is a knowledge with vast implications for mankind, and therefore vast responsibilities. *When nobody else knows, we do know* where the wild and significant areas are, we know what needs to be saved and why, and only we know what is threatened with extinction.[4]

Consider, finally, an assessment of global conservation by Michael Soulé which complains that the language of policy documents has "become more humanistic in values and more economic in substance, and correspondingly less naturalistic and ecocentric." Soulé seems worried that in theory—though mercifully not in practice!—some national governments and international conservation organizations (ICOs) now pay more attention to the rights of human communities. Proof of this shift is the fact that "the top and middle management of most ICOs are economists, lawyers, and development specialists, not biologists." We have here a sectarian plaint, a trade-union approach to the problem, spurred by an alleged "takeover of the international conservation movement by social scientists, particularly economists."[5]

Soulé's essay, with its fear of conspiracies and takeover bids, well illustrates the paranoia of a community of scientists which has a huge influence on conservation policy but yet wants to be the sole arbiter. A scholar acclaimed by his peers as the "dean of tropical ecologists" has expressed this ambition more nakedly than most. I have already quoted from a paper by Daniel Janzen in the *Annual Review of Ecology and Systematics*; I now quote from his 1986 report on a new national park in Costa Rica whose tone and thrust perfectly complements that of his ostensibly scientific essay. "We have the seed and the biological expertise: we lack control of the terrain," he says. This situation he was able to remedy by raising enough money to purchase the forest area needed to create the Guanacaste National Park. One can only marvel at Janzen's conviction that he and his fellow biologists know all while the

[4] Hugh Iltis, "Whose Fight is the Fight for Nature," *Sierra Club Bulletin*, vol. 9, no. 9, 1967, pp. 36–7, emphasis added.

[5] Michael Soulé, "The Tigress and the Little Girl," manuscript of a book since published, chapter 6: "International Conservation Politics and Programs."

inhabitants of the forest know nothing. He justifies taking over the forest and dispossessing forest farmers by claiming that "today virtually all of the present-day occupants of the western Mesoamerican pastures, fields and degraded forests are *deaf, blind and mute* to the fragments of the rich biological and cultural heritage that still occupies the shelves of the unused and unappreciated library in which they reside."[6] Janzen once told an admiring interviewer that he wanted to plan "protected areas in a way that will permanently accommodate solitude-seeking humans as well as jaguars, tapirs, and sea turtles . . ." These solitude-seeking humans might include backpackers, deep ecologists, and biologists, but not it appears indigenous farmers or fishermen.[7]

Again, in an editorial written for the prestigious journal *Conservation Biology*, Janzen asked his fellow biologists—professors as well as graduate students—to devote 20 percent of their funds and time to tropical conservation. He calculated that the 500 million dollars and the 20,000 man-years thus generated would be enough to "solve virtually all neotropical conservation problems." He asks: "What can academics and researcher committees do," and offers this answer: "Significant input can be anything from voluntary secretarial work for a fund-raising drive to a megamaniacal effort to bootstrap an entire tropical country into a permanent conservation ecosystem." His assumption is that money plus biologists suffice to solve the conservation problems of the tropics. Janzen's self-assurance is such that he is unlikely to have been struck by an alternative solution, namely that biologists would do better to throw themselves into a megamaniacal effort to bootstrap but one temperate country—Janzen's own—into living off its own resources.[8]

What we have here is an ecologically updated version of the white man's burden. The biologist, replacing the colonial civil servant or military official, knows it is in the native's "true" interest to abandon his hearth and home, leaving field and forest clear for the new rulers of his domain—not the animals with which he once coexisted but the

[6] Daniel H. Janzen, *Guanacaste National Park: Tropical Ecological and Cultural Restoration* (San Jose: Editorial Universidad Estatal a Distancia, 1986), p. 11, emphasis added.

[7] See David Rains Wallace, "Communing in Costa Rica," *Wilderness*, no. 181, Summer 1988.

[8] See *Conservation Biology*, vol. 1, no. 2, October 1988.

biologists, park managers, and wildlifers who now collectively determine how his territory is to be managed. For Costa Rica we only have Janzen's word for it; for other areas we are better placed to challenge the conservationist's point of view. A remarkable book on African conservation has laid bare the imperialism, unconscious and explicit, of Western wilderness lovers and biologists working on that continent. I cannot summarize the massive documentation of Raymond Bonner's *At the Hand of Man*, but here is a sampling of his conclusions:

> Above all, Africans [have been] ignored, overwhelmed, manipulated and outmaneuvered—by a conservation crusade led, orchestrated and dominated by white Westerners.

> Livingstone, Stanley and other explorers and missionaries had come to Africa in the nineteenth century to promote the three C's—Christianity, commerce and civilization. Now a fourth was added: conservation. These modern secular missionaries were convinced that without the white man's guidance, the Africans would go astray.

> [The criticisms] of egocentricity and neo-colonialism . . . could be leveled fairly at most conservation organizations working in the Third World.

> As many Africans see it, white people are making rules to protect animals that white people want to see in parks that white people visit. Why should Africans support these programs? . . . The World Wildlife Fund professed to care about what the Africans wanted, but then tried to manipulate them into doing what the Westerners wanted: and those Africans who couldn't be brought into line were ignored.

> Africans do not use the parks and they do not receive any significant benefits from them. Yet they are paying the costs. There are indirect economic costs—government revenues that go to parks instead of schools. And there are direct personal costs [i.e. of the ban on hunting and fuel collecting, or of displacement].[9]

And now consider the remark of a Zambian biologist on the same lines:

> Many conservation policies in Africa tended to serve foreign interests, such as tourism and safari hunting, and largely ignored African environmental values and cultures. In fact, the only thing that is African about most

[9] Raymond Bonner, *At the Hand of Man: Peril and Hope for Africa's Wildlife* (New York: Alfred A. Knopf, 1993), pp. 35, 65, 70, 85, 221.

conventional conservation policies is that they are practiced on African land.[10]

Bonner's book focuses on the elephant, one of the half dozen or so animals that have come to acquire "totemic" status among Western wilderness lovers. Animal totems existed in most pre-modern societies but, as the Norwegian anthropologist Arné Kalland points out, in the past the injunction not to kill totemic species applied only to members of a group. Hindus do not ask others to worship the cow, but those who love and cherish the elephant, seal, whale, or tiger try and impose a worldwide prohibition on their killing. No one, they say, *anywhere*, *anytime*, will be allowed to touch the animal they hold sacred even if—as with the elephant and several species of whale—scientific evidence has established that small-scale hunting will not endanger its viable populations and will, in fact, save human lives put at risk by the expansion (as a consequence of total protection) of the *lebensraum* of the totemic animal. The new totemists also insist that their species is the "true, rightful inhabitant" of the ocean or forest, and ask that human beings who have coexisted for hundreds of years with the animals be taken out and sent elsewhere.[11]

The rise of conservation biology in the late twentieth century has an uncanny similarity to the rise of scientific forestry in the late nineteenth century. Both disciplines lay claim to the same territory—uncultivated parts of the globe that are covered with what one group of scientists defines as "forest," the other as "wild." The parallels in their methods and aims are striking. As foresters did once, biologists now use alarmist and hyperbolic language to canvass public support. As foresters talked once of threats to social stability and economic growth posed by the non-availability of natural resources, biologists speak now—again in apocalyptic tones—of the dangers to civilization posed by the loss of

[10] E.N. Chidumayo, "Realities for Aspiring Young African Conservationists," in Dale Lewis and Nick Carter, eds, *Voices from Africa: Local Perspectives on Conservation* (Washington: World Wildlife Fund, 1993), p. 49.

[11] Arné Kalland, "Seals, Whales and Elephants: Totem Animals and the Anti-Use Campaigns," in *Proceedings of the Conference on Responsible Wildlife Management* (Brussels: European Bureau for Conservation and Development, 1994). Also idem, "Management by Totemization: Whale Symbolism and the Anti-Whaling Campaign," *Arctic*, vol. 46, no. 2, 1993.

biodiversity. This rhetoric is a prelude to the privileging of their own knowledge: the argument is that only they have the expertise to deal effectively with the problem to which they direct our attention. Biologists have followed foresters in forming professional associations and professional journals to advance their interests: *Conservation Biology* and the Society for Conservation Biology being analogs of the Society of American Foresters and the *Journal of Forestry*, products of the scientific crusades of an earlier age. Finally, like foresters, biologists disparage and diminish other forms of knowledge, in particular the knowledge of local people and communities.

III

To turn now to a controversy in my own bailiwick. The Nagarhole National Park in southern Karnataka has an estimated forty tigers, the species toward whose protection enormous amounts of Indian and foreign money and attention have been directed. Now Nagarhole is also home to about 6000 tribals who have been in the area longer than anyone can remember, almost as long perhaps as the tigers. The state Forest Department wants the tribals out, claiming they destroy the forest and kill wild game. The tribals answer that their demands are modest, consisting in the main of fuelwood, fruit, honey, and the odd quail or partridge. They do not own guns: only affluent coffee planters living on the edge of the forest do. Maybe these planters poach big game? In any case, they ask the officials, if the forest is only for tigers, why have you invited India's biggest hotel chain, the Taj Group, to build a resort inside it while you plan to throw us out?

Into this controversy jumps a green missionary passing through Karnataka. Dr John G. Robinson works for the Wildlife Conservation Society in New York, for whom he oversees 160 projects in 44 countries. He conducts a whistlestop tour of Nagarhole and hurriedly calls a press conference in the state capital, Bangalore. Throwing the tribals out of the park, he says, is the only means to save the wilderness. For the biologist this is not a one-off event in relation to Nagarhole, but a sacred and universal principle. So Robinson claims that "relocating tribal or traditional people who live in these protected areas is *the single most important step towards conservation.*" Tribals, he explains, "*compulsively hunt for food,*" and compete with tigers for prey. Deprived of food, tigers cannot survive, and "their extinction means that the balance of the ecosystem is upset and this has a snowballing effect."[12]

One does not know how many tribals Robinson met, very likely none. Yet the Nagarhole case is depressingly typical. All over India the management of parks has sharply opposed the interests of poor tribals who have traditionally lived in them against the interests of wilderness lovers and urban pleasure seekers who wish to keep parks "free of human interference." This means, of course, free of other humans whose presence will dilute their pleasure. These conflicts are being played out in the Rajaji sanctuary in Uttar Pradesh, in Simlipal in Orissa, in Kanha in Madhya Pradesh, in Melghat in Maharashtra and in numerous other locations.[13] Everywhere, Indian wildlifers have ganged up behind the Forest Department to evict tribals and rehabilitate them far outside the forests. In this they have drawn sustenance from Western biologists and conservation organizations who have thrown the prestige of science and the power of the dollar behind the campaign to kick the original owners of the forest out of their homes.

To be sure, as the Sanskritist Robert Goldman reminds us, in the Indian subcontinent the dispute between those who have an aesthetic appreciation of nature and those who seek to use nature for subsistence goes back a very long way. In fact the epic Ramayana has its origins in just such a conflict. Its putative first author, the poet Valmiki, on a stroll through the forest, admiringly watches "an inseparable pair of sweet-voiced *kraunca* birds wandering around," when a "Nisada hunter, filled with malice [*sic*] and intent on mischief [*sic*], struck down the male of the pair." When the fallen bird "uttered a piteous cry," Valmiki curses the hunter with an early death, and does so in a verse of perfect metrical quarters, "each with a like number of syllables, and fit for the accompaniment of stringed and percussion instruments." Hearing the poet convey his *soka*, or grief, in such an exquisitely crafted *sloka*, or verse, Brahma appears and commands him to tell the story of the great king Rama in that form.[14] So, perhaps, Valmiki was the original

[12] *The Deccan Herald*, Bangalore, November 5, 1995, emphasis added.

[13] A useful countrywide overview is provided in Ashish Kothari, Saloni Suri, and Neena Singh, "Conservation in India: A New Direction," *Economic and Political Weekly*, October 28, 1995.

[14] See Robert Goldman, ed. and transl., *The Ramayana of Valmiki: An Epic*

ecotourist, and that Nisada the first subsistence hunter to fall foul of an authoritarian form of conservation. Their conflict certainly gave us an imperishable epic in verse. For the present-day victims of authoritarian conservation there is, alas, no such consolation.

Green missionaries today are possibly as dangerous, and certainly more hypocritical, than their commercial and religious counterparts. The globalizing advertiser and banker works for a world in which everyone, regardless of class or color, is in an economic sense an American: driving a car, drinking Pepsi, owning a fridge and washing machine. The missionary, having discovered Christ, wants all pagans to share the discovery. The conservationist wants to protect the tiger or whale for posterity yet expects *other* people to make the sacrifice.

Moreover, the processes unleashed by green imperialism are more or less irreversible. The consumer titillated into eating Kentucky Fried Chicken can always say "once is enough." The Hindu converted to Christianity can decide later to revert to his original faith. But the poor tribal, thrown out of his home by the propaganda of the conservationist, is condemned to the life of an ecological refugee.

A partisan of the tribal might answer Dr Robinson and his ilk in various ways. He might note that tribals and tigers have coexisted for centuries; it is the demands of cities and factories that have of late put unbearable pressures on the forest, with species after species being put on the endangered list. Tribals are being made scapegoats while the real agents of forest destruction—poachers, planters, politicians, profiteers—escape notice. As Dr Robinson flies off to the next project on his list of 160 such, he might reflect on his own high-intensity lifestyle which puts a greater stress on the world's resources than dozens, perhaps hundreds, of forest tribals. The tribal partisan will point out the glaring inequity in the fact that even as plans were afoot to evict tribals from Nagarhole, the Taj Group was welcomed in to build a posh hotel. Meanwhile, the Forest Department has applied for American money to build seven patrol stations and a network of roads connecting them. This, it is claimed, is necessary for greater vigilance against poachers, when what it will in fact do is further open the forest to external and

of Ancient India: Volume I: Balakanda (Princeton: Princeton University Press, 1985), pp. 127–9.

privileged penetration. Our tribal partisan might argue, finally, that a policy which treats forest dwellers as enemies rather than partners can only be counterproductive. What this policy will encourage, in time, is poachers and smugglers of ivory and sandalwood who can count on tribal acquiescence in the battle against the common enemy, the Forest Department.[15]

All this was said more eloquently many years ago by Verrier Elwin. Unlike Dr Robinson, he was no foreigner in a hurry but, as we saw, a Western scholar who made his home among the tribals and forests of India. Writing in 1963, after some thirty years of experience, Elwin deplored the "constant propaganda that the tribal people are destroying the forest." He asked pointedly how tribals "could destroy the forest. They owned no trucks; they hardly had even a bullock-cart; the utmost that they could carry away was some wood to keep them warm in the winter months, to reconstruct or repair their huts and carry on their little cottage industries."

Who then is the real culprit? Elwin tells us of the

> feeling amongst the tribals that all the arguments in favour of preservation of forests are intended to refuse them their [rights]. They argue that when it is a question of industry, township, development work or projects of rehabilitation, all these plausible arguments are forgotten and vast tracts are placed at the disposal of outsiders who mercilessly destroy the forest wealth with or without neccesity.[16]

IV

The main difference between Elwin's time and ours is the growing influence of wildlife fanatics. In the past the tribal was expected to give way to the juggernaut of "development," so that his forest abode could be claimed by iron mines, steel plants, and large dams. That mission is now joined by the gospel of total conservation in which the interests of the tiger are always elevated above the interests of the tribal.

That Elwin reversed this order of priority is, of course, not unrelated

[15] Cf. "Tribals Ready for Confrontation over Nagarhole Resort," *The Times of India* (Bangalore edition), August 30, 1996.

[16] Verrier Elwin, *A New Deal for Tribal India* (New Delhi: Ministry of Home Affairs, 1963), pp. 54–5.

to the fact that his profession, anthropology, tends to place the concerns of humans, especially vulnerable humans, above all else. But the issue is too serious to be reduced to a matter of which discipline privileges which species. Culturally sensitive biologists have, from time to time, also uttered warnings about the dangers of neglecting, in programs of wilderness and wildlife conservation, the rights of communities who live in and around protected areas. Three such, writing in 1949, 1977, and 1994 respectively, illustrate my point. First, the botanist M.S. Randhawa, notable here for his alertness to farmers' interests even if he uses the now discarded distinction between "useful" and "harmful" species:

> With the liquidation of the feudal order . . . the problem of wildlife preservation has acquired a new significance. Whatever may be the faults of princes and rajahs, it must be said to their credit that they preserved the wild animals and forests of their states rather well. With the growing demands of cultivators who want to save their crops from harmful animals, there is need of clear formulation of policy. There is immediate need of initial survey of all proposed National Parks areas. While there is necessity of maintenance of good vegetational balance and preservation of rich flora and fauna in the National Park areas, the general wildlife policy must be such as will not prejudice the use of developed agricultural land. The interests of the cultivator and the lover of nature must be harmonized. The apprehensions of farmers that the National Parks and Nature Reserves will develop into uncontrolled sanctuaries where pests and weeds will be allowed to flourish, and which will spread into surrounding agricultural lands, must be allayed. The biologist must give lists of harmful and useful birds and animals. While the friends of the cultivator should be encouraged in the National Parks, the enemies must be exterminated. The biologist should also give a finding whether campaigns should be started for the destruction of wild boars, porcupines, monkeys, bats and parrots who cause enormous damage to crops and gardens. Before any such campaigns are started, it should be ascertained whether wholesale destruction of certain birds or animals may not have harmful repercussions, on account of the upsetting of [the] balance of power between various organisms.[17]

[17] M.S. Randhawa, "Nature Conservation, National Parks and Bio-Aesthetic Planning in India," Presidential Address, Section of Botany, in *Proceedings of the Thirty-Sixth Indian Science Congress* (Allahabad: 1949), pp. 87–103.

A second example is the great ornithologist Sálim Ali, who comes straight to the point without recourse to the dubious division between good and bad species:

> No conservation laws or measures can succeed fully unless they have the backing of informed public opinion, which in our case means the usually illiterate village cultivator. In other words, unless we can make the villager understand, and convince him of the logic in expecting him to preserve the tiger or leopard that has deprived him of maybe his sole worldly possession—the cow which moreover provided the meagre sustenance for himself and his family—how can we induct his willing cooperation? Similarly, how can we expect him to see any sense in being asked not to destroy the deer or pig that have ravaged the crops which he has toiled for months to raise, and on which all his hopes are banked? Admittedly this is going to be a very difficult task, but I believe it is not impossible if we could but find the right approach. We have never really tried enough. Devising a realistic strategy is now a challenge to all conservationists.[18]

Finally, I give below some remarks by the ecologist Raman Sukumar, whose work on the Indian elephant has highlighted conflicts—as manifest in incidents of manslaughter and the destruction of crops—between large animals protected in national parks and farmers who live on the periphery:

> It is both unrealistic and unjust to expect only a certain section of society, the marginal farmers and tribals, to bear the entire cost of depredatory animals. We have to work towards ameliorating the impact of wildlife on people if conservation of wildlife and their habitats is to gain acceptance among such people who interact with these in their daily lives . . . Today the local people see sanctuaries or national parks as simply the pleasure resorts of the affluent. There is urgent need to reorient management of our wildlife reserves so as to pass on economic benefits to local communities . . . If an adequate proportion of the income derived from tourism is retained by the local economy there would be increased motivation for people to value wildlife and their habitats . . . It is time we take bold new approaches towards reconciling economic development with conservation.

[18] Sálim Ali, "Presidential Letter: Wildlife Conservation and the Cultivator," *Hornbill,* April–June 1977.

In relation to the elephant–human conflict in South India, Sukumar has outlined several "bold new approaches." He has urged just compensation for the loss of life (which at present varies, depending on the province, from a niggardly Rs 2000 to Rs 15,000, that is, from $45 to $350) and for damage to crops. He also believes that, in some cases, trenches and electric fences dissuade elephants and other large mammals from trespassing into habitations and fields. Most radically, he states that "wildlife populations that come into severe conflict with human interests may have to be directly managed to keep their levels below [in]tolerable limits." He goes on to explain what the euphemism "directly managed" actually means:

> It is clear that the adult male elephants are inherently more predisposed to raiding crops as a consequence of social organization. The removal of an adult male elephant from the population would have a far greater effect in reducing crop-damage (by a factor of 20 in economic terms) and saving human lives than the removal of an elephant from a family herd. Our understanding of demographic processes in such polygynous species also shows that the loss of a certain proportion of males is not likely to affect the intrinsic rate of growth of the population. The removal of females from the population would certainly reduce its growth rate. Hence, the selective culling of male elephants identified as inveterate crop raiders or rogues would be the best form of population management.[19]

Sukumar's recommendations are the outcome of years of careful and patient scientific work, yet they have run up against the brick wall of the dominant wilderness fanaticism which currently drives policy. Most conservationists remain uninterested in working toward a "realistic" strategy. Forest departments will not pay tribals and forest dwellers proper compensation, claiming it will open the floodgates for all kinds of rustics making all sorts of forged claims. Other biologists, and wildlife lovers in general, will not countenance talk of culling, either on

[19] R. Sukumar, "Wildlife–Human Conflict in India: An Ecological and Social Perspective," in Guha, ed., *Social Ecology*. The empirical research from which these recommendations flows is reported in Raman Sukumar, *The Asian Elephant: Ecology and Management* (Cambridge: Cambridge University Press, 1989); cf. also the thesis on which the book is based: "Ecology of the Asian Elephant and its Interaction with Man in South India," Centre for Ecological Sciences, Indian Institute of Science, Bangalore, 1985.

moral grounds—all life is sacred—or on instrumental ones—which species will we have to manage next?[20]

And so the tension around national parks continues. Angered by conservationists, villagers in Karnataka and Tamil Nadu were more than willing to aid the notorious sandalwood and elephant smuggler Veerappan, who at least took care of their stomachs. So, elephants raided crops and killed the occasional villager while Veerappan cheerfully eluded thousands of security personnel, who took nearly two decades to catch and kill him.

Conflicts such as these have led the more thoughtful Indian ecologists to reject the notion that species and habitat protection can succeed only through the punitive approach favored by the majority of wildlife conservationists, domestic and foreign. Biologists like Sukumar have sought to actively resolve conflicts between large mammals and humans, while sociologists such as Ashish Kothari, who have rich field experience, plead for a more democratic system of park management in which the voices of local communities can be heard loud and clear.

These conservationists wish to indigenize and democratize wildlife management, such that (to paraphrase Dietrich Brandis) it ceases to possess the character of a foreign plant. By no means do they wish to see a world completely dominated by cows, corn, and those who raise them. They have time for the tiger and the rainforest, and they want to protect islands of nature not yet fully conquered by man. Their plea is, rather, to put wilderness protection in its place, to recognize it as a distinctively North Atlantic brand of environmentalism whose export and expansion must be done with caution, care, and above all humility. For, in the poor and heavily populated countries of the South,

[20] Culling goes contrary to the ideology of deep ecology that provides philosophical cover to authoritarian biologists and conservationists. Another unfortunate case concerns crocodiles raised near Madras by Romulus Whitaker and his colleagues. They have successfully bred thousands of crocodiles in captivity, but they await permission from the Government of India to harvest a species that they have convincingly demonstrated is no longer endangered. The permission has not been forthcoming despite the fact that it will generate substantial amounts of foreign exchange to the state (from the sale of leather bags and the like), and provide employment and income to the Irula tribals with whom Whitaker works.

protected areas cannot be managed with guns and guards. It is imperative here that we take full cognizance of the rights of the people who lived in, and often cared for, the forest before it became a national park or a World Heritage Site.[21]

The present philosophy and practice of conservation is flawed also in a scientific as much as social sense.[22] In much of the Third World, national park management is heavily imprinted by the American experience. In particular, it takes over two axioms of wilderness thinking: the monumentalist belief that the only real wilderness is "big, continuous wilderness," and the claim that *all* human intervention is bad for the retention of diversity. These axioms have led to the constitution of large sanctuaries, each covering thousands of square miles, and a total ban on human ingress in the core areas of national parks. At the same time, little or no thought has been given to the conservation of diversity outside these protected areas.

These axioms, "giganticism" and "hands off nature," though sometimes cloaked in the jargon of science, are simply prejudices. If it is realized that the preservation of *plant* diversity is possibly more important than the preservation of large mammals, a decentralized network with many small parks makes far greater sense. Such a network might build on the numerous sacred groves that still dot the Indian landscape. Yet modern wilderness lovers are averse to this, for they are in principle opposed to local control and prefer centralized management. Belief in an absolute ban on human intervention is equally misguided, for studies show that the highest levels of biological diversity are often found in areas with some (though not excessive) intervention. By opening up new niches occupied by insects, plants, and birds, partially disturbed ecosystems often have greater diversity than untouched areas.

[21] For thoughtful ideas and suggestions on how the interests of wild species and poor humans might be made more compatible, see M. Gadgil and P.R.S. Rao, "A System of Positive Incentives to Conserve Biodiversity," *EPW*, August 6, 1994.

[22] The following three paragraphs draw on my essay, "The Two Phases of American Environmentalism: A Critical History," in Frederique Appfel-Marglin and Stephen Marglin, eds, *Decolonizing Knowledge: From Development to Discourse* (Oxford: Clarendon Press, 1996).

The dogma of total protection can have tragic consequences. In the celebrated Keoldeo Ghana bird sanctuary in Bharatpur in 1982, scientists forbade villagers from exercising traditional grazing rights. When the villagers protested, the police opened fire, killing several of them. When the ban was enforced in subsequent years, the population of key bird species, for example waterfowl and the Siberian crane, declined because cattle grazing, by keeping down the tall grass, had helped these bird species forage for insects. Grazing was thus beneficial for the park, but the pill was too bitter to swallow, and scientists have refused to lift the ban.[23]

V

The mirror image of the "authoritarian biologist" is a personality type we might call the "anthropocentric socialist." This type believes that the interests of humans, especially poor humans, must always take precedence over animals, even gravely endangered animals. A leading human rights activist in India likes to cite the Chenchus, a community of hunter-gatherers who were asked to make way for a tiger reserve in the southern Indian state of Andhra Pradesh. The problem, writes K. Balagopal, is that these tribals "have to pay for the protection of tigers while no one pays for the conservation of their communities." As one Chenchu told a visitor from the state capital, "If you love tigers so much, why don't you shift all of them to Hyderabad and declare that city a tiger reserve?"[24]

Making the same point, albeit in more gentle language, are villagers in the Indonesian island of Timpaus. As reported by Harald Beyer Broch:

> Some islanders have heard that foreign organizations work for protection of crocodiles, and that they succeed to the point that it is difficult to sell crocodiles in Indonesia today. Many of the present villagers said they would

[23] Personal communication from Madhav Gadgil. In the famous Valley of Flowers, high up in the Himalaya, a ban on grazing has reportedly led to the local extinction of several species for much the same reason: personal communication from Mahendra Singh Kunwar.

[24] K. Balagopal, "A Little More of the Same," *Seminar* (New Delhi), no. 412, December 1993.

like these protectionists to live in villages where crocodiles are a threat, as they were in Timpaus some twenty years ago. That experience would prob-ably have made them change their opinion. It might be easier to want to protect animals that you never encounter, than those that may eat you next day.[25]

The authoritarian biologist and the anthropocentric socialist re-present two extremes of the spectrum. Through much of the 1980s the wildlife debate was conducted between votaries of these antinomies. Then there came along the "pragmatic scientist," who sought to har-monize the imperatives of species conservation with the interests of farmers and herders living around protected areas.

The distance between the pragmatic scientist and the authoritarian biologist is very nearly the distance between Raman Sukumar and Daniel Janzen. The former wants to marry conservation to economic development, to reconcile the rights and needs of humans and ani-mals. He is willing to talk to, and learn from, anthropologists and human rights activists. The latter, on the other hand, thinks that the conservation biologist must have a completely free hand in the design and management of nature reserves.

However, there is also a fourth participant in the debate, a type we may call the "democratic scientist." This type moves beyond his "pragmatic" colleagues in at least three ways. First, in being more ecumenical with regard to scale, whereby small patches of refugia, such as sacred groves and ponds, are given the some loving attention as large areas of wilderness. Second, in being more ecumenical with regard to species, with rare plants, including cultivated plants, and insects being valued along with large mammals. Third, in respecting not just human rights but also the knowledge systems of local communities so that folk ecological knowledge is incorporated within the management of conservation regimes.

These ideas, and others akin to them, underlie a fascinating study of India's biodiversity co-ordinated by the pioneering environmental group Kalpavriksh. Covering all of India's states and union territories,

[25] Harald Beyer Broch, "Local Resource Dependency and Utilization: Environmental Issues as seen from Timpaus, Indonesia," paper presented at the Workshop on Environmental Movements in Asia, Leiden, October 27–29, 1994.

this was the most participatory exercise in environmental planning ever undertaken in the country's history: it is also, most likely, without parallel elsewhere in the world.

Kalpavriksh worked with state and central governments, NGOs, scientists, and peasant and tribal communities to produce nearly a hundred plans grouped under political regimes, ecological zones, and subject themes. Each report aimed at integrating the *ecological security* of the region or state with the *livelihood security* of humans most critically dependent on its biodiversity. It studied and critically assessed biodiversity in the wild as well as in cultivated areas and placed special focus on the rights of women and children—the main cultivators and collectors of this biodiversity.

The final technical report, summarizing all the others, recommended that, in matters pertaining to biodiversity management, "the State [should] become a facilitator rather than a ruler" by nurturing "a decentralized natural resource governance structure." It argued that a viable long-term policy must "strengthen and support community conservation areas . . . across the entire rural land/waterscape."

The Kalpavriksh report is a deeply interesting document best viewed, from the perspective offered here, as a state of the art presentation of the democratic scientist's point of view.[26]

VI

Early in 2005 a vigorous debate broke out within India about the status of the country's national animal, the tiger. Reports began appearing in the press suggesting that there had been an alarming drop in the animal's numbers. In several formally notified "Project Tiger" sanctuaries,

[26] *Securing India's Future: Final Technical Report of the National Biodiversity Strategy and Action Plan* (Pune: Kalpavriksh, 2005). This mammoth exercise was originally commissioned by the Ministry of Environment and Forests, Government of India, in January 2000. When it was completed, five years later, the ministry refused to endorse the report. No reasons were offered, but it was widely believed that the decision was taken because the report was deemed to be not friendly enough to market and industrial interests. Cf. also chapter 8 below, which analyzes in detail the work and ideas of a paradigmatic "democratic scientist."

such as Sariska, no tigers had been spotted for weeks on end. Anecdotal evidence from other parks—particularly those in North India—also confirmed the decline. This fresh manifestation of a tiger crisis led to the prime minister constituting a Tiger Task Force, and, beyond this, to a wider public debate, on the best means of preventing the tiger from sliding into extinction.

As it happens, with this debate on the tiger began a debate on the rights of adivasis in forest areas. This was sparked by a new legislation proposed by the Ministry of Tribal Affairs, seeking to correct the "historic wrong" of British rule denying tribals their traditional rights. The draft bill noted that, even after independence, the government had "continued with [these] colonial legislations." The error was now to be rectified by "giving a permanent stake to scheduled tribes" living in forests and associating them with their own protection and conservation.

Among the rights to be granted under this bill were small plots of land for cultivation and the conversion of "forest villages" into "revenue villages," a change which would permit their inhabitants to claim educational and health facilities from the state. However, the bill also vested its beneficiaries with certain duties: it said that the state would not countenance "any form of unsustainable or destructive practices." It insisted that alongside rights went the "responsibility and authority for sustainable use, biodiversity conservation and maintenance of ecological balance." It identified among the specific "duties" of the forest rightholder the duty to guard against any activity that "adversely affects the wildlife, forest and the biodiversity in the local area."

The professed reason for the bill was that it aimed at correcting a historical injustice. But—although this was left unsaid by the government—the bill was also a response to the growing presence of Naxalites, India's Maoist revolutionaries, in forest areas. These had shrewdly stoked the discontent of tribals against the state in general for not providing them schools, hospitals, and gainful employment. Against the Forest Department they had incited a more particular discontent: the denial of access to forest produce in the name of "scientific forestry" and "wildlife conservation." As one forest officer was constrained to admit: "In the absence of any government support and the apathetic attitude of the forest management departments towards the livelihood of forest-dependent communities, the Naxalites have found fertile ground to proliferate . . ."[27]

Whatever its motivations, the bill raised a storm of protest among wilderness protectionists. Without reading its cautionary caveats—or perhaps ignoring them deliberately—they warned that this new legislation was intended to deliver a body blow to conservation. Articles were written and speeches delivered claiming that if the act passed into law not a single tiger would be left in India, and perhaps not a single tree either.[28]

In this controversy, as so often in the past, the most vocal spokesman for the tiger has been a man named Valmik Thapar. Now in his early fifties, Thapar comes from a very well-known Delhi family, among whom there have been influential generals, editors, professors, and television hosts. Thapar has devoted his life to the study of a single animal, the tiger, mostly in a single location, the Ranthambore National Park in Rajasthan. Over the past twenty years he has written a series of popular and beautifully illustrated books on the species and made many documentary films on the subject.[29]

Thapar is part of a wider group of elites who have exercised a major influence on wildlife policy in India. Others include Billy Arjan Singh of the Dudhwa National Park in the Terai, and Belinda Wright who works in the Central India tiger sanctuary of Kanha. Also to be counted as part of this group is M.K. Ranjitsinhji, a hunter-turned-conservationist who, when he was a senior civil servant, drafted the Wildlife Preservation Act of 1972. Such individuals are not trained biologists, but nor are they simple urban pleasure-seekers. They are a bit of both and something more besides. Their love for the tiger is deep, even perhaps obsessive. It is, literally, their life.

Because of their passion and social connections this group was able to shape the evolution of Project Tiger in its early years. Hunting was banned altogether in the sanctuaries, as were timber felling and

[27] D. Mukherji, "If You Look After Forest People, You Kill Naxalism," *The Asian Age*, June 28, 2005.

[28] Cf. Ramachandra Guha, "Tribal Pursuits," *Hindustan Times*, June 16, 2005.

[29] Among his recent books are *The Secret Life of Tigers* (Delhi: Oxford University Press, 1999) and *The Cult of the Tiger* (Delhi: Oxford University Press, 2004).

fuelwood collection in each sanctuary's core area. Villages were relocated outside the park, usually with little or scant compensation. At first it appeared these methods were working. When Project Tiger was launched in 1973 the all-India population of the species was estimated at 1800. Two decades later it was closer to 3000. But in the last few years the numbers began to drop alarmingly. One reason was that there had clearly been an overestimation in the tiger census. A second was the loss of forest land to mining, industry, and large dams. A third was that the hunting of tigers had re-started, not in the shape of licensed shikar by the wealthy but via killings by armed gangs of poachers who were sometimes aided by disaffected villagers.

There had been poaching in the past as well, which had serviced the desires and fantasies of Europeans wanting a tiger skin on their living room wall. However, from the late 1980s, it had become clear that the main impetus for these fresh killings was the new love for tiger skins among Arab sheikhs, and, more crucially, the growing market for tiger parts in Communist China: the bones of the tiger, ground to a fine powder, are an important ingredient in traditional Chinese medicine. Also deemed valuable is the tiger's penis, a rare delicacy in traditional Chinese cuisine. According to an article published in 1997, the powder from tiger bones was valued at $500 a gram, a bowl of penis soup at $300, and the skin itself at $15,000.[30]

For these and other reasons the population of the tiger began to decline: hence the constitution of the Tiger Task Force, of which Valmik Thapar was a member. He put his views most forcefully before this official body, and also in the press. Speaking to a newspaper in Bangalore in the last week of June 2005 he insisted:

> One thing is very clear—tigers have to be saved in undisturbed, inviolate landscapes. You can't have villages, cities, railway, transmission lines and everything else that fragments forests. You either create landscapes that are undisturbed, or you don't save tigers. As far as I'm concerned, *tigers and human beings—forest dwellers or tribal peoples—cannot coexist.* There's no cuddly ideology here.

Later, when the question of tribal rights was raised, Thapar replied with an apparent show of magnanimity: "I'm not saying that every

[30] Peter Matthiessen, "The Last Wild Tigers," *Audobon*, March–April 1997.

forest should have only tigers and there should be no tribal or local people. Let the country decide. You want 500 tigers, 1000? Decide on the landscapes. Close [them]."[31]

Thapar's views represent those of a cohort of tiger lovers. The first thing to say about them is that they are profoundly unhistorical. For, in fact, tigers and tribals have coexisted for centuries in India. True, in some parts they compete for survival and subsistence. But the reason for this competition is that the living space and natural resources of *both* have shrunk on account of economic processes powered by privileged humans who have little time for tigers and none for tribals. The shrinking of the tiger's habitat and numbers is the result of such things as large dams, iron ore mines, and menus in Beijing and Taipei's restaurants. It would be fair to say that because of these processes the tribal has been almost as much a victim as the tiger. The solution urged by Thapar is to punish one victim in order, ostensibly, to save the other.

The second thing about Thapar's argument is that it is unapologetically authoritarian. Who will decide how much land to set aside exclusively for the tiger, and where will this be located? Implicit in Thapar's statement is that he and others like him will make these decisions. Like the American biologists quoted earlier, he believes he and his ilk "should provide leadership in the [tiger] preservation movement," for "when nobody else knows [what land to set aside and how best to protect it], we do know." Thapar has on several occasions been warmly nostalgic about Indira Gandhi's "Emergency," those twenty months of authoritarian rule in India when power was concentrated in the persons of Prime Minister Indira Gandhi and her son Sanjay, for both of whom a professed love of nature went hand in hand with disregard for democratic procedure in general and human rights in particular.[32]

The third thing to say about the views of Thapar and his ilk is that they seem to be deeply hypocritical. As with the Western biologists, within this group certain exceptions are always made for the "no humans in wilderness areas" rule. While seeking the removal of tribals, Indian wildlifers are never quite so hard on themselves or on urban

[31] *The Hindu*, Bangalore edition, June 28, 2005, emphasis added.

[32] Cf. Valmik Thapar, "Revamp Forest Bureaucracy," *The Times of India*, June 27, 2005.

pleasure-seekers. Rather than oppose the latter group, they actively canvass them, hoping that support from the wealthy and politically powerful will convince the state to pursue the coercive conservation policies they themselves prefer. The outstanding environmentalist and nature lover Ashish Kothari has written with feeling of "the fact that conservationists pointing to the destructive potential of millions of adivasis getting forest rights, conveniently hide under their carpet their own destructive lifestyles." For, in India as elsewhere, the typical wilderness lover drives an SUV that emits greenhouse gases, flies around the world in ozone-depleting planes, consumes power that comes from dams that submerge forests, and builds houses made from materials originating in strip mines. Speaking for a community of which he is a part, Kothari writes that "we bemoan the potential loss of India's forests due to the granting of adivasi rights, but are happy to carry on our own lifestyles that are the cause of far greater destruction than what forest dwellers could ever cause . . . As a conservationist, I have to say that I am truly ashamed at such blindness and hypocrisy."[33]

Whether through blindness or hypocrisy, the authoritarian conservationist seeks to condemn tribals for "crimes against nature" far less brutal than those committed by modern man. The tribal's battles against nature are conducted with a bow and a snare; ours are waged with chain saws, oil drills, automobiles, and bombs. It is *we*, the allegedly civilized, who have decimated forests and the wildlife that previously sustained both tiger and tribal. With our rifles and quest for trophies we first hunted wild species to extinction; now we disguise ourselves as conservationists and complain that adivasis are getting in the way.

The perspective of the traditional wildlife conservationist is based on faulty history, flawed science, and anti-democratic politics. It is based on genuine and deep love, but a love that is blind. Years of personal identification with a particular animal have blinded the lover to the wider world in which not just he, but also his beloved tiger, must coexist.

As it happened, in the Tiger Task Force, Thapar found himself in a minority of one. The other members were the distinguished ecologist

[33] Ashish Kothari, "Bungle in the Jungle," *Seminar*, no. 552, August 2005, pp. 68–9.

Madhav Gadgil (the subject of Chapter Eight), the experienced park manager H.S. Panwar, and the former civil servant Samar Singh—an enthusiastic proponent of participatory approaches to forest and wildlife management. The committee was chaired by Sunita Narain, Director of the Centre for Science and Environment in Delhi. Over-ruling Thapar's objections the Task Force recommended a shift from "exclusive" to more "inclusive" methods of national park management. They deplored the tendency of "tiger lovers . . . to band together into a select group that would control policy and programme formulation" in the "belief that the tiger can only be protected by building stronger and higher fences against 'depredators.'" In contrast with this centralizing perspective the Task Force drew attention to the vulnerability and suffering of underprivileged Indians who "share their resources with the tiger, without getting any benefits in return . . . To succeed, tiger conservation . . . has to bring benefits to [these] poor people."

How may this be accomplished? One way is to turn those who live in and around national parks "into the frontline defenders of the forests and protected areas, rather than see them as antagonists." Their knowledge and skills can be used to guide researchers and eco-tourists rather than poachers. Rather than ban all human use of forests the state could encourage the sustainable extraction of non-timber forest produce, such as honey—as was in fact being done very successfully in some parks in South India. The choice was between working with local people "to create situations in which they can live within the rules of the protected areas and in fact to strengthen [their] protection," or working against them "so that they increasingly turn against the protected areas and animals." If the latter alternative comes to be preferred, the state would have to "invest more and more into [wilderness] protection—more fences, guns and guards. Maybe we will win. But it is more likely we will lose."

The inclusion of local communities in the management process was but one of several collaborative processes recommended by the Task Force. It called for a closer working relationship between the central government and the states; for co-operation between the Forest Department (the agency in physical control of parkland) and independent researchers who were often better informed about its wildlife ecology; and for trans-disciplinary links between the natural and the social sciences. Beyond national borders, it urged that India "find strategies of engaging with China" and "work to build its bilateral relationships" with the country where the trade in tiger parts originated.[34]

Toward the end of their report the Tiger Task Force invoked Joint Forest Management and its ideal of reciprocity between state and citizen. Given its inclusive and dialogic approach, one might be tempted to see the reproduction, in the sphere of national park management, of the stages through which the forestry debate has passed. Perhaps *conflict* has been succeeded by *blame* which has given way to *negotiation*—now, can *collaboration* be far behind? This could be an unduly optimistic view. For one thing, those who uphold the old-style, authoritarian paradigm of park management continue to exercise much influence. And they have powerful allies. One is the Forest Department, which, having already conceded so much discretionary power through JFM regimes, is loath to give up its near-complete control over national parks. A second is the international conservation community, which stands squarely behind the group identified here as wilderness fanatics. The Western media is saturated with articles and books in which this group is presented in heroic and even near-mythic mode. The stories here are deeply unsympathetic to forest dwellers, who are seen as misguided at best and malevolent at worst. In these accounts it is only the rich urban Indian wilderness lover who is presented as enlightened, and as standing between the tiger and apocalypse.[35]

It would be foolish to deny that a crisis exists. The fate of a wonderful animal, the Indian tiger, does indeed hang in the balance. Prediction is not the business of the historian, but no historian can rule out the possibility that this glorious creature may one day be as dead as the dodo: perhaps in or around the year 2050 the last tiger will perish, at least in the wild. When that happens, some will say it was because the means devised for the tiger's protection were far too authoritarian. Others will say they were not authoritarian enough. No one is likely to ask, at that point in time, how many forest dwellers have been dispossessed, driven out of their homes, and done in for the cause—the undeniably noble cause—of saving the tiger.

[34] Anon., *Joining the Dots: The Report of the Tiger Task Force* (New Delhi: Union Ministry of Environment and Forests, 2005).

[35] See, for instance, Matthiessen, "The Last Wild Tigers;" Ruth Padel, *Tigers in Red Weather: A Journey Through Asia* (London: Time Warner Books, 2005).

CHAPTER 6

The Historical Social Ecology
of Lewis Mumford

Whenthe Western environmental movement broke out in the early 1970s, a young British journalist called Anne Chisholm wrote a book profiling scientists whose work had a direct bearing on the ecological predicament. Not surprisingly, her roster was dominated by university dons with impeccable scholarly credentials, including Réne Dubos, Raymond Dasmann, Estella Leopold, and Kenneth Boulding. Yet she chose to begin her celebration of ecological pioneers with a man without any formal training in ecology—indeed, without any formal intellectual training whatsoever (the man's only university, as he was to recall in his autobiography, was the city of Manhattan). But for Chisholm this man had the most visible influence on contemporary environmental thought: "of all the wise men whose thinking and writing over the years has prepared the ground for the environmental revolution, Lewis Mumford, the American philosopher and writer, must be preeminent."[1]

Chisholm's judgment would have found strong support within the scientific community, for Mumford had already been chosen to sum up the deliberations of two seminal scientific symposia on ecological change.[2] Yet, in the three decades since Chisholm wrote her book,

---

[1] Anne Chisholm, *Philosophers of the Earth: Conversations with Ecologists* (London: Sidgwick and Jackson, 1972). Mumford's invocation of the city as his university is in his *Sketches From a Life: The Autobiography of Lewis Mumford: The Early Years* (New York: The Dial Press, 1982), esp. chapter 11.

[2] See W. L. Thomas, ed., *Man's Role in Changing the Face of the Earth* (Chicago: University of Chicago Press, 1956); F. Fraser Darling and John P. Milton, eds,

Mumford's reputation as an ecological thinker has suffered an extraordinary eclipse. Meanwhile, the environmental movement has grown enormously, and, in the manner of a mature and self-confident social movement, has begun to construct its own genealogy and pantheon of heroes. The prehistory of environmentalism has been documented most abundantly for Mumford's own country, the USA, yet nowhere is ignorance of Mumford's environmental writings more acute. That, at any rate, is my conclusion from a reading of some of the most authoritative histories of American environmentalism, for example those written by Roderick Nash, Stephen Fox, and Samuel Hays.[3]

The commonly acknowledged patron saints of American environmentalism, this reading further tells me, are the naturalist and nature lover John Muir, and the forester and biologist Aldo Leopold. Why American environmentalists can make Muir and Leopold cultural icons while neglecting Mumford is a fascinating question that I will turn to toward the end of this chapter. For the moment let me only say that I find Mumford's ecological thought as congenial as did Chisholm, who is also an outsider to American environmentalism. This chapter is, then, primarily an essay in rehabilitation: its analysis of Mumford's ecological ideas is aimed especially at American environmentalists who have failed to recognize, and seldom even acknowledge, one of their own most authentic voices.

II

Mumford's appreciation of nature came, in the first instance, from boyhood summers spent in Vermont. Toward the end of his life he remembered those early encounters in the wild with skunks, woodchucks, and deer and river trout as having "deepened my native American roots."[4] In this, Mumford's experience was perfectly in tune with a long line of American environmentalists from Henry Thoreau to

---

Future Environments of North America (Garden City. N.Y.: Natural History Press, 1966).

[3] See Roderick Nash, *Wilderness and the American Mind*; Stephen Fox, *The American Conservation Movement*; Samuel P. Hays, *Beauty, Health and Permanence*.

[4] Lewis Mumford (hereafter LM), *Sketches from a Life*, p. 90.

Edward Abbey whose love of nature followed directly from their experience of the diversity and beauty of the North American wilderness.

But had Mumford's ecological horizons remained confined to the wild, he would merit no more than a footnote in any history of environmental ideas. What distinguishes him from the pantheon of American wilderness heroes—and why I am writing about him in the first place—is his fundamentally ecological understanding of the ebb and flow of human history. Unlike Muir, Leopold, and a dozen other cultural icons, he refused to disembed individual attitudes to nature from their social, cultural, and historical contexts. This more inclusive ecological approach he owed to the only man Mumford acknowledged as his teacher—the maverick Scotsman Patrick Geddes, whose work is described in Chapter Two of this book.

Mumford inherited from Geddes both a fundamentally ecological approach and a repertoire of neologisms—paleotechnic/neotechnic, conurbation, megalopolis, etc.—that he put to remarkably innovative use, especially in his authoritative histories of technology and the city. He also owed to Geddes his respect for pre-modern technologies and patterns of resource use. Notably, it was Geddes who drew the disciple's attention to the work of that forgotten American conservationist George Perkins Marsh. And, as Mumford noted in an early appreciation, it was Marsh who first treated man as an "active geological agent," who could "upbuild or degrade," but who was, one way or another, a "disturbing agent" who upset the harmonies of nature and overthrew the stability of existing arrangements and accommodations, extirpating indigenous vegetable and animal species, introducing foreign varieties, restricting spontaneous growth, and covering the earth with "new and reluctant vegetable forms and with alien tribes of animal life."[5]

[5] LM, *The Brown Decades: A Study of the Arts in America* (1931; rpnt New York: Dover Publications, 1955), pp. 76–7. Years later Mumford speculated that he was invited to co-chair the 1955 Werner-Gren Conference on "Man's Role in Changing the Face of the Earth" because of his memoir on George Perkins Marsh in *The Brown Decades*—and, as Geddes had introduced him to Marsh, in effect he owed that invitation to his master (see LM, *Sketches from a Life*, p. 408). The proceedings of the Wenner-Gren symposium, edited by W.L. Thomas (cited in note 2 above) were dedicated to Marsh.

Marsh himself had focused on the destruction of forest cover. Deforestation was but one example of the many ways in which Americans, in "the very act of seizing all the habitable parts of the earth," had "systematically misused and neglected our possessions."[6] The ecological implications of early American economic development were fleshed out by Mumford in a remarkable and unjustly forgotten series of essays on regionalism, published in *The Sociological Review*, a journal edited by Patrick Geddes's close associate Victor Branford. *The Sociological Review* essays constitute Mumford's first systematic attempt to apply the Geddesian ecological framework to historical phenomena.[7] This regional approach to social analysis, which the Indian sociologist Radhakamal Mukerjee was also developing at the same time, took off from Geddes's conceptual trinity of Folk/Work/Place (itself borrowed from the work of the French sociologist, Frederick Le Play).[8]

In his *Sociological Review* essays Mumford used the regional framework to analyze the ecological crimes of American pioneer civilization (the epitome of "irregionalism") and outline the prospects for a more sustainable economy and culture (what he termed "regionalism").[9] The refusal to base industry and institutions on regional endowments had led on the one side to enormous ecological devastation, and on the other, to a parasitical relationship between city and hinterland: "In America during the last century," wrote Mumford, "we mined soils, gutted forests, misplaced industry, wasted vast sums in needless transportation, congested population and lowered the physical vitality of the community without immediately feeling the consequences of our actions." During this period, "it has suited us to ignore the basic realities of the land: its contours and landscape, its vegetation areas, its power [and] mineral resources, its industry, its types of community . . ." This was a "miner's kind of civilization" exalting the miner's cut-and-run attitude to nature, as exemplified by timber mining and the relentless skimming of soils. This civilization's cities were likewise

[6] LM, "Regionalism and Irregionalism," *The Sociological Review*, vol. 19, no. 4, 1927, p. 277.

[7] Ibid.; LM, "The Theory and Practice of Regionalism," *The Sociological Review*, vol. 20, nos 1 and 2, 1928.

[8] For Mukerjee's work see chapter 2 above.

[9] The following paragraphs are based on the essays cited in note 7 above.

unmindful of ecological realities: bloated in their proportions, they become "prime offenders in their misuse of regional resources." He did not fail to notice, either, the proliferation of slums and slagheaps within city boundaries.

Mumford characterized the processes—of what he, following Geddes, called the paleotechnic age—as

> doubly ruinous: they impoverish the earth by hastily removing, for the benefit of a few generations, the common resources which, once expended and dissipated, can never be restored; and second, in its technique, its habits, its processes, the paleotechnic period is equally inimical to the earth considered as a human habitat, by its destruction of the beauty of the landscape, its ruining of streams, its pollution of drinking water, its filling the air with a finely divided carboniferous deposit, which chokes both life and vegetation.[10]

But, he warned, the day of the pioneer had passed; American economic development could no longer afford to neglect regional realities. For, if one thought not discretely of products and resources but of the region as a whole, it would be clear "that in each geographic area a certain balance of natural resources and human institutions is possible, for the finest development of the land and the people." In America, the "regionalism" movement (notably the Regional Planning Association which Mumford had helped initiate) had emphasized the conservation of natural resources, but only in a more inclusive framework. Thus, regionalism "must not merely, through conservation, prevent waste: it must also provide the economic foundations for a continuous and flourishing life." In particular, regionalism would seek to harmonize urban living with the countryside by making the city an integral part of the region. Here, Mumford drew attention to Ebenezer Howard's Garden City Movement (also strongly influenced by Geddes)—the creation of cities limited in size, surrounded by farmland,

[10] Mumford rarely missed an opportunity to berate the pioneer for his crimes against nature. As late as 1962 he was still complaining that "even when the pioneer didn't rape Nature, he divorced her a little too easily: he missed the great lesson that both ecology and medicine teach—that man's great mission is not to conquer nature by main force but to cooperate with her intelligently but lovingly for his own purposes" (LM, "California and the Human Prospect," *Sierra Club Bulletin*, vol. 47, no. 9, 1962, pp. 45–6).

with easy access to natural areas, and in other ways in organic unity with their hinterland.[11]

These early and penetrating essays illustrate Mumford's deepening interest in the ecological infrastructure of human life. Shortly afterward, he wrote that the three main threats to civilization were the continuing destruction of forest cover and soil erosion, the depletion of irreplaceable mineral resources, and the destructive potential of modern warfare.[12] The *Sociological Review* series acted as a trailer for his masterly histories of technology, *Technology and Civilization* (1934), and of the city, *The Culture of Cities* (1938). These—Mumford's most celebrated books, written at the height of his powers—need to be read as essentially ecological histories of the rise of modern Western civilization.

Both books outline a three-stage interpretation of the development of industrial civilization. These successive but overlapping and interpenetrating phases Mumford termed "eotechnic," "paleotechnic," and "neotechnic." The last two terms he owed to Geddes; he added the first to designate the preparatory stage in which most of the technical and social innovations of the modern world had been anticipated.[13]

Studies of Mumford's histories usually neglect their ecological underpinnings. Yet, those underpinning are clear: "each of the three phases of machine civilization has left its deposits in society. Each has

[11] In the event, American economic development has continued to ignore regional realities. But ecological disaster has been forestalled through the drawing in of natural resources from all over the globe. At the time of Mumford's *Sociological Review* series, the USA was still largely relying on its own resources. But, especially since the Second World War, the development of its consumer society has rested on a fundamentally exploitative relationship with the rest of the world. Consumers in the high centers of industrial civilization can take for granted the continued supply of mink from the Arctic, teakwood from India, and ivory from Africa, without being in the slightest degree responsible for the environmental implications of their lifestyles. This theme is further explored in chapter 9.

[12] LM, "Science on the Loose," review of Robert Millikan's *Science and the New Civilization*, *The New Republic*, August 6, 1930. See also the section entitled "Pre-1970 Ecology," in LM, *My Works and Days* (New York: Harcourt, Brace and Jovanovich, 1979), pp. 29–32.

[13] Cf. L.M., *Technics and Civilization* (New York: Harcourt, Brace and Co., 1934), p. 109.

changed the landscape, altered the physical layout of cities, used certain resources and spurned others, favored certain types of commodity and certain paths of activity and modified the common technical heritage." Viewed from the point of view of characteristic inputs of energy and materials, "the eotechnic is a water-and-wood complex, the paleotechnic phase is a coal-and-iron complex, and the neotechnic phase is an electricity-and-iron complex."[14]

In a strictly ecological sense the eotechnic phase was largely benign. The resources it most heavily relied on—wood, water, and wind— were all renewable. It created exquisite landscapes and did not cause pollution. The "energy of the eotechnic phase did not vanish in smoke nor were its products thrown quickly in junkheaps: by the seventeenth century it had transformed the woods and swamps of northern Europe into a continuous vista of wood and field, village and garden . . . ." The ecological impact of this phase could be regarded even more favorably when set against the record of its succeeding phase, the paleotechnic era of "carboniferous capitalism."[15]

After 1750 industrial development "passed into a new phase, with a different source of power, different materials, different social objectives." The new source of energy was coal; the dominant new material iron; the overriding social objectives power, profit, and efficiency. Widespread dependence on coal and iron meant that for the first time in human history societies were living not on current income from nature but on nature's capital. At the same time, the characteristic byproducts of carboniferous capitalism were polluted air, water, and homes; abominable living conditions made worse by the concentration and congestion brought about by factory production and modern urban living. The newer chemical industries also introduced dangerous substances into air and water. And that handmaiden of industrial capitalism, the railroad, "distributed smut and dirt . . ." Indeed, the "reek of coal was the very incense of the new industrialism," and the rare sight of a "clear sky in an industrial district was the sign of a strike or a lock-out or an industrial depression." These varied and often deadly forms of environmental degradation were a consequence of the values of a money economy, in which the environment was treated as

[14] Ibid., pp. 110, 268.
[15] Ibid., pp. 111, 118, 147.

an abstraction, and air and sunlight, "because of their deplorable lack of value in exchange, had no reality at all."[16]

Despite all this, Mumford was hopeful that the paleotechnic phase was but "a period of transition, a busy, congested, rubbish strewn avenue between the eotechnic and neotechnic economies."[17] The neotechnic phase which Mumford saw emerging would rely on a new and non-polluting source of energy—hydroelectricity—and devise long-lasting materials (alloys) and synthetic chemical compounds. Mumford was also hopeful, even in the 1930s, for a push in the direction of solar energy. As water was readily available in Africa, South America, and Asia, the arrival of electricity would also tend to displace Europe and North America from its position of industrial dominance. As far as pollution was concerned, the "smoke pall of paleotechnic industry begins to lift: with electricity the clear sky and the clean waters of the eotechnic phase comes back again." Meanwhile, the renewed utilization of human excrement and the development of nitrogen fixing fertilizers would arrest the soil erosion caused by the miner's civilization of the earlier phase.[18] The neotechnic phase, when it fully came into its own, would restore three vital equilibria: equilibrium in the environment between humans and nature; equilibrium between industry and agriculture; and equilibrium in population through the balancing of birth rates and death rates.[19]

Mumford's magisterial history of the city also closely follows a three-stage interpretation: of environmental use, abuse, and renewal. He begins with the medieval city (corresponding to the eotechnic phase) against which, he claimed, modern writers had developed a violent but largely unfounded prejudice. In Mumford's reconstruction the pre-modern city blended easily with its rural surroundings, while the extent of usable open space within contrasted sharply with the "notorious fact of *post*-medieval overcrowding." Again, the waste materials of city life were largely organic and hence easily decomposable. In essence, the medieval city was more than adequate "on the biological side," with its sights, smells, and sounds infinitely more

[16] Ibid., chapter 4. Quotation from pp. 151, 168–9.
[17] Ibid., p. 211.
[18] Ibid., chapter 5. Quotation from p. 255.
[19] Ibid., pp. 429–31.

pleasurable than those of its modern successor. Indeed, architecturally speaking, "the town itself was an omnipresent work of art."[20]

Mumford's evocation of a harmonious and organic past was, once again, preparatory to his condemnation of the living present, the "insensate industrial town" of the paleotechnic era. In the urban complex which superseded the medieval city, the factory and the slum were the two main elements. Whereas the effluents of a single factory could often be absorbed by the surrounding landscape, the characteristic massing of industries in the paleotechnic city polluted "air and water beyond remedy." Meanwhile, in the congested living quarters of the slum, "a pitch of foulness and filth was reached that the lowest serf's cottage scarcely achieved in medieval Europe." Sanitation and waste disposal also fell far short of minimal hygienic standards. As "night spread over the coal-town," wrote Mumford dramatically, "its prevailing color was black. Black clouds of smoke rolled out of the factory chimneys, and the railroad yards, which often cut clean into the town, mangling the very organism, spreading cinders everywhere." To the historian of the paleotechnic city, it was "plain that never before in recorded history had such vast masses of people lived in such a savagely deteriorated environment."[21]

The way out lay in the growing movement for regionalism. With the epoch of land colonization coming to a close, Mumford thought he discerned a change in attitudes toward the earth, with the parasitic and predatory attitudes of the pioneer being supplanted by the more caring values of the emerging biotechnic regime. In European countries the regionalist movement had fought against excessive centralization, reclaimed the folk heritage, and fostered the growth of co-operatives. In the United States the conservation movement, under the romantic impulse, had helped set aside large areas of wilderness; now under a more scientific guise it was also actively promoting the conservation of raw materials. Meanwhile, Ebenezer Howard's Garden City movement, which stressed the creation of balanced urban communities within balanced regions, was growing in influence.[22]

[20] LM, *The Culture of Cities* (New York: Harcourt Brace and Co., 1938), chapter 1. Quotations from pp. 49, 51.

[21] Ibid., chapter 3. Quotation from pp. 162, 164, 191, 195.

[22] Ibid., especially chapters 5 and 6.

The common analytical framework of Mumford's two great eco-logical histories has a markedly Hegelian ring: the stages of eotechnic/paleotechnic/neotechnic being analogous to the dialectic of thesis/antithesis/synthesis.[23] While his philosophical frame may have been inherited, his ecological sophistication is, for its time and place, quite remarkable. The major organizing principles of his histories are truly ecological in nature: the use of energy and materials as indices of tech-nical and environmental change; the mapping of resource flows with-in and between regions characteristic of different stages; the forms of environmental degradation and movements of environmental redress typical of different epochs; and the role of values in creating the "money economy" of destruction and the (future) "life economy" of renewal. Underlying it all is a commitment to environmental conser-vation as a positive force, contrasting the negativism with which en-vironmentalism, then as now, was beset. In a passage which is strikingly contemporary in tone, Mumford wrote in 1938 that

> originating in the spectacle of waste and defilement, the conservation movement has tended to have a negative influence: it has sought to isolate wilderness areas from encroachment and it has endeavored to diminish waste and prevent damage. The present task of regional planning is a more positive one: it seeks to bring the earth as a whole up to the highest pitch of perfection and appropriate use—not merely preserving the primeval, but extending the range of the garden, and introducing the deliberate cul-ture of the landscape into every part of the open country.[24]

III

The optimism of Mumford's ecological histories of the 1930s will surprise anyone acquainted only with his later writings. At the time he was hopeful that the emerging values of the neotechnic economy would humanize and domesticate the machine. From the standpoint

[23] Hegel is mentioned only once in *Technics and Civilization* and not at all in *The Culture of Cities*. However, Mumford had read Marx closely, and perhaps his stages approach unconsciously drew upon Marx's interpretation of the Hegelian dialectic. Marx's theory of history is open to both evolutionist and cyclical readings: while Marxists have usually preferred the former, Mumford would have undoubtedly been more comfortable with the latter.

[24] *The Culture of Cities*, p. 331.

of democracy, too, neotechnic technology—in particular, hydroelectricity—worked in favor of decentralization and the human scale, in direct contrast to the giantism and concentration of the paleotechnic epoch. Mumford even has something positive to say for the automobile. Although he deplored its reliance on gasoline, he believed its growing displacement of the railroad meant that humans would no longer crowd around railheads, pitheads, and ports.[25]

Mumford's early ecological philosophy was, therefore, deeply historicist in nature. He believed that the forces of history were themselves moving in the direction of a cleaner environment, a more benign technology, a more democratic social order. Meanwhile, his association with the regionalist movement—probably the only time in his long career as a public intellectual that he participated in collective action—also favored a more optimistic outlook on social change.

All this sits oddly with Mumford's more common reputation, based on his later writings, as a prophet of doom. Locating this transition in time, it appears that the aftermath of the Second World War fundamentally altered his faith in the forward movement of history. The carpet bombing of German cities, the dropping of atomic bombs on Japan, and the paranoia of the Cold War all deeply affected him. No longer could history be relied upon to usher in the neotechnic age; for technology, and the "gentlemen" who controlled its development, had gone mad.

This change in outlook is captured in a preface Mumford wrote in 1973 for the reprint of a book first published nearly thirty years earlier. He defended the book's support of John Stuart Mill's theory of the "steady state" in opposition to the Victorian belief in progress and the expansionary thrust of modern Western civilization; the book represented a continuation of the call in *Technics and Civilization* for a dynamic equilibrium between human and nature, and industry and agriculture. But, he noted significantly, "the chief effect of the regressive transformations that have taken place in the last quarter of a century [i.e. since the end of the Second World War] has been to change my conclusions from the indicative to the imperative mood; not 'we

[25] LM, *Technics and Civilization*, pp. 221–3, 247, 250, 267; "The Theory and Practice of Regionalism," p. 19.

shall' achieve a dynamic equilibrium but '*we must*'—if we are not to destroy the delicate ecological balance upon which all life depends.' "[26]

In this more somber, reflective phase, Mumford's social and environmental values remained steadfast: yet he was considerably less sanguine about their wider acceptance. Nonetheless, scattered through his writings one can see the elements of an ecological philosophy that is at once analytic and programmatic. No doubt it is difficult to find a compact or authorized statement of his views in the post-war period: there is no canonical text comparable to *Technics and Civilization* or *The Culture of Cities.* Rather, his perspective on ecology, culture, and politics must be reconstructed from his diverse writings, particularly his neglected periodical essays and articles.

Let us first examine Mumford's reconsideration of modern technology, beginning with his criticisms of atomic energy and culminating in the full-scale attack in *The Pentagon of Power* (1970). Abandoning the hope that modern technology would develop in a benign direction, he now believed that modern science and technology bore the impress of capitalism—with "the capitalist's interest in quantity—his belief that there are no natural limits to acquisition" being "supplemented in technology by the notion that quantitative production had no natural limits either."[27] Where "the machine takes precedence of the man," he wrote, "and where all activities and values that sustain the human spirit are subordinated to making money and privately devouring only such goods as money will buy, even the physical environment tends to become degraded and inefficient."[28] Mumford reserved his strongest strictures on technology for atomic energy, which to him exemplified the one-sided, life-denying development of modern technics. He argued for this technology to be put on "strict probation," refusing to accept the "sedative explanations" of the Atomic Energy Commission that pollution would be negligible and easy to control. Such reassurances gave him no confidence, for the history of industrial pollution

[26] LM, "Preface," *The Condition of Man* (1944; rpnt New York: Harcourt, Brace, and Jovanovich, 1973), p. viii.

[27] LM, "Technics and the Future of Western Civilization," in idem, *In the Name of Sanity* (New York: Harcourt, Brace, and Jovanovich, 1954), p. 47.

[28] "California and the Human Prospect," p. 43.

showed "our childish shortsightedness under the excitement of novelty, our contempt for health when profits are at stake, our lack of reverence for life, even our own life, [we] continue to poison the atmosphere in every industrial area, and to make the streams and rivers, as well as the air we breathe, unfit for organic life."[29]

Mumford's faith in science and technology was also shaken by its role in the Second World War and the arms race which followed. He was an early and percipient critic of the atomic bomb and urged America to share its nuclear knowledge with the Soviet Union rather than embark on meaningless and costly competition. The development of atomic energy and the perfection of weapons of mass destruction, he argued, undermined democracy by fostering secrecy by and within the state.[30] And the military-industrial complex was itself only part of a wider denial of democracy, in that large areas of central government had passed out "of all popular surveillance and control, operating in secret, defiantly withholding or adulterating the information needed by democracy in order to pass judgment on the work of its officers."[31] He compared the state of American democracy unfavorably to the USA of a century earlier, when there had indeed been a great diffusion of property, wealth, and political power. In calling for a renewal of democracy, Mumford was putting forward a cyclical theory of political structures curiously similar to his (by now modified) cyclical theory of technical development: a harmonious but irretrievable past, an abominable present, and a future that had yet to be claimed.[32]

Two elements of Mumford's democratic vision bear highlighting. First, he stressed that citizens must have control over public programs that vitally affect their lives. For Mumford, high among Geddes' revolutionary contributions to planning—which set him apart from

[29] LM, "Prospect," in Thomas, ed., *Man's Role*, pp. 147–8.

[30] See for example his essays "Gentlemen! You are Mad!" *Saturday Review of Literature*, March 2, 1946; "The Morals of Extermination," *Atlantic Monthly*, October 1959; and the collection *In the Name of Sanity*. Cf. also Paul Boyer, *By the Bomb's Early Light: American Thought and Culture at the Dawn of the Atomic Age* (New York: Pantheon, 1985), esp. pp. 284–7.

[31] LM, "The Moral Challenge to Democracy," *Virginia Quarterly Review*, vol. 35, no, 4, 1959, p. 565,

[32] Ibid., esp. pp. 562–7.

the archetypal administrator, bureaucrat, or businessman—was his "willingness to leave an essential part of the process to those who are most intimately connected with it—the ultimate users, consumers, or citizens."[33] Mumford also inherited Geddes' high regard for folk, or pre-modern, knowledge. In the early days of the most savage war in human history, he hoped for a time when the "mechanically more primitive cultures . . . may influence and civilize their European conquerors; may restore to them some of that deep organic sense of unity with the environment, some of that sensuous enrichment and playful enjoyment that Western man has so often forfeited in his aggressive conquest of the environment . . ."[34]

These sentiments were perfectly consistent with Mumford's larger plea for what we would now call "cultural and biological diversity." The machine world, he complained,

> has insulated its occupants from every form of reality except the machine process itself: heat and cold, day and night, the earth and the stars, woodland, crop land, vine land, garden land—all forms of organic partnership between the millions of species that add to the vitality and wealth of the earth—are either suppressed entirely from the mind or homogenized into a uniform mixture which can be fed into the machine.

Against this deadly uniformity, Mumford called for us to cherish history by "promoting character and variety and beauty wherever we find it, whether in landscapes or in people."[35]

Chapter Three of this book has argued that the three generic environmental philosophies are wilderness thinking (or primitivism), agrarianism, and scientific industrialism. Mumford is rare, possibly unique, among environmental philosophers in his ability to synthesize and transcend partisan stances on behalf of wilderness, countryside, and city. As his close associate Benton Mckaye pointed out, the primeval, the rural, and the urban were all environments necessary for the full development of humans. Consequently, a regionalist program had to incorporate all three elements: the preservation of the primeval

[33] LM, *My Works and Days*, pp. 115–16.

[34] LM, "Looking Forward," *Proceedings of the American Philosophical Society*, vol. 83, no. 4, 1940, p. 541.

[35] "California and the Human Prospect," pp. 45–7.

wilderness, the restoration of the stable rural landscape, and the salvaging of the true urban.[36]

The humanizing of technology and the protection of diversity were both contingent on a fundamental change in values. As Mumford's biographer has perceptively noted, while other radicals "expected such a value change to occur after the revolution, for Mumford this value change *was* the revolution."[37] In the machine age, the disintegration of the human personality had reached an advanced stage, as the pathologies of the civilized world bore witness. So, as Mumford told a gathering of international scientists in 1955, "if we are to achieve some degree of ecological balance . . . we must aim at human balance too."[38] In an address first delivered at the centenary meeting of the American Association for the Advancement of Science, and published coincidentally, but appositely, on Mahatma Gandhi's birthday, he called for a greater human element in technics—for technics to fully engage the human personality. At a deeper level he went on to call for a dethroning of technics from its superior place in modern society. In this larger task of cultural renewal—

> Not the Power Man, not the Profit Man, not the Mechanical Man, but the Whole Man, must be the central actor in the new drama of civilization. This means that we must reverse the order of development which first produced the machine; we must now explore the world of history, culture, organic life, human development, as we once explored the non-living world of nature. We must understand the organics of personality as we first understood the statics and mechanics of physical processes; we must center attention on quality, value, pattern, and purpose, as we once centered attention on quantity, on physical relationships, on mass and motion.[39]

[36] Benton Mckaye to Lewis Mumford, December 3, 1926, quoted in John L. Thomas, "Lewis Mumford, Benton Mckaye and the Regional Vision," in Thomas P. Hughes and Agatha C. Hughes, eds, *Lewis Mumford: Public Intellectual* (New York: Oxford University Press, 1990).

[37] Donald L. Miller, *Lewis Mumford: A Life* (New York: Weidenfeld & Nicolson, 1989), p. 166.

[38] LM, "Prospect," p. 1146.

[39] LM, "Let Man Take Command," *The Saturday Review of Literature*, October 2, 1948, p. 35.

Even more than values, individuals and societies need viable myths. Mumford hoped for the overthrow of the myth of the machine, which had, for such an extended period, held Western man in thrall. For sanity, stability, and survival the myth of the machine had to be replaced with "a new myth of life, a myth based upon a richer understanding of all organic processes, a sharper insight into man's positive role in changing the face of the earth . . . and above all a deeply religious faith in man's own capacity to transform and perfect his own self and his own institutions in cooperative relation with all the forces of nature, and above all, with his fellow men."[40]

IV

If the second section of this chapter closely followed Mumford's ecological histories, the third reconstructed his environmental philosophy from the social commentaries he contributed to American periodicals. I now explore, more tentatively, the outlines of how Mumford might have chosen to be remembered as a social and ecological thinker. Here I use three appreciations Mumford wrote of other people—namely, his son, an ecological pioneer, and a nineteenth-century polymath whom he greatly admired. None of these tributes are at all well known. Yet it is in these apparently ephemeral works that we glimpse hints of Mumford's self-image, and his uncertainties regarding his place in history.[41]

Mumford's only son, named for Patrick Geddes, died in action at the age of nineteen, in the Second World War. The loss of his son shattered the father and was to contribute significantly to his deepening pessimism about the direction of Western civilization. Yet, in the brave memoir he wrote after Geddes Mumford's death, the writer was able to celebrate in his son the attitudes toward the land and people that Mumford himself had so long cherished.

[40] "California and the Human Prospect," pp. 58–9.

[41] It is, of course, not at all uncommon for writers to project their hopes, prejudices, and aspirations in their tributes to other people. For Orwell's identification with Dickens, see John Rodden's suggestive study, *The Politics of Literary Reputation: The Making and Claiming of "St. George" Orwell* (New York: Oxford University Press, 1989), esp. pp. 181–2, 238–9.

In a strongly pastoral chapter, "The Land and the Seasons," Mumford called his son a "true countryman." Through his deep feelings for the countryside, Geddes Mumford "was renewing the spirit Thoreau had brought to the American landscape. . . . Geddes responded in every fiber to Thoreau's question: 'who would not rise to meet the expectations of the land.'" In a later chapter, "Country Ways and Country Neighbors," also written in a pastoral vein, Mumford remembered his son liking to work with his hands and as having an intense dislike of the machine. An illustration of his "antipathy toward the machine" was Geddes's preference, expressed to his mother when he was a child, for a horse to plow the fields. When his mother suggested that a tractor could do the job just as well, Geddes replied in amazement: "But, Mommie, you'd never use a tractor on the *ground* would you? Have you ever seen the fields after a tractor has gone over them? A tractor doesn't care what it does: it digs right into the earth and hacks it up. A horse goes gently. I'd never use a tractor."

Moreover, "Geddes' feelings for the country included country people." Here, Mumford wrote evocatively of a smallholder farming neighbor of theirs, Sam Honour. Of English stock, Sam was "full of country love . . . and nearer to the peasant than any other American I have ever met." In his person Sam was "a living specimen of an older and homelier America, which was closer to Geddes' ideal than the one he was part of."[42]

If Mumford's love of the land, like his son's, derived from a youthful exposure to the country, his mature ecological consciousness owed itself, as we saw, to Patrick Geddes and the great American geographer to whom the latter had introduced him, George Perkins Marsh. In *The Brown Decades* (1931) Mumford had alerted the American public to the significance of this forgotten writer; so when a full-length biography appeared a quarter of a century later Mumford was uniquely placed to write a further appreciation. Marsh's *Man and Nature* was unquestionably a "comprehensive ecological study before the very word ecology had been invented." Mumford was also quite justified in claiming that Marsh would have opposed in general "the vast

[42] LM, *Green Memories: The Story of Geddes Mumford* (New York: Harcourt, Brace and Co., 1947), pp. 114–15, 126–8.

program of pollution and extermination that has been engineered in our country in the name of scientific progress," and, in particular that he would have spoken out, were he alive, against the production of nuclear energy with its potential for "permanently crippling" the human race and making the planet unfit for habitation.

It is in setting Marsh's thought in perspective that Mumford truly reveals himself. It was not that "Marsh undervalued science or the products of science," he wrote, "but he valued the integrity of life even more. . . ." For, the Vermonter's "unique contribution was his combination of the naturalist's approach with that of the moralist and the humanist; he supplied both the intellectual tools and the moral direction necessary." His "type of mind was the exact opposite of the German-trained specialists who began to dominate America in the 1880s, when Marsh died; for the latter narrowed their life experience and segregated their specialized interests." But, ironically, it was Marsh's very ability to transcend narrow spheres of thought which "made his work suspect to the following generation, who dodged the task of evaluating his genius by ignoring it."[43]

This uncharacteristically defensive tone also crept into Mumford's appreciation of William Morris, the nineteenth-century genius whose achievements were even more wide ranging than the versatile Vermonter's. Morris, wrote Mumford, was not merely a "dreamer of dreams" but also a "resolute realist, who refused to take the sordid Victorian triumphs of mechanical progress as the ultimate achievements of the human spirit." He was not, as is commonly supposed, a revivalist but rather what Henry Russel Hitchcock called a "New Traditionalist, seeking not to revive the past but to nourish and develop what was still alive in it." Morris had undoubtedly devoted immense time and energy to the recovery of traditional techniques being rendered superfluous in the machine age—indeed Morris, "a whole generation before the anthropologists began their belated work of salvage with surviving stone age and tribal communities, performed a similar task for the arts and crafts of the Old World past." But "if he had been more

[43] LM, "Marsh's Naturalist-Moralist-Humanist Approach," review of David Lowenthal, *George Perkins Marsh: Versatile Vermonter*, in *Living Wilderness*, vol. 71, Winter 1959–60, pp. 11–13.

sympathetic with the peculiar triumphs of his own age, he might not have had the copious, concentrated energies to perform this necessary salvage operation."

Nor did Morris want to abolish all machines: he thought they could do the necessary work and leave other, more joyous tasks to be done by human beings themselves. Morris was in effect an early appropriate technologist who, instead "of accepting either megatechnics or mono-technics as inevitable . . . sought to keep alive or if necessary to restore those forms of art and craft whose continued existence would enrich human life and even keep the way open for fresh technical achieve-ments."

In challenging the stereotype of Morris as an impractical dreamer Mumford also discussed his engagement with socialism. Although it came rather late, Morris' life-work was strengthened immeasurably by the socialist vision which "bestowed a fuller social content and a larger human purpose on all his private achievements as an artist, and gave him the confidence to work for a future in which all men might know the joys of creative labor that he himself had experienced."[44]

Written nearly ten years apart, and on two very different nine-teenth-century thinkers, there are nonetheless striking similarities in Mumford's tributes to Marsh and Morris. In both he appears to project himself, and more notably, *society's preferred evaluation of himself,* on to a kinsman in ideas and action, albeit of an earlier generation. He anticipates and contests the criticism that Marsh was against science and goes on to attribute his neglect to his refusal to be trapped within narrow specialisms. Mumford had faced the first criticism himself, and was coming to terms with the neglect of his counsel in the intellectual and political forums where he might have expected to be given a hear-ing. His defense of Morris can likewise be understood as a product of close personal identification. Morris, he argues, was not blindly against technology; he knew how to use the past without being a revivalist; he was as much a "realist" as a "dreamer;" and he was guided to a deeper social vision by his engagement with socialism. In writing this tribute Mumford may possibly have been conscious of how his

[44] LM, "A Universal Man," *New York Review of Books,* May 23, 1968, pp. 8, 10, 12, 15.

defense of Morris was at once a defense of his own life and work. He was seventy-three years old at the time, almost at the end of his active career, and profoundly unsure of how history would judge him.

V

We return to where we began—with the reception, or more accurately the non-reception, of Mumford's environmental writings in his own society. Illustrative in this regard is a major round table on environmental history organized by the prestigious *Journal of American History.* In his keynote essay Donald Worster recalls Aldo Leopold's call in *A Sand County Almanac* for an "ecological interpretation of history," commenting that it has "taken a while for historians to heed Leopold's advice," but that at long last the field of environmental history "has begun to take shape and its practitioners are trying to build on his [Leopold's] initiative."[45]

Now, I have nothing against Leopold, and considerable admiration for Worster: not only is Worster the most brilliant of American environmental historians, he is also among the most wide-ranging. More, he once seriously contemplated writing a doctoral dissertation on the subject of this chapter. Why, then, would he invoke Leopold's call for an ecological history, made in passing and in a wholly different context, rather than the work of the man who may justly be regarded as having founded the field in America? For Mumford was using the term "ecological history" as early as 1917, outlining an ecological theory of history in his brilliant essays on regionalism of the 1920s, and writing two full-blown ecological histories in the next decade.[46] As I have shown, he continued to write on environmental themes until the end of his life.

While Worster's preference can be explained positively rather than negatively, that is, as a positive identification with Leopold in which Mumford's more weighty contributions get obscured, it is nonetheless emblematic of the wide neglect of Mumford's ecological writings

[45] Donald Worster, "Transformations of the Earth: Toward an Agroecological Perspective in History," *Journal of American History*, vol. 76, no. 4, 1990, p. 1087.

[46] Miller, *Lewis Mumford*, p. 87.

by American environmental historians, environmental philosophers, and environmental activists. Leopold and Muir appear to be far more congenial to the mind and heart of the American environmentalist. Both were remarkable human beings, acute observers of the natural world, and powerful moralists. But neither had Mumford's historical sweep, sociological sensibilities, or philosophical depth.

This neglect needs to be explained, and I would like to offer a preliminary interpretation. First, a primary influence has been the dominance of wilderness thinking in the American environmental movement. Like Muir and Leopold, Mumford valued primeval nature and biological diversity, but unlike them he focused simultaneously on cultural diversity and relations of power *within* human society. Moreover, his subtle, nuanced, and complex philosophy cannot be reduced to Manichaean oppositions, black and white, good and evil, to which environmentalism, like other social movements, has so often succumbed. Wrenching Muir and Leopold's thought out of context, radical environmentalists can reduce it to the polar opposition of biocentric/anthropocentric. That easy option is foreclosed by the nature of Mumford's thought. There is little hint in Mumford's oeuvre of a scapegoat "out there," whether capitalist or shallow ecologist. Rather, the burden of his work is toward internal social reform, of recognizing that the enemy is "us."

Second, Mumford is not a narrow nationalist. Several writers have noted the historical interpenetration of environmentalism and nationalism in the USA. The wilderness movement itself began as a nationalist crusade to preserve "monuments" of nature not found in Europe; it has since been closely identified with the need to challenge the world's identification of American culture with materialism.[47] Politically, Mumford always opposed American nationalism and its most

---

[47] Cf. Alfred Runte, *National Parks*. Mumford had anticipated Runte's critique of monumentalism when he deplored the tendency of American planners of the past to "single out the most striking forms of landscape." He went on: "If the culture of the environment had yet entered deeply into our consciousness, our aesthetic appreciations would not stop short with stupendous geological formations like the Grand Canyon of Arizona: we should have equal regard for every nook and comer of the earth, and we should not be indifferent to the fate of less romantic areas." *The Culture of Cities*, p. 332. This is yet another striking

egregious expression, isolationism.[48] Intellectually, the internationalism of his outlook is indisputable. Deploring the "false tribal god of nationalism," he was clear that "cultural advances usually work by cross-fertilization," a credo to which his own thought bore such eloquent testimony.[49]

Mumford's political beliefs must also have worked against the wider cultural acceptance of his thought within the USA. An early critic of Stalinism, he was nonetheless a lifelong socialist. He deplored the tyranny and continuing worship of technology in Soviet Russia but recognized that the promise of equality underlying communism, though perverted in practice, was wholly in keeping with the spirit of the age. The task of democracy, he pointed out, was to show that there were better ways of promoting economic and political equality than tyranny and thought control.[50]

Finally, Mumford was perhaps too much of a polymath. He made fundamental contributions in so many fields that it is easy to overlook the ecological underpinnings of his thought. Two major works on Mumford—Donald Miller's authorized biography and the collection of essays edited by Thomas and Agatha Hughes—are both models of sympathetic and rigorous scholarship. They carefully appraise Mumford's contributions to architecture, technology, urban history, regional planning, and literature, but contain little awareness of his ecologically oriented writings.[51] And so Mumford continues to be neglected by American environmentalists.

---

example of Mumford's prescience, for only in the last decade or so has the wilderness movement begun to shift its priorities toward the protection of overall biological diversity and away from a narrow emphasis on the spectacular.

[48] See, for instance, his controversial essay, "The Corruption of Liberalism," *The New Republic,* April 29, 1940. For a conservative critique of Mumford as anti-patriotic, see, Edward Shils, "Lewis Mumford: On the Way to the New Jerusalem," *The New Criterion,* vol. 9, no. 1, 1983.

[49] "Let Man Take Command," p. 8; "Looking Forward," p. 545.

[50] See LM, "The Bolshevist Religion," *The New Republic,* April 1, 1928; LM, "Alternatives to the H-Bomb," *The New Leader,* June 28, 1954.

[51] One reason is probably the writers' own lack of interest in ecology; another is their methodological reliance on Mumford's books and private papers, ignoring the periodical essays that I have so heavily relied upon here. I should add that

And yet Mumford continues to speak powerfully to environment-alists from other cultures. The noted green thinker (and former German green) Rudolf Bahro came upon Mumford's thought rather late but immediately recognized that his work "has the same significance for the ecological movement as the achievement of Marx once had for the labor movement."[52] What the visionary Bahro knew intuitively I have tried to demonstrate painfully, with the apparatus of scholarship, in this chapter. Perhaps I should have been more than ordinarily prepared for the phenomenon of a prophet with little honor in his own country who is deeply respected outside. For, what else has been the fate of the greatest Indian of modern times, Mahatma Gandhi, and the greatest Indian who ever lived, Gautama Buddha?

---

my own reconstruction of Mumford's ecological philosophy is based on a deliberately restricted focus: I have completely ignored his writings in American Studies and architecture, two fields in which his reputation is assured.

[52] Quoted in Kirkpatrick Sale, "Lewis Mumford," obituary notice in *The Nation*, February 19, 1990. Although he has never written at length on Mumford, Sale is rare among American environmentalists in frequently expressing admiration for the man. Cf. his *Dwellers in the Land: The Bioregional Vision* (San Francisco: Sierra Club Books, 1985).

CHAPTER 7

The Subaltern Social Ecology
of Chandi Prasad Bhatt

In the first week of June 1981 I began a secular pilgrimage deep into the Alakananda valley. My destination was Gopeshwar, a town that clings to a hill somewhat short of that holy Hindu shrine, the temple of Badrinath. The living deity I wished to pay tribute to here was Chandi Prasad Bhatt, founder of the Chipko movement, whom I mentioned at the start of this book as fundamental to the beginnings of my interest in environmental history.

From Dehradun, where I lived, I took an early morning bus to Rishikesh and then another to Gopeshwar. The route was redolent with mythology and history, and the landscape diverse: pine forests on one hill, skillfully cut terraces on another, bare and exposed soil on a third. The bus stayed on the left bank of the Ganga until Devprayag, after which we crossed the now divided river to follow the Alakananda. Around noon we reached Srinagar, the ancient capital of Garhwal. This lay in a low valley and was hot and dusty and altogether unappealing—such decent buildings as it ever had had disappeared in a flood, back in 1894. I had lunch in a bazaar that was home to a million flies and got back into the bus. Except it wouldn't start. I got out once more. After a brief subterranean inspection the driver gave his verdict: the radiator had burst and the passengers had now better look out for themselves.

With three or four others I got into a white taxi. We passed a series of hamlets situated on the union of sundry lesser rivers with the mighty

Alakananda. After one such confluence, at Sonprayag, we turned a corner and saw a shepherd boy approaching us, driving his flock. He wore a tightly buttoned-up tunic and had a felt cap on his head. In his right hand was a stick with which to discipline his sheep. As we passed him he flung out his left hand at the taxi and yelled: "H.N. Bahuguna!"

I can still see, as I write this, the boy and his vivid gesture. But at this distance in time I should perhaps explain his yell.

That summer, after decades of self-imposed exile, the veteran politician Hemavati Nandan Bahuguna had returned to his native Garhwal to fight a by-election against a nominee of the Congress Party. Bahuguna had once been a Congress Chief Minister of Uttar Pradesh, as well as a national General Secretary of India's leading (and then also ruling) political party. But now he had left Congress and come back to the hills, he said, so that he could fight for its victimized folk against the fat cats of the plains. One can't be sure he spoke for himself—Bahuguna was a great opportunist who had made his career in the plains— but he certainly spoke for his constituents, as for instance that little shepherd. For, in the India of the 1980s, a private taxi represented almost the apex of consumer society. Anyone who sat in a taxi was certifiably from the plains. Had the bus not broken down and had we passed the flock of sheep and its tender in it, there would have been no hand flung accusingly at us, no invocation by name of a born-again rebel politician.

I hope the shepherd boy had also heard of Chandi Prasad Bhatt, a man born in the hills who had chosen to stay: stay there and serve. To him Garhwal and Garhwalis were not an exploitable resource to be turned to when one's political career was in the doldrums. Bhatt's life-work had been to make his people self-reliant: self-reliant economically, socially, ecologically. But the relevance of his work was by no means restricted to the Himalaya. The movement he started and the ideas it generated were to exercise a powerful appeal among the people of the Indian plains—indeed for rural people everywhere.

Chandi Prasad Bhatt was born on the June 23, 1934, in a family of priests who tended the temple of Rudranath, which nestles in a forest at 13,000 feet. Rudranath is part of the "Panch Kedar," the five Himalayan temples dedicated to Shiva, the most venerated of which is Kedarnath. As a boy Chandi Prasad went up often to the family shrine, the journey also alerting him to local traditions of folk ecology. When he walked through the *bugiyal*, or alpine pasture, he had to take off his shoes so as not to harm the flowers. In one four-kilometer stretch above the Amrit Ganga there was a ban on spitting, coughing, and pissing: on anything that might lead to the pollution of the river below. There were taboos on plucking plants before the festival of Nandasthmi, which took place in September, after which the restraint was removed so that the plucking of now-ripened flowers released their seeds.

Once, on the walk to Rudranath, Chandi Prasad met a shepherd burning flowers of the sacred and beautiful *brahmakamal*. He asked the shepherd why. It was the week of Nandasthmi, and the shepherd answered that he wouldn't have normally, except that his stomach ached horribly and he knew the extract of the flower would cure him. But, the offender quickly added, I broke off the plant with my mouth, like a sheep, so that the deity would think it was nature's natural order rather than the mouth of man.

The elements of ecology that Chandi Prasad learned were acquired informally from the landscape and peasants and pastoralists who made their living within it. Meanwhile, he also studied in schools in the small hill towns of Rudraprayag and Pauri but stopped short of taking a university degree. To support his mother—his father had died when he was very little—he taught art to children for a year before joining a local transport company, the Garhwal Motor Owners Union (GMOU), as a booking clerk. With the GMOU he was posted up and down the Alakananda in large villages, with names as lovely as Pipalkoti and Karanprayag. His years selling bus tickets, he says, alerted him to the social diversity of India, for many of his customers were pilgrims from different parts of the country, practicing various trades and professions.

How did an obscure transport clerk become an influential social worker? In Bhatt's telling the transformation started with his attending a public meeting in Badrinath in 1956. The star speaker here was Jayaprakash Narayan (JP), a hero of the freedom struggle who, after independence, had left politics to do social service as part of the "Sarvodaya" (Service-for-All) movement started by the Gandhian spiritualist Vinoba Bhave. Another speaker was the local Sarvodaya leader

Man Singh Rawat. The young man was deeply impressed by both: now, he would seek out news of JP or Vinoba Bhave and their Sarvodaya movement. When the time came to take his annual holiday he spent it with Man Singh Rawat in the interior villages of Uttarakhand. Rawat's brother owned three buses of the GMOU. If this (by local standards) rich man can abjure his inheritance for Sarvodaya, thought Chandi Prasad, why not I?

Between 1956 and 1960 Chandi Prasad spent his leave learning about Sarvodaya from Rawat and his wife Sashi Behn, who had been trained by the legendary social worker Sarla Behn at the Laxmi Ashram in Kausani. Like Mira Behn (whom we met in Chapter Four), Sarla Behn had been born an Englishwoman, originally named Catherine Mary Heilman; like her, she had joined Gandhi, gone to jail for his cause, and then begun rural work under his inspiration. In the 1930s she had set up an ashram in rural Kumaon which focused particularly on education and employment for women. Many Gandhian activists had been trained by her, among them Man Singh and Sashi Behn Rawat.

During his apprenticeship as a Sarvodaya worker Bhatt took educative treks with the Rawats and also one, in 1959, with Vinoba Bhave. China was now making menacing moves on the frontier. This other Asian giant's challenge, said JP, was not merely military but also ideological. A call for more volunteers was answered by Bhatt who, in 1960, left his job to join the Sarvodaya movement. It was a considerable sacrifice, for he was now married and had a child.

With a few friends Bhatt first ran a labor co-operative that helped repair houses and build roads, its members sharing the work and wages equally. Then, in 1964, was founded the Dashauli Swarajya Seva Sangh (DGSS), which has justly been called the "mother organization of the Chipko movement." That movement lay a full decade in the future. Still, it is worth noting that the foundation stone of the DGSS was laid by a woman—Sucheta Kripalani, Chief Minister of Uttar Pradesh—while the land was donated by another woman, Shyama Devi.

My account of Bhatt's early years and initiation into Sarvodaya comes from an extended interview he granted me in September 2001: the first time, I believe, that this reticent and consistently self-effacing man chose to speak to an outsider about such things.[1] With the found-ing of the DGSS, however, we enter the domain of the public man, that is, of "Bhatt" rather than "Chandi Prasad." The DGSS's emphasis was on local employment generation through the promotion of weaving, bee-keeping, herb collection, and cottage industries that would sus-tainably use forest produce. In 1968 JP and his wife Prabhavati visited Gopeshwar: seeing the work of Bhatt and his fellows they said they were reminded of the spirit of sacrificial heroism that had marked Gandhi's movement.

The activities of the DGSS occasionally brought it into conflict with government. The clashes were usually minor and usually resolv-ed, until in 1973 the Forest Department refused to allot it a batch of hornbeam trees from which to make agricultural implements. As we saw earlier (in Chapter Two), to their dismay the same trees were then auctioned off to a sports goods company in distant Allahabad. The DGSS's feelings were echoed more strongly by the residents of Man-dal, the village that lay adjacent to the disputed forest. At Bhatt's sug-gestion the villagers threatened to hug the trees rather than allow the loggers in. Chipko's first historian, Anupam Mishra, notes that the term originally used by Bhatt was the Garhwali *angalwaltha*, meaning "embrace," a word more resonant with local feeling than the Hindi word "chipko," meaning "to stick to."[2]

The protest at Mandal was followed by several such actions against commercial forestry in the villages of the Alakananda valley. One such protest, at Reni in the spring of 1974, was the work wholly of women, led (as recounted in Chapter Two) by Gaura Devi. Meanwhile, the other great Gandhian of Garhwal, Sunderlal Bahuguna, broke off his trek through Uttarakhand to be with and celebrate the protesters. What he saw was conveyed in articles he wrote in the respected nation-alist weekly of Dehradun, *Yugvani*. Bahuguna hailed Chandi Prasad Bhatt as the "chief organizer" (*mukhya sanchalak*) of the Chipko ando-lan. This, he added, was not an economic movement that would

[1] The interview was conducted at the Lal Bahadur Shastri National Academy of Administration in Mussoorie, where both Bhatt and I had come to speak to young men and women who had just joined the Indian civil services.

[2] See Anupam Mishra and Satyendra Tripathi, *Chipko Movement* (New Delhi: Gandhi Peace Foundation, 1978).

subside once its demands were met: on the contrary its main aim was the fostering of love for trees in the hearts of humans. Safeguarding the hill forests was only Chipko's first step toward transforming the relationship between humans and nature.[3]

The early Chipko protests earned Bhatt the lasting enmity of timber contractors. For decades they had enjoyed free sway over the Himalayan forests, helped by a state policy that granted them leases at rates well below market price. Huge fortunes were made by merchants, practically none of whom were hill men: most hailed from the towns of the Uttar Pradesh plains. The Chipko movement was also opposed by powerful local officials who saw it as a threat to their own authority. They joined with the contractors to malign the Chipko leader; as one journalist reported, "frustrated businessmen and magistrates are spreading the rumour that Bhatt is a Chinese agent."[4]

Chipko was born in the Alakananda valley; its midwives were Bhatt and his co-workers in the DGSS. Later it moved eastward to Kumaon where protests against commercial forestry were co-ordinated by left-wing students of the Uttarakhand Sangharsh Vahini; as well as westward to the Bhagirathi valley where the movement was led by Sunderlal Bahuguna and his associates. Within its original home the movement had entered its second phase: that of reconstruction. Under Bhatt's leadership the DGSS organized dozens of tree planting and protection programs, motivating women in particular to revegetate the barren hillsides that surrounded them. Within a decade this work had begun

---

[3] Bahuguna's essays were printed in *Yugvani* in May and June 1974. The references to Bhatt as the main organizer of Chipko were dropped from the book version of Bahuguna's trek report, *Uttarakhand mein Ek Sau Bis Din* (One Hundred and Twenty Days in Uttarakhand) (Silyara: Navjivan Ashram, 1974). Later, when Bahuguna began organizing Chipko-style agitations in his own region of Tehri Garhwal, he wrote articles dating the origins of Chipko variously to 1930—when a group of hill peasants was killed by the police after a mass protest against forest regulations—or to the seventeenth century, when a group of Rajasthani pastoralists were, according to local myth, martyred for the same reason. This writing out of Bhatt from early Chipko history, and the denial that he was the movement's main founder and inspirer, was then continued by Bahuguna's acolytes, as for example Vandana Shiva in her book *Staying Alive*. The subject has been been a source of lasting bitterness between the two men.

[4] Anon., "The Mahatma's Legacy," *Newsweek*, December 13, 1982.

to show results. A study by S.N. Prasad of the Indian Institute of Science, conducted in 1984, showed that the survival rate of saplings in DGSS plantations was in excess of 70 percent, whereas the figure for Forest Department plantations was much less, between 20 percent and 50 percent.[5]

In the early 1980s the DGSS became the DGSM, with "Mandal" replacing "Sangh." By any name it remains an exemplary organization. Its work has been lovingly described in a booklet written by the journalist Ramesh Pahari, who has known Bhatt for three decades. Pahari writes of Bhatt's "simplicity and modesty, but [also his] firmness of ideas and decisions." He quotes a low-caste member of the DGSM committee, Murari Lal, to the effect that "Bhattji has fought bigger battles for removal of social inequities, than for environmental protection." It was in Murari Lal's village that the first tree-planting program was organized. This one-time construction worker has been an inseparable associate of Bhatt for thirty-five years. Their relationship is based on mutual respect, the only irritant being the Gandhian's objection to Murari Lal's love of tobacco.[6]

Bhatt has little time for writing, but when he has put pen to paper his words convey both understanding and wisdom. Twenty years ago, in the journal *Pahar*, he wrote a soberly argued critique of large dams. He has also written insightfully on forest conservation, urging a creative synthesis between the "practical knowledge" of peasants and the "latest scientific knowledge" of the state.[7]

Some Indian environmentalists tend to demonize modern science, seeing in it the basic source of all forms of violence and exploitation in our time.[8] Chandi Prasad Bhatt has a more discriminating and, dare

[5] Personal communication from Dr S.N. Prasad.

[6] Ramesh Pahari, *Dashauli Gram Swarajya Mandal* (Dehradun: Peoples Science Institute, 1997).

[7] Chandi Prasad Bhatt, *Eco-System of the Central Himalayas and Chipko Movement: Determination of Hill People to Save their Forests* (Gopeshwar: Dashauli Gram Swarajya Sangh, 1980); idem, *The Future of Large Projects in the Himalaya* (NainiTal: Pahar, 1992). This is an English translation of an essay first published in Hindi in 1983.

[8] Cf. the essays in Ashis Nandy, ed., *Science, Hegemony, and Violence: A Requiem for Modernity* (New Delhi: Oxford University Press, 1989).

one say, more subtle perspective on the dominant forms of modern knowledge. He can analyze and critique the ways in which science has both centralized power and caused environmental degradation. Indeed, he has been in the forefront of the opposition to monocultural forestry and large dams, both state schemes which have claimed the mandate of science. Yet Bhatt also sees that technical knowledge, when informed by an ecological sensibility and attention to social deprivation, can and has been put to humane use. He has long called for a decentralized approach to planning, and has himself pioneered the dissemination of "appropriate" rural technologies such as biogass plants and micro-hydel projects. While keen to listen to and learn from the people, he doesn't romanticize folk wisdom either. It isn't just science which has to be reformed, he argues, but also local practices which, in an altered ecological and demographic context, have become unsustainable. He notes that in the hills terracing on very steep slopes and free-range grazing are no longer viable for either society or nature.[9]

Postmodern critics of science like to invoke Mahatma Gandhi: that invocation is mistaken, if not somewhat opportunistic. Bhatt's understanding of the limits and possibilities of modern science is, I believe, far closer to Gandhi's position. That position was stated with characteristic clarity in a speech the Mahatma delivered to a group of college students in Trivandrum in March 1925:

> It is a common superstition in India, and more so outside India—because that is what I find from my correspondence in Europe and America—that I am an opponent, a foe, of science. Nothing can be further from the truth than a charge of this character. It is perfectly true, however, that I am not an admirer of science unmixed with something I am about to say to you. I think we cannot live without science, if we keep it in its right place. But I have learnt so much during my wanderings in the world about the misuse of science that I have often remarked, or made such remarks, as would lead people to consider that I was really an opponent of science. In my humble opinion there are limitations even to scientific search, and the limitations that I place upon scientific search are the limitations that humanity imposes upon us.

[9] Cf. Chandi Prasad Bhatt, *Himalaya Kshetra ka Niyojan* (The Amelioration of the Himalaya) (Gopeshwar: Dashauli Gram Swarajya Mandal, 1984).

Gandhi went on to say that he appreciated the urge that led scientists to conduct basic research, to do "science for the sake of science." But he worried that scientists and science students in India came overwhelmingly from the middle class—which also usually meant the upper castes—and hence knew only how to use their minds and not their hands. His view was that it would be "utterly impossible for a boy to understand the secrets of science or the pleasures and the delights that scientific pursuits can give, if that boy is not prepared to use his hands, to tuck up his sleeves and labour like an ordinary labourer in the streets." However, if "hands go hand in hand with your heads," then you could properly place science in the service of humanity. "Unfortunately," said Gandhi

> we, who learn in colleges, forget that India lives in her villages and not in her towns.
>
> India has 700,000 villages and you, who receive a liberal education, are expected to take that education or the fruits of that education to the villages. How will you infect the people of the villages with your scientific knowledge? Are you then learning science in terms of the villages and will you be so handy and so practical that the knowledge that you derive in a college so magnificently built—and I believe equally magnificently equipped—you will be able to use for the benefits of the villagers?[10]

It is very unlikely that Bhatt has read this speech. Yet through his wanderings in the world and his deeply developed moral sense he has arrived at an understanding of modern science strikingly congruent with Gandhi's. In his own more modest way Bhatt has also influenced the direction of scientific research and application. He has worked with some greatly esteemed Indian scientists—among them the ecologist Madhav Gadgil (the subject of the next chapter) and the agricultural scientist M.S. Swaminathan. He has inspired younger scientists to put their knowledge to the service of India's villagers. One of his early efforts was to persuade a young engineer to work on upgrading the indigenous water mill (*gharat*). Traditionally used to grind grain, this device suitably refined was now able to generate electricity for local needs. Reporting this experiment Bhatt remarked that "the hills want

[10] "Speech in Reply to Students' Address, Trivandrum," March 13, 1925, in *Collected Works of Mahatma Gandhi*, vol. 26, pp. 299–303.

exactly this type of technology. But to produce it, engineers and scientists would have to first become rustics and devote themselves to the Himalayas to understand exactly what they want."[11]

Bhatt is a great pioneering environmentalist, an actor and thinker of remarkable range and achievement who, by virtue of innate modesty and lack of command over English, remains much less known and honored than he should be. He has no trumpet nor any trumpeters. One really has to go to Garhwal to get the measure of his work, and that of his colleagues. To me these words of Ramesh Pahari seem almost exactly right:

> A variety of issues being discussed all over the world today—the advancement of women and dalit [downtrodden] groups and their participation in decision-making, ecology, environment, traditional rights of people, the indigenous knowledge of people, basing development processes on successful experiences and self-reliant economics—have first been worked on by DGSM thirty-odd years ago; and without any fanfare.

I think one can quietly repeat that last clause: *without any fanfare.*[12]

II

Let me return to that bus-and-taxi journey twenty-five years back when that shepherd boy shouted "H.N. Bahuguna." Later that same evening I reached Gopeshwar. After depositing my bags in a government guesthouse I made for the DGSM office. I had just begun research toward a social history of the Himalayan forests, a project in which Bhatt's work would naturally figure rather heavily. I hoped over the course of the next few days to interview him at length about Chipko and, with luck, scrutinize the files of the DGSM as well.

That evening, however, someone else had got there before me. This was a doctoral student from the University of Roorkee who had come to consult Bhatt about *his* project. He wished to choose twenty villages, with one set of ten situated more or less on a motor road, and another

---

[11] Chandi Bhatt, *Eco-system of the Central Himalayas*, pp. 39–40. The remarks date from 1978. This technology is now fairly widespread in Garhwal, as also in neighboring Himachal Pradesh and Nepal.

[12] Pahari, *Dashauli Gram Swarajya Mandal.*

set of ten located more than five kilometers away from the road. In these villages he would administer a questionnaire on the availability of various goods and services to test the hypothesis that access to roads was crucial to rural uplift.

The Roorkee economist wanted to survey twenty villages: but which twenty? He had never been to Garhwal before and no reliable maps juxtaposing villages with roads existed. So his sample came to be constituted by Bhatt.

Bhatt spoke in chaste Hindi, accented here and there by his native tongue (soft s's, as in *pasupalan*, and the occasional substitution of vowels, as in *kohte hain* for *kehte hain*). From the storehouse of his memory he drew out the names of twenty villages; ten right by the road, ten distant from it. But that wasn't enough: he also provided the economist directions, and useful contacts. So he said, for example:

> Take the bus to Chopta. Get down at Hanumangarhi. Walk on for a kilometer, past an oak forest, and then take the path leading up the hill to the left. This leads to the village of Bemru, which I am sure is more than five kilometers from the roadhead. Ask for the school-master: his name is Pran Nath. Tell him I have sent you. He will help you with the question-naire.

It was a command performance, extending for over an hour and conducted for an audience of two. This fellow, I thought, must have trekked across every hill and every valley in upper Garhwal and very nearly talked to every man, woman, and child there. As I walked back to my room that night I was reminded of an episode from the epic Mahabharata. Bhatt, I felt, was Krishna, and the Roorkee boy and I Duryodhana and Arjuna, respectively, come here to garner his drops of wisdom. I would have to wait until the next day to get what I wanted from him: his work with forests and Chipko. I trusted I would put that to more creative use, for, as I saw it, my rival's project seemed rather to trivialize Bhatt's awesome knowledge of the geography of Garhwal.

Over the next week, with the economist safely away in his villages, I talked at length to Bhatt and went over the documents he showed me. These I later juxtaposed with interviews conducted and documents read elsewhere in the hills. What I finally learnt about Chandi Prasad Bhatt, Chipko leader, is narrated in my book *The Unquiet Woods*. Here

I'll stick with the man. He was, and indeed still is, very handsome: of medium height but erect and beautifully proportioned, an oval face clothed in a neat beard, dark bright eyes looking directly at you. In his native heath he exudes a quiet confidence and dignity; not always outside it, however. Thus in October 1983 I saw him in the Kumaon town of Pithoragarh releasing the first issue of a research annual on the Himalaya. Inside a fairly large conference room this pioneer of Chipko was not comfortable facing the crowd. He clutched the microphone hard with both hands for assurance, whereas a practiced speaker would have stood away from it. The next day, however, he spoke more naturally in the open. This was at the village of Chandak-Sikhrana, at the time badly battered by magnesite mining.

In September 2001 I heard Bhatt speak in Mussoorie in honor of P. Srinivas, a brave forest officer who was killed searching for the legendary bandit and elephant poacher Veerappan. Bhatt still spoke softly and with shy sincerity but he seemed more at ease now with the appurtenances of modern technology: mike, slides, a slide projector. With their aid he took an audience of aspiring civil servants through a magisterial ecological history of the Himalaya: the glaciers, the rivers, the forests, the fields. The slides came from his own travels and the language he used to gloss them was exquisitely clear: as clear, indeed, as his description of a free-flowing hill river: "*shishe jaise chamakta hua jal*" (water transparent as a pane of glass). He documented the degradation caused by humans but also their potential for ameliorative action. Responsible environmentalism, he said, could be of the P. Srinivas kind or of the Chipko kind. It could come from upright officials or from concerned citizens, or, better still, from the two working in combination.

The first question from the audience dealt not with the Himalaya but the Narmada Bachao Andolan (NBA). The questioner claimed the NBA was motivated by foreign agents who wished to hold up India's development. Bhatt gently reminded him of the historical experience of displaced people in India. He said, "*doob shetra wale log ko chinti ké bhi neeche samjha jata hai*" (the oustees of dams are treated even worse than ants). Characteristically, he moved from criticism to construction. An estimated 47,000 hectares were to be irrigated by the Sardar Sarovar dam. Why shouldn't 10 percent of this be alloted to those displaced by the project? He had spoken of this when he visited Gujarat after the earthquake of January 2001 and thought it a solution the NBA could fruitfully pursue.

The case can be made for Bhatt as the first environmentalist of the poor whose work with Chipko anticipated similar struggles led by the likes of Brazil's Chico Mendes and Kenya's Wangari Maathai. Yet, ironically, this global pioneer is not even very well known in India. Those who know Bhatt and his work have long felt that—from the English language press at any rate—he has never got his just deserts. The Chipko movement that he and his colleagues started was in fact a definitive moment in the history of world environmentalism. Before Chipko it was thought, *pace* Lester Thurow (see Chapter One), that the poor were too poor to be green. After Chipko, indeed through Chipko, it was demonstrated that peasants and tribals had a greater stake in the responsible management of nature than had aesthetically-minded city dwellers. Then again it was Bhatt who first taught Indian environmentalists it was not enough to righteously protest at destruction of one kind or another: they must also set about the process of reconstruction. Seeking always to improve the lives of the poor, Bhatt has sought to humanize modern science rather than reject it, to democratize the bureaucracy rather than too quickly demonize it.

Bhatt doesn't care very much for media attention. He would value far more the impact of his work on the village women of Garhwal. Through his example he has also had considerable influence on social workers elsewhere in India. When I wrote a profile of Bhatt in the press I received this letter from an activist working in the tribal districts of Andhra Pradesh—the letter bears witness both to the quality of Bhatt's mind and to his style of working:

Dear R. Guha

I read your coverage on Sri Chandiprasad Bhatt in *The Hindu*. Sri Bhatt visited our place Rampachodavaram in the tribal area in East Godavari of Andhra Pradesh in 1987 to find out the reasons for the severe floods of river Godavari in 1986. I started a NGO, SAKTI, in 1985 after completing [my] Ph.D. on tribal knowledge systems of this area. A common friend brought Bhatt to me. He toured for seven days and his report came in *Jansatta* [a Hindi daily] with the title "Godavari ke god me ab toot kar girenge pahad" [the mountains will soon fall into the Godavari river]. His visit inspired me to take a different course of action, litigation, to check the deforestation, since the hold of Naxalites [Maoist revolutionaries] is intense in these areas and they are also part of the nexus. We were able to check state sponsored deforestation by forcing the closure of [a] plywood factory felling the wild mango trees, felling of thick forest by cultivation *pattadars* [farmers] and mining by non-tribals, etc. . . .

On my request Mr Bhatt again visited our place in 1990 when Visakha district tribal area was devastated by [a] cyclone in the summer of 1990.

[The noted environmentalist] Anil Agarwal was visiting Hyderabad in 1992. We were discussing Sri Bhatt. Anil was telling me that Bhatt mobilized the people and afforestation was taken up in the Reserved Forests without caring for any permission from the [forest] department. This information inspired me to take up afforestation mobilizing tribals . . .

So far, I could not go to Sri Bhatt's place. Though the interaction with him is very brief the insight and impetus he gave me is everlasting and unfolded a new era in the history of resource management in the tribal areas of Andhra Pradesh. I hope you will cover such efforts of Sri Bhatt in outreaching other areas and his other facets of constructive work.

Regards

P. Sivaramakrishna
SAKTI

I have the most cherished memories of talking with Bhatt myself. But let me end with another memory, of simply passing him on a road. One evening in New Delhi, I was driving past a row of very high-voltage institutions bunched together: the India International Centre (IIC), the World Wildlife Fund, the Ford Foundation, the World Bank, and the United Nations Development Program. There, on this road redolent with power and privilege, I passed two middle-aged men clad in khadi, talking. I turned into a side lane and watched them for a while. They were Bhatt and Anupam Mishra, Bhatt's fellow green Gandhian of integrity and achievement, the early chronicler of Chipko and the author of masterly surveys of water management in Rajasthan. They continued talking till a bus came along, they hopped into it and were lost to me.

Then, and now, I speculate on where these two men were coming from. From a meeting at the WWF, perhaps? In that case, there should have been other people around them. Or maybe some of these other people had gone off to the IIC for a drink, still others to the World Bank pool for a swim. Even were they to have had the necessary memberships, I cannot imagine Chandi Prasad Bhatt and Anupam Mishra exercising either of those options. In them lives a spirit of quiet service that once existed freely in Indian politics and activism.

This is a spirit that, certainly in India, has been completely excised from the political sphere and is gravely threatened in the world of activism. Even for these two basic reasons, if for no other, there is more to be said for the life and example of Chandi Prasad Bhatt than for the myriad new environmentalists whose activism is inseparable from a life of privilege and the desire for publicity.

CHAPTER 8

The Democratic Social Ecology
of Madhav Gadgil

In no city of modern India is scholarship and social reform so interwoven as Pune. Here have lived and worked the pioneers of the
Indian liberal tradition—Jotiba Phule, Gopal Krishna Gokhale,
Tarabai Shinde, D.K. Karve, B.R. Ambedkar, and others—those who
brought to wider attention the need for women's education, caste uplift, social service, and liberal values more generally. These were the
luminaries, but ranking slightly below them is a range of other Punai-
kars (Pune citizens) who combined pursuit of knowledge with the
desire for action. One such was the economist, sociologist, and institu-
tion-builder Dhananjaya Ramachandra Gadgil.

Born in 1902, Gadgil was educated at the universities of Bombay
and Cambridge. At the latter he wrote an M.Litt. dissertation which
became a classic. Published in 1923 as *The Industrial Evolution of India
in Recent Times*, it stayed in print a full seventy years. Among his other
contributions to scholarship were many essays on economic policy and
planning, and a landmark study of the sociology of business communities. Among his contributions to society were his founding of the
Gokhale Institute of Politics and Economics and the nurturing of
farmers' cooperatives in Maharashtra. From 1967 to 1970 he served as
Deputy Chairman of the Government of India's Planning Commission, a post generally regarded as the summit of achievement for an applied economist in India.

D.R. Gadgil was a man of learning and courage. In 1946 he and the brilliant civil servant A.D. Gorwala were asked by the Government of Bombay to recommend measures to assure a fairer distribution of food in times of scarcity. While they deliberated Mahatma Gandhi announced that there was no need for state intervention in the distribution of food. Gadgil and Gorwala insisted that non-intervention by the state would promote hoarding and blackmarketing. In this time of crisis, they argued, only rationing and fair price shops could bring grain within reach of the poor. To disagree with Gandhi took courage; but then Gadgil had plenty of that. As the columnist D.F. Karaka put it:

> It would be difficult to find a truer picture of all that is best in the ancient Indian tradition than Gadgil. A slim, gaunt man, argumentative and aggressive on the right occasions, full of courage and with a wisdom grounded in deep knowledge of both theory and facts, Gadgil had devoted himself for many years to the building up of a true school of politics and economics, eschewing all profitable pursuit. On occasion after occasion he had turned down offers of employment by the government. He joined the Board primarily because he felt the situation in the country was so critical that a right lead was essential and without the right lead it might become disastrous. [1]

II

About ten years after D.R. Gadgil took on Mahatma Gandhi he was visited by Wassily Leontief, the Russian exile and founder of input–output analysis who is widely regarded as one of the greatest economists of the twentieth century. Leontief was giving a series of lectures at the Gokhale Institute and was a house guest of the Gadgils. One day the visitor struck up a conversation with his host's youngest son, a boy of thirteen named Madhav. "Young man, what will you do when you grow up?," asked Leontief. "I want to become a biologist," answered Madhav. "Wonderful, excellent!," commented the economist: "Never do what your father does—especially if your father is any good at what he does."

It is a pity that so few Indians follow this advice. Consider how the reputations of the politician Indira Gandhi, the musician Anoushka

---

[1] D.F. Karaka, *Betrayal in India* (London: Victor Gollancz, 1950), p. 217.

Shankar, and the cricketer Rohan Gavaskar have been so clouded by the vastly greater reputations of the parent who preceded them in the same profession. D.R. Gadgil agreed implicitly with Leontief and was partly responsible for orienting his son away from economics. He had an amateur's interest in nature, in birds particularly, and was a subscriber to the *Journal of the Bombay Natural History Society*. His son Madhav read the journal as it came to the house and juxtaposed its contents with what he saw in the wider world.

Even today, Pune has acres of green grass amidst all the concrete. There is, for example, the verdant campus of the University of Pune (formerly the residence of the Governor of Bombay), rich in trees and butterflies and birds. There are also large open spaces colonized by nature in the army cantonment. Fifty years ago Pune was greener still. Then, as now, it lay within easy range of the Western Ghats, otherwise known as the Sahyadri mountains.

Once, on a hilltop in Italy overlooking Lake Como, I heard Madhav Gadgil speak to a band of international scholars about his lifelong love affair with the Sahyadris. He later expressed it in print: "Describing King Raghu's conquest of the four corners of India, Kalidasa likens the Western Ghats to a comely young maiden, her head near Kanyakumari, her feet near [the river] Tapi. I fell in love with this damsel at a tender age, maybe of three or four, and with time have grown more and more fond of her."[2]

By his early teens Madhav Gadgil had decided to become a biologist. Toward this end he took a first degree in science from Ferguson College, Pune, and then a masters in zoology from Bombay University. In 1965 he proceeded to Harvard to enrol for a doctorate in ecology. With him was his newly wedded wife, Sulochana, a Pune girl who had been admitted to Harvard for a PhD in mathematics.

In the 1950s and 1960s a distinguished member of the Harvard biology department was James Watson. Watson thought the future of biology, indeed of all science, lay in the laboratory. He had contempt for the field biologist, whom he saw as an unfortunate throwback to the world of the amateur naturalist. One of those at the receiving end of Watson's scorn was Edward O. Wilson.[3] By the time Madhav Gadgil

[2] Madhav Gadgil, "In Love with Life," *Seminar*, September 1993.

[3] As recalled with some feeling in Wilson's memoirs, *Naturalist* (Washington, DC: Warner Books, 1994).

arrived at Harvard, however, Watson had left Harvard and evolutionary ecology was coming into its own. E.O. Wilson was one of the Indian's early mentors. His dissertation work, however, was done with W.H. Bossert on life history strategies. This was a pioneering attempt at applying mathematical modeling to ecology. One of the papers that grew out of this work became a "citation classic."[4]

Two conversations I had in the late 1980s testify to the impact that Gadgil's early work had. One was in Delhi, with an Indian biologist of his generation, who claimed, or complained rather, that the math in that classic paper was the work of Gadgil's wife.[5] The second conversation was in Berkeley, with an up and coming American biologist, who was disbelieving when I told him that Gadgil was based in India. For how could a man who did such cutting-edge work live anywhere but in the USA?

In fact the Gadgils had decided to return home shortly after completing their PhDs. This was unusual, but more striking was their decision not to have children in America, this perhaps a deeper mark of their patriotism, for Indians who choose to come back still usually have their children in America so as to give them an early escape route to the West.[6]

In 1971 the Gadgils returned to their native Pune. Gadgil joined the Maharashtra Association for the Cultivation for Science. There was no teaching and the laboratory facilities were meager, so he decided to resume his acquaintance with the mountains around Pune. On a field trip in the Ghats he came across a small patch of primeval forest protected by the peasants as a sacred grove. However, the Forest Department wanted to acquire this grove preparatory to axing it.

The intensity of the villagers' feelings over that patch of forest led Gadgil to look for other such groves across Maharashtra. With his

---

[4] M. Gadgil and W.H. Bossert, "Life Historical Consequences of Natural Selection," *American Naturalist*, no. 104, 1970.

[5] This the complainant saw as an unfair advantage, particularly as he himself was married to a housewife. (But then that was his choice.) While it is not relevant where the math came from, one must note nevertheless that Sulochana and Madhav Gadgil are the only Indian husband and wife team who are both top quality scientists. Sulochana is Professor of Atmospheric Sciences at the Indian Institute of Science in Bangalore and a world authority on the monsoon.

[6] One more indication of this patriotism is that after coming back Gadgil has chosen to publish much of his best work in Indian journals.

teacher V.D. Vartak he traveled the countryside, enumerating and studying the sacred groves that remained. Like Dietrich Brandis a century before him (see Chapter Four), Gadgil came to see these groves as examples of indigenous conservation. They were richer in plant and animal diversity than the surrounding vegetation, particularly with regard to climbers and epiphytes. "With the felling of forest all around them, the sacred groves have become the last refuge of many plant species." Thus, their conservation was "desirable both from a practical and an aesthetic point of view."[7]

In 1973 Sulochana Gadgil was offered a position at the Indian Institute of Science (IISc) in Bangalore. She had her husband's c.v. with her; in the event, both were asked to join the institute's newly established Centre for Theoretical Studies. The IISc is without question the leading center of scientific and technological research in India. The quality of its research and teaching has never been in dispute, though its relevance to society sometimes has: the world-class mathematicians, physicists, and biologists on its staff are oriented largely toward publication in Western journals that are little read in India, while the dozens of PhDs they annually produce more often than not end up in an American university, part of India's ever growing "brain drain."

The IISc is, for the most part, an island of West-centered excellence in an ocean of Indian poverty and drudgery. However, the year after the Gadgils joined, there arose a movement to "correct the urban bias" in the programs of the institute by fashioning a science for the rural poor. This led to the creation of the Centre for Appropriate Science and Technology for Rural Areas (ASTRA), whose prime mover was A.K.N. Reddy, Professor of Chemistry at the IISc.

Through the 1970s and 1980s ASTRA developed and widely disseminated a range of environmentally sound, low cost, decentralized technologies, as for example mud-block houses, biogass plants, and improved cooking stoves. On a more academic plane it conducted studies of the flow of energy and biomass in village ecosystems, mapping how peasants fulfilled material requirements from local environments.

---

[7] Madhav Gadgil and V.D. Vartak, "Sacred Groves of India: A Plea for their Continued Conservation," *The Journal of the Bombay Natural History Society*, vol. 72, no. 2, 1974.

Reddy himself was an early exponent of environmentally sound development. An essay of 1978 by him identified the goals of "eco-development" as, first, the satisfaction of basic needs, especially of poorer segments of the population; second, endogenous self-reliance, both in terms of using local raw materials and through social participation and control; third, harmony with the environment so as to ensure the long-term sustainability of the development process. In its work ASTRA was also alert to the sociological dimension; to the interplay of caste and gender within the village and to factors that constrained or promoted the social adoption of new technologies.[8]

Like the folks at ASTRA, Gadgil was a scientist whose temperament took him away from the laboratory into the field. While still in Pune he had begun working with the anthropologist Kailash Malhotra on a study of the pastoralists of peninsular India. This, truly, was a marriage of disciplines, with concepts of territoriality and niche diversification used to understand the human ecology and foraging strategies of shepherds and herders.[9]

Fieldwork by Gadgil and Malhotra revealed that different endogamous groups living in the same region minimized competition through resource partitioning and exclusion. Thus, individual castes, and often individual families or lineages within them, were by custom assigned a monopoly over a particular resource in a particular territory. This reduced competition, fostered prudence, and helped maintain the stability of the system in the long run.[10]

---

[8] Among A.K.N. Reddy's writings, see especially "The Transfer, Transformation and Generation of Technology for Rural Development," in K.D. Sharma and M.A. Qureshi, eds, *Science, Technology and Development: Essays in Honour of A. Rahman* (New Delhi: Sterling Publishers, 1978); and *Technology, Development and the Environment: A Reappraisal* (Nairobi: United Nations Environment Program, 1979). Cf. also K.S. Jagadish, "Generating Appropriate Rural Technologies: The ASTRA Experience," in Vijay Padaki, ed., *Development Intervention and Programme Evaluation: Concepts and Cases* (New Delhi: Sage Publications, 1995).

[9] Madhav Gadgil and and K.C. Malhotra, "Ecology of a Pastoral Caste: The Gavli Dhangars of Peninsular India," *Human Ecology*, vol. 10, no. 2, 1982.

[10] Idem, "Adaptive Significance of the Indian Caste System: An Ecological Perspective," *Annals of Human Biology*, vol. 10, no. 5, 1983.

The work of Gadgil and Malhotra represented a cross-disciplinary collaboration unprecedented in the Indian academy. Ecologist and anthropologist, respectively, they were akin in their penchant for fieldwork and in their facility with languages—both speak superb Marathi and Hindi, and each speaks at least two other languages. Both were scientists with immense curiosity, interested in knowledge for knowledge's sake, but also public intellectuals keen that the fruits of such knowledge find application in social policy.

In 1980 the duo were asked by the newly established Department of Environment to survey the major environmental problems facing India. Characteristically, they went to the field to find out. They spent five weeks traveling around the countryside, visiting the Western Ghats and the Himalaya, the Rajasthan desert, the Central Indian forests, and the farmlands of the Deccan. They stayed away from the towns, choosing instead to talk to and stay with peasants, pastoralists, and fisherfolk. The report they wrote provided a masterly overview of various forms of environmental degradation in contemporary India. Among the cases highlighted were waterlogging in the Narmada valley, pollution by chemical factories in Goa, and deforestation in the Himalaya. There was, they noted, widespread "overexploitation by commercial interests" who had a "tendency to externalise costs," with the burden of these depradations being borne by "impoverished masses eking out a subsistence." Among the corrective measures they suggested were the democratization of natural resource management by involving local communities, and the assessment of large development projects by a comprehensive "techno-environmental-socio-economic" framework rather than by financial criteria alone. The Gadgil–Malhotra report was a precocious attempt at charting the elements of an environmentalism of the poor.[11]

III

I first met Gadgil in the same summer that I first met Chandi Prasad Bhatt. He had come to the Forest Research Institute in Dehradun,

[11] Madhav Gadgil and K.C. Malhotra, *A People's View of Eco-Development*, Report to the Committee to Recommend Legislative Measures and Administrative Machinery for Environmental Protection, Government of India, September 1980 (New Delhi: World Wildlife Fund, 1982).

where my father worked, to speak on social behavior among elephants. After he had finished I went up and introduced myself. We had something to talk about for I had just begun research on the history of forest policy in India. It was a subject about which Gadgil knew a great deal.

Looking back at Gadgil's career after he returned from Harvard, I am tempted to divide it into three distinct phases: (i) indigenous conservation systems in the 1970s; (ii) forest policy in the 1980s; (iii) biodiversity and related issues in the 1990s.

As we saw earlier, through the 1970s his work was mainly on indigenous conservation systems, as exemplified by sacred groves and traditions of prudent resource use in the Deccan countryside.

In the 1980s, his second phase, Gadgil came to focus on forest policy. One of his first PhD students, S.N. Prasad, had written a dissertation on the disappearing bamboo stocks of northern Karnataka. This alerted Gadgil to serious biases in Indian forest policy caused in the main by the pressures of industrial demand. Thus, as Gadgil and Prasad discovered, bamboo was supplied by the state to paper mills at the subsidized rate of Rs 1 (about 2 cents) per ton. Basket weavers, meanwhile, had to buy the bamboo they needed in the open market, where the price prevailing was Rs 5000 (about $110.00) per ton. This was not merely unjust but, from an ecological point of view, deeply irrational. Offered a massive subsidy, and not sure how long the offer would last, paper mills were encouraged to raid the bamboo forests and fell clumps, regardless of what this might mean for bamboo regeneration.[12]

Through the 1980s Gadgil wrote a series of seminal papers on forest policy and forest management. These combined the perspectives of sociology and ecology, looking both at the scientific limitations of forestry as it was practiced and its wider implications in terms of social equity. On the historical side Gadgil's studies demonstrated the failures of sustained-yield management in the tropics. Whatever it may have been in its original home, Germany, scientific forestry in India was a pseudo science, lacking both the empirical base and the theoretical frame required to make sense of the diverse ecosystems which it

[12] S.N. Prasad and M. Gadgil, *Conservation of Bamboo Stocks in Karnataka* (Bangalore: Karnataka State Council for Science and Technology, 1980).

faced. On the ecological side, Gadgil mounted a powerful critique of the destruction of mixed tropical stands and their replacement by monocultures of exotics like eucalyptus and tropical pine. In one case, in his beloved Western Ghats, the eucalyptus had been attacked by a fungal disease, converting rich tropical forest into a man-made desert. On the sociological side Gadgil showed that forest management in India had discriminated against the interests of peasants, pastoralists, and artisans, whose requirements of forest produce were always sub-servient to industrial demand.

Where other critics of forest policy were content merely to criticize, Gadgil sought ways in which these policies could be changed so as to harmonize competing demands. He identified three major claims on the forest: those of ecology, equity, and efficiency. These, he argued, could best be met through a tripartite physical demarcation. Some forest areas should be managed principally for maintaining biological diversity, other forest areas for meeting the long-neglected subsistence requirements of peasants, tribals, pastoralists, and artisans. As for the market demand for timber, this should be shifted wholly away from natural forests. Private farmers could be encouraged to grow commercial tree species on their holdings and supply direct to paper and plywood factories, ideally through the medium of marketing co-operatives. Rural producers might also be encouraged to undertake some wood processing. This would lead to a fairer distribution of market gains between city and countryside while allowing natural forests to regenerate without the threat of excessive pressure from commercial interests. These policies would also reduce corruption within the Forest Department—by reducing the discretionary power of its officials to award contracts for timber felling.[13]

To be fair, Gadgil was by no means the only scholar working in this field. The 1980s witnessed an intense, acrimonious, but in the end

[13] Probably the most authoritative of Gadgil's statements on forest policy is his foundation day address to the Society for Promotion of Wastelands Development, published as *Deforestation in India: Patterns and Processes* (New Delhi: SPWD, 1989). Among the numerous other essays authored or co-authored by Gadgil, see especially Madhav Gadgil, Rauf Ali, and S. N. Prasad, "Forest Policy and Forest Management in India: A Critical Review," in Walter Fernandes and Sharad Kulkarni, eds, *Towards a New Forest Policy* (New Delhi: Indian Social Institute, 1983).

productive debate on forest policy in India. Contributors to this debate included sociologists, foresters, lawyers, activists, and even some
industrialists. But in my view it was Gadgil who provided the most
original and insightful analyses of what was wrong in the forest sector.
It was also the work of Gadgil that, in the end, had a lasting impact.
The National Forest Policy, issued by the Government of India in
1988, bears the mark of his studies and recommendations, not least in
its ecological focus (with clearfelling being explicitly prohibited), as
well as in its relative sensitivity to tribal and rural interests.

IV

In the winter of 1987–8 a coalition of NGOs in peninsular India hosted a "Save the Western Ghats March" (SWGM). The idea, originally,
was Kalanand Mani's. Mani was an activist from Bihar who had cut his
teeth working with Jayaprakash Narayan's anti-corruption movement
of the 1970s and had since settled in Goa. Groups all along the Ghats
joined in, from socialists in Maharashtra active on the range's northern edges, to the Kerala Sastra Sahitya Parishad (KSSP)—a popular
science movement that had long worked on the Ghat's southern ex-
tremities. The chairman of the "central advisory committee" for the
SWGM was Gadgil's co-author, the anthropologist K.C. Malhotra.
Also active in the march's planning was Gadgil.

In November 1987 one group of marchers began its walk from
Nawapur in Maharashtra. Simultaneously, another group began its
way up the peninsula from its southernmost tip at Kanyakumari.
Three months later they met at the town of Ponda in Goa. Each group
covered in excess of 2000 kilometers, mostly on foot, except where the
terrain grew too harsh, at which point buses and motorcycles were
deployed. A dozen marchers from the south, and seventeen from the
north, went the whole hog, being accompanied in segments by hundreds of other volunteers, these variously students, scientists, activists,
and villagers. They walked, they watched, and they observed, keeping
track of forms of environmental degradation, seeking to analyze causes
and, where possible, the best ways of stopping or stemming this degradation.[14]

[14] See Mahesh Vijapurkar, "Lessons from a March," *Frontline*, February 20–
March 4, 1988.

Gadgil spent several weeks on the march. At the plenary meeting in Ponda he presented a magisterial paper on the ecology and biodiversity of the Western Ghats. This analyzed its soil structure, hydrology, and vegetation, as well as the threats posed to its integrity by the demands of industry, mining, plantations, and commercial agriculture.[15] Based on the feedback he received at this meeting, Gadgil then formulated a "follow-up action plan" for the marchers. He outlined a range of thirteen specific programs to be taken up, covering both "ecological objectives" such as biodiversity conservation, and "social objectives" such as equitable access. This plan sought to accommodate the diversity of ideologies represented at Ponda, with some marchers seeking return to a rural past, but others in favor of encouraging modern industry with adequate environmental safeguards.

Gadgil's own preference was for an inclusive approach, "with a broad involvement of all cross sections of the society" and the environmental ideologies that matched these. He suggested the formation of an umbrella group, to be called the "Consortium of Voluntary Agencies for Sustainable Development of Western Ghats" perhaps, or—a shorter Indian alternative—"Paschimadri Parisara Samudaya." By whatever name, any such consortium had to work with a range of other institutions. These could include local schools and colleges, which at present had "little to do with problems either of their immediate environment or of the society," yet which "have however great potential for constructive work;" local representative bodies such as village and district councils; the armed forces and industry, which had "an overwhelming impact on the environment and the society of the Western Ghats;" and local farmers whose practices were not always benign in their impact on the environment.[16]

Gadgil prefaced his proposal with a warning: any follow up, he said, must "consider not only what is desirable but also what is feasible." This was a coded, or perhaps not so coded, reference to the "purism"

[15] Madhav Gadgil, "The Western Ghats of India: An Ecodevelopment Approach," in *Save the Western Ghats* (Ponda, Goa: Central Organising Committee of Save the Western Ghats March, 1988), pp. 4–35.

[16] Madhav Gadgil, "Save the Western Ghats March: Towards a Follow-Up Action Plan," discussion paper, Centre for Ecological Sciences, Indian Institute of Science, Bangalore, 1988.

of the environmental movement, its tendency to postulate impractical and utopian solutions, its inability to get along with other groups in society and, on occasion, even with its own diverse constituents. The catholic and collaborative approach recommended by Gadgil was, it appears, deeply uncongenial to the majority of the marchers. The follow-up action plan he had so thoughtfully articulated came more or less to naught. The coalition that had been imaginatively put together through the 4000-kilometer march once more dissolved into its sectarian components.

V

The aftermath of the SWGM must have been deeply disappointing for Gadgil, but his love affair carried on regardless. In the first week of June 1992 I accompanied him on a trip down and up the Ghats. By now he and I had been collaborators for more than a decade: a book of ours had just been published; a sequel was in the process of being written. We had had countless conversations in Calcutta, Delhi, and Bangalore at the IISc.

I am by nature and temperament a creature of the city. As a scholar, too, I am more comfortable conversing with "dead" documents than living people. The archives I consult are located in state and national capitals. At the time, my field experience was restricted to a few weeks in the Himalaya, when I was working on my doctoral dissertation. I felt this lack keenly, but Gadgil felt it more keenly still.

Thus it was that, in June 1992, I found myself accompanying him on one of his regular visits to northern Karnataka. It was, as it happens, the very week of the Earth Summit in Rio de Janeiro, and it was typical of the man that where other Indian "environmentalists" made certain of their plane tickets to Rio, Gadgil chose to spend his customary one week a month in the fields and forests of the Western Ghats.

Our first night was spent in the Talgoppa Express which took us from Bangalore to the crest of the Ghats. From the railhead we descended down the Agahasini valley to the coastal town of Kumta. The drive was for the most part through degraded evergreen forests, a marker of whose condition was the weed eupatorium, a sun-loving plant a couple of meters high that had colonized many clearings. Of Latin

American origin, this weed apparently reached Kerala on the backs of Malayali soldiers retreating from Burma during the Second World War. How it got to Burma we don't know, but after it came to Kerala it spread rapidly northward and now covered large areas of coastal Karnataka as well.

Our drive through these disturbed forests provoked Gadgil into a discourse on the history of exotic plants in general. There was the coconut, which had contributed so greatly to Indian cuisine and culture. There were weeds like eupatorium which must be reckoned unwelcome intruders. Yet others had both benefits and costs, as in the various species of eucalyptus imported into India from Australia.

With its Australian cousin *Acacia auriculiformis*, eucalyptus had become ubiquitous in parts of the Western Ghats. These species were widely favored by the state Forest Deparment for they were not grazed by cattle, making it easier for officials to meet their planting targets. As we found, however, local villagers had mixed feelings about them. These trees provided fuelwood, but no fruit, fodder, or medicines.

These monocultural plantations newly raised made a striking contrast to the original vegetation of the Ghats. Specimens of these earlier forms dotted the area, chiefly in the form of sacred groves, this being of particular interest to Gadgil and being studied by one of his students, M.D. Subash Chandran.

Chandran, originally from Kerala, now taught at the Dr A.V. Baliga College in Kumta. We stayed with him and his wife, and in between splendid meals cooked by them—rich in fish caught in the estuary—we walked the sacred woodlands he had studied. In one patch twenty-five kilometers square he had identified as many as fifty-four sacred groves still protected by peasants. These served vital ecological functions, giving shelter to plants and animals and protecting water sources. Sadly, they had been bypassed altogether in official conservation efforts which privileged state action over popular knowledge and participation.

After a quick tour through the estuarine island of Masur-Lukkeri (where Gadgil once lived for extended periods, and where a schoolteacher had taught him the Kannada script), we left Kumta for the town of Sirsi, perched on top of the Ghats. Sirsi and its neighborhood are dominated by Havik Brahmins who specialize in horticulture. Their majestic spice gardens depend vitally on leaf manure taken from nearby forests. A hundred years of unregulated use had left the forests badly depleted until, in 1979, a local environmental group stepped in. We spoke to its members—mostly enlightened Havik farmers—and learned how they planned to regulate lopping and rehabilitate the forests.

From Sirsi we turned further inland across the Carnatic Plateau and into the district of Dharwad. We were traveling from an area of lush vegetation and abundant rainfall toward a more arid terrain. From a social point of view this was signaled by our first sight of nomads, returning with their sheep to their villages before the monsoon began. From an ecological viewpoint the transition was marked by the substitution of eupatorium by parthenium, another weed of Latin American origin.

Of this plant's entry into the region Gadgil had an even more interesting story to tell. It had first arrived in India with a consignment of American wheat which was stored in a godown near his home town, Pune. This godown lay downstream of the Panshet dam, and when that dam burst in 1961 its flood waters carried away the parthenium. The weed subsequently spread all over the Deccan. In Karnataka it was known derisively as Congress grass because, with its white flower atop a lean stalk, it rather resembled a Congress politician with his khadi cap.

Our drive ended in Ranibennur, where we had come to honor the great writer Shivaram Karanth and celebrate an environmental victory. A local NGO, the Samaj Parivartan Samudaya (SPS), had long opposed the destruction caused by a local factory owned by the house of Birlas, Harihar Polyfibres Ltd. This factory polluted the Tungabhadra river and preyed on the natural resources of the district.

The state government had taken the side of the factory. Together they had formed Karnataka Pulpwoods Ltd (KPL), to which had been alloted 75,000 acres of common land used extensively by villagers. When KPL bulldozed the existing vegetation and started replacing it with eucalyptus, SPS swung into action. They organized a series of satyagrahas and also took the case to the Indian Supreme Court. That process had begun in 1984; now, eight years later, the court had ruled against KPL, forcing it to shut down.[17] Better still, SPS had been awarded the Indira Gandhi Pariyavaran Puruskar (a prestigious environmental awareness prize) by the Ministry of Environment and Forests in New Delhi, the award signifying a wider recognition of the justice of its struggle.

Gadgil and I had been associated with SPS for some time. So too had Shivaram Karanth who was, in fact, the first petitioner in the Supreme Court case. So this celebration was a dual one, and suitably happy, with songs and dances and a moving speech by the writer, where he told us that in living to the age of ninety he had consumed far too much of the earth's resources himself.

Ranibennur was our last stop. That night, after the meeting, we took the Kittur Express back to Bangalore. For Gadgil this was a week like any other but for me it had been richly educative. Over this time we drove or walked through evergreen forests and estuaries, arecanut gardens and treeless plateau. We met farmers trying to manage their resources sustainably, biologists reconstructing ecological history, activists opposing the ravages of industry. We encountered Latin American weeds and Australian trees, testimony to trans-national ecological encounters in the centuries before the Rio Summit.

Through all this I talked little, being content to look around and listen to excerpts from my companion's vast stock of knowledge. He was pleased that I had come, and so too would have been my hero Marc Bloch—the historian who once said historians needed thinner notebooks and thicker boots.

VI

By the time of our trip through the Western Ghats, Gadgil's life was dominated by biodiversity rather than by forests narrowly conceived. This, the third stage of his work in India, was in some ways an

[17] The KPL case is analyzed in greater detail in Ramachandra Guha, "The Environmentalism of the Poor," in Richard G. Fox and Orin Starn, eds, *Between Resistance and Revolution: Cultural Politics and Social Protest* (New Brunswick: Rutgers University Press, 1998).

integration as well as transcendence of the first two. His early work on sacred groves had alerted him to the need to protect small patches of refugia. Later, working on elephants in the large nature reserve of Bandipur, he had noticed how the management of the park was completely indifferent to the interests of villagers living in the vicinity. In 1982 he had written a thirty-seven page document, "An Indian Conservation Strategy," that sought to harmonize the claims of biodiversity conservation with the imperatives of social justice. This is a remarkable essay, anticipating Western debates on the subject by a decade or more. India, he noted, "surpasses in its biological wealth every other land mass of comparable size." But Indians had "unfortunately, done little to nurture this biological heritage;" to the contrary, they had "lost a greater proportion of it than any other land mass of comparable size."

The essay began with an overview of the ways in which modern Indians had decimated the biological diversity they had inherited from their forefathers: through the destruction of forest cover, the simplification of crop regimes, the building of large dams, the profit urges of industry. And yet despite the ravages of man there was much that remained: rich biological communities in upland and lowland, in deserts and along the coasts. How, asked Gadgil, "do we then go about salvaging what is still left of our magnificent biological heritage?" His answer lay in a shift away from "the traditional approach that emphasizes the protection of a few striking species of wild animals such as the rhinoceros or the tiger." Instead, argued Gadgil a full twenty years back, we should "reorient our choice of [protected] communities to try to achieve the maximum preservation of overall biological diversity." Small fragments disdained by conservationists obsessed with size could often be the last remaining samples of their ecotype. Remarkably, it was in a sacred grove in Kerala that scientists found a woody climber of the genus Kunstleria, previously unrecorded in India.

The orthodox approach to nature conservation, argued Gadgil, was flawed in an ecological sense, and from a social point of view as well. Thus, wildlife managers were instructed to "keep people away by force of arms." But this was "neither feasible nor desirable." There was a moral imperative to provide gainful employment as well as fuel and fodder to villagers living in and around protected areas. At the same time, "where such nature reserves attract economic activity such as tourism, we should ensure that the benefits from it flow entirely to the local population."[18]

This essay of 1982 provided an uncanny anticipation of global debates on biodiversity as they unfolded in the 1990s and beyond. These are debates to which Gadgil has enormously contributed. He has looked at the legal and international aspects of the problem, providing critical analyses of the implications of the Dunkel Draft, the WTO negotiations, and the Convention on Biological Diversity. He has written on the optimal size of nature reserves, on the impact of human intervention on species diversity, and on the relation of local communities to protected areas. He has popularized the notion of "Peoples Biodiversity Registers" which document and demonstrate the indigenous knowledge of formally unlettered people. All told, to my knowledge no scientist worldwide has done as much as Gadgil to deepen and democratize the idea and ideal of biodiversity conservation.[19]

VII

Over a decade utterly formative for my intellectual development, Gadgil and I worked together. To begin with, our intellectual energies were pooled toward researching and writing an ecological history of India. But we also both had a keen interest in the developing environmental movement, in the struggles of forest-dependent peasants, dam-displaced tribals, and trawler-affected artisanal fisherfolk. These struggles, we hoped, would lead to suitable changes in public policy, such that the state would promote laws and technologies more sensitive to the environment and the needs of rural communities.

Gadgil and I wrote two books together, the second moving beyond history toward prescription. The books are in the public domain; they

[18] Madhav Gadgil, *Towards an Indian Conservation Strategy* (New Delhi: Indian Social Institute, 1982).

[19] The best summation of his work in the field is in Madhav Gadgil and P.R. Seshagiri Rao, *Nurturing Biodiversity* (Ahmedabad: Centre for Environmental Education, 1998). But see also Madhav Gadgil, "Poverty and Biodiversity," in *Encyclopaedia of Biodiversity*, vol. 4 (New York: Academic Press, 2001).

have been sometimes praised and sometimes very vigorously criticiz-ed.[20] However, while cleaning up some papers recently I found a more activist document that we had coauthored and which apparently was never published. It was written toward the end of 1989, just after the fall of the Berlin Wall, just after the defeat of Rajiv Gandhi's Congress government in the general elections of that year. The Congress regime had been widely accused of corruption, of being soft on industry, and of a creeping authoritarianism. This last was manifest especially in a "Defamation Bill" that sought to impose strict curbs on the function-ing of India's free press.

The Congress had been replaced by a regime called the National Front, an alliance of populist, socialist, and regional parties which pro-mised clean government as well as a more rural and Gandhian policy orientation. It was a minority government propped up by the support of the Communists on the left and the Bharatiya Janata Party (BJP) on the right. As changes of regime usually are, it was accompanied by a fairly extended honeymoon period when intellectuals and activists hoped for some *real* change from the new rulers: in part this was be-cause the National Front had been voted out of power in several of the states it had previously controlled, and the hope was that this would drive home to them the importance of good governance.

Such was the background for the document which Gadgil and I wrote, and which we circulated to a wide variety of colleagues in the environmental community with the hope that with their criticisms and comments we could prepare a better statement still which could then be presented as a collective charter from India's greens. It drew upon a decade of research on my part, and two decades of research on his part. But it also drew on the many conversations the two of us—and Gadgil especially—had with scientists, social scientists, public of-ficials, and activists working in the environmental or natural resource management field. In so far as it embodies this collective thinking of certain sections of the Indian environmental movement, *c*.1989, the document seems relevant and is reproduced below in full.

[20] See Madhav Gadgil and Ramachandra Guha, *The Use and Abuse of Nature*, omnibus edition incorporating *This Fissured Land* and *Ecology and Equity* (New Delhi: Oxford University Press, 2000), Introduction.

ECOLOGY FOR THE PEOPLE
(*written* circa *November 1989*)

1. India stands at the crossroads. That is the message of the elections just conducted. People everywhere have voted for a change in the way the affairs of the country are being run today; in states ruled by Congress as well as by constituents of the National and Left Fronts. That was also the message of the tens of thousands gathered at [the anti-big-dam rally] at Harsud in Madhya Pradesh. Obviously, there is a search on for an alternative path to development, for a strategy that would be sustainable, that would reverse the current trend of growing social and economic disparities.

2. Fortunately, there are hopeful signs of an emerging national consensus on many elements of such an alternative strategy. Above all these include the need to decentralize decisionmaking, to create rural employment as a matter of the highest priority and to provide a much more open, accountable system of governance. All these areas are of great relevance to the concerns of environmentalists, for it is the centralized, bureaucratic decision-making with little public accountability that has been driving much of the short-sighted, destructive development. It is also such a process of development that has led to cornering of the benefits of development by a narrow elite, exacerbating social and economic disparities and creating acute problems of rural poverty rooted in unemployment and underemployment.

3. This development process has emphasized immediate intensification of resource use with little thought for long-term consequences, or for efficiency of resource use. In the event resources have been used exceedingly wastefully, which has entailed substantial environmental and social costs. These costs have been passed on to the bulk of our population which remains poor, disorganized, and illiterate, and of course to unborn generations. The gross neglect of problems of rehabilitation of project refugees is one way in which such costs are inflicted on the weaker sections of society; alienation of the masses from any control over the resources of their locality and dedication of these resources to meet commercial needs is another. The same pattern of centralized, bureaucratic development

has meant that the ongoing rural employment programmes have contributed little to the rehabilitation of degraded local environments.

4. Acknowledging the right of all citizens to know all that is going on in the country, to put in place monitoring of development programmes independently of the machinery adminstering these programmes, and ensuring that a narrow elite cannot impose decisions without a wide consensus involving all segments would be important steps toward eliminating these distortions. Full information regarding all development programmes as well as defense programmes involving rehabilitation (barring only specifically identified security-related matters) should be accessible to all citizens quite openly; indeed there should be strict penalties prescribed for anybody obstructing access to information and rewards for those who make special efforts to communicate it. Social and environmental benefit–cost analyses of all development projects must be taken up concurrently with the preparation of the Detailed Project Reports [DPRs]. While project authorities should have the responsibility for ensuring that such analyses are conducted, they should be obliged to organize them through independent agencies which are provided full access to all relevant information, and which in turn must be obliged to involve all concerned citizens in the exercise through public hearings in the relevant localities. Programmes for rehabilitation of refugees from the project, programmes of compensatory afforestation, treatment of catchment areas, etc. should also be formulated as an integral part of all development projects along with the preparation of DPRs and their environmental and social cost–benefits should be similarly assessed by independent agencies in a process involving public hearings.

5. Such open scrutiny should also characterize all other government programmes at all scales ranging from gully plugging of small streams and selection felling from reserved forests to subsidizing smokeless *chulas* [wood stoves]. Decisions as to the desirability of such activities should necessarily involve local people; ideally the entire population in the form of *gram sabhas* [village councils]; as well as other institutions such as schools, voluntary agencies and of course *mandal panchayats* [local councils] and *zilla parishads*

[district councils]. The key to bringing about such involvement would be complete access to all relevant government records to citizens, with strong disincentives for denial of access.

6. Granting the right to productive work would be an important step in conferring dignity to the large numbers of our poorer citizens. But it is important to ensure that the work they undertake shall focus on sustainable development of natural resources and on eco-restoration as far as possible in their own localities on state-owned, common and private lands. Only such an effort would ensure that in the long run these people could come to enjoy a better quality of life. To ensure that the work generated is carried out properly instead of in a shoddy, eco-degrading fashion, and that the workers do get paid due wages, the pertinent records should be open to public scrutiny. Furthermore, such employment programmes should also be subject to an independent monitoring by local voluntary agencies and educational institutions.

7. Finally, the local government at the village level should come to focus on good management of the local resource base of land, water, vegetation, and animal life. It is the poorer people in rural areas who suffer most from the degradation of this resource base and who could be best motivated to take good care of its health. Unfortunately they have today become its worst enemies, driven as they are by day-to-day compulsions of making two ends meet. A properly organized right to work programme should remove these compulsions. But that would not be enough, as another important component of the resource base—common lands and waters—has in many areas become no man's property. At the time of taking over these community resources the British insisted that while local people may have some privileges of their use, they shall have no rights. Therefore the local community today cannot keep out non-members nor regulate the behavior of their own group members in the use of the commons. While setting up *panchayati raj* [decentralized] institutions it is therefore essential that a new framework be developed for conferring both authority and responsibility on local people for good management of the commons. The most appropriate social unit for taking on such responsibility would be a

village/hamlet where everybody is in regular face to-face contact. Each such unit should be assigned its own common land and water to be ultimately governed by the whole community. The commons should remain state property with regulations even more stringent than the forest conservation act to assure its integrity [i.e. to prevent its diversion to commercial or industrial uses], but it should be first dedicated to meeting local subsistence needs, and only when these are fully met to supplying outside demands. In the long run local communities should maintain the resources of the commons with inputs of their own labor, and where necessary cash, helped only through the right to work programmes. The mandal panchayat structure should be appropriately designed to facilitate such management by villages/hamlets making up the panchayat area.

8. We believe that the time is right in the country to establish a number of such initiatives through a broad national consensus, initiatives that would go a long way toward reversing the current trends of environmental degradation and worsening of social disparities. We hope that the many strands involved in the environmental movement will come together to persuade parties of all political persuasions to implement these policies.

Although it is impossible to be certain from this distance in time, my surmise is that the inspiration and ideas in this document must mostly have been Gadgil's. Anyway, the file where I came across this old document also had an array of responses, some approbatory, willing to sign the statement as it was, others thoughtfully critical. The sociologist Gail Omvedt pointed out that in her state, Maharashtra, the current right-to-work schemes tended to focus on "the hated rock-breaking." Perhaps, she said, there was also a need for "the right not to work or at least to be freed from inhumane work. . . ." The ecological economist Anil K. Gupta suggested that we recommend discontinuing the massive subsidies enjoyed by the urban middle class. By making them pay a fair price for education as well as water and power, one might create a "resource replenishment" fund that could be directed toward enhancing the capabilities and life chances of the rural poor, particulary those living in high-risk environments prone to drought or floods. The socialist A.K. ("Dunu") Roy—himself a pioneer of social-ecological research—saw in our proposal "the absence of an analysis of the nature of the political economy."[21] He thought that

> *even* if the Right to Know, the Right to Work, and Panchayati Raj were to
> be legislated for by the present government, it would barely hamper the
> "development" process. The class forces would ensure that these rights get
> amalgamated into the general trend of impoverishment on one hand and
> enrichment on the other . . . [T]he only way to upset this apple-cart . . . is
> by calling and organising for economic and social equality too. In other
> words, by wresting control of the economic process and resources from the
> rich. And this cannot be done by people like us who are themselves allied
> to the rich. It has to be done by the poor. We can only assist.

Dunu Roy concluded that "perhaps this document is a first step in a long road." Gadgil and I would have agreed. However, the whole process ran aground when the National Front abandoned its "alternative development agenda" in favor of narrow caste politics. This took the form of implementing the Mandal Commission Report which demanded higher representation in the public services of "backward castes" dominant in the countryside, these constituting the backbone of the regionalist parties that made up the Front. In response, the BJP withdrew its support, seeking instead to renew its campaign to build a Ram temple in the town of Ayodhya.

For the next decade and more the politics of India was dominated by the divisive tendencies of caste and religion. Only in May 2004, with the defeat of the BJP and the coming to power of a Congress-led coalition supported by Left parties, did questions of rural development re-enter the domain of political debate. A Right to Information Bill has been passed by parliament, inspired by a bill in the state of Rajasthan, itself the product of a sustained campaign led by a remarkable group called the Mazdoor Kisan Shakti Sanghatan (MKSS). Also passed by parliament is a National Employment Guarantee Act, which, like the Information Bill, is deeply inspired by the MKSS.

The MKSS campaigns, as also their intellectual articulations by the respected economist Jean Dreze (Belgian-born but long resident in India and now an Indian citizen) have focused on the importance of

---

[21] Cf. A.K. Roy, *et. al.*, *Planning the Environment* (New Delhi: Department of Science and Technology, 1981).

these two bills in ensuring public accountability, deepening political democracy, and enhancing social equity. These are all admirable ends but to them can easily be added one more, compatible with and complementary to the others—that of environmental sustainability. In that extension the work, old and new, of Madhav Gadgil can provide a very handy starting point.[22]

VIII

As one who has so closely known Gadgil for a quarter of a century, let me single out and summarize what I see as the distinguishing features of his work.

First, there is his deep knowledge of his land and its people. I have spoken already of our field trip together. On another occasion, we got talking about the Western Ghats in the corridors of the Centre for Ecological Sciences at the IISc. Around us lay framed photographs taken by the botanist Cecil Saldanha and from a recent exhibition featuring his work. I asked Gadgil to identify the locations. This he did with little difficulty. This photograph appeared to have been taken north of Siddapur; that one was most likely from somewhere close to the Karnataka–Goa border; the one on the far wall was certainly from the catchment of the Sharavathi river.

While he retains a special affection for his native Sahyadris, Gadgil

[22] As the process is still unfolding, there is as yet no serious scholarly work on these various campaigns. However, there is a vigorous debate being conducted in the press which can perhaps be traced by Googling "Employment Guarantee," "Right to Information," "Mazdoor Kisan Shakti Sanghatan," and "Aruna Roy," the last being the gifted and charismatic MKSS leader and recipient of the Magsaysay Award. Although based for many years in a village in Rajasthan, Aruna Roy started her career as a civil servant and can be said to know the system inside out. In this public debate Jean Dreze has contributed prolifically to the press. Of slightly more distant relevance, but relevant nonetheless, are Dreze's three books with Amartya Sen on development issues: *Hunger and Public Action* (1989), *India: Economic Development and Social Opportunity* (1995), and *India: Development and Participation* (2002), all published by Oxford University Press, Delhi. Finally, despite the passing of these legislations their long-term impact on poverty remains uncertain. Some economists think that they represent an excessive burden on the state exchequer. Some socialists, *pace* Dunu Roy, think that in the absence of a realignment of class forces they will have little material impact. The proponents, naturally, are more optimistic.

has traveled extensively through rural India. In 1992, when we decided to write a constructive sequel to our depressing ecological history *This Fissured Land*, Gadgil said he had first to visit the north-east, the part of India he knew least. Fortunately a student of K.C. Malhotra's was doing a dissertation on shifting cultivators in Manipur. So Gadgil took his backpack and walked two weeks with this student, asking him about the ecology and social structure of the tribals and their hills, in exchange passing on a great deal of information new to the younger man.

Second, there is his profound intellectual originality. This is manifest in his work on forms of indigenous or non-modern conservation systems, in his analysis of different societies in terms of their "modes of resource use," in his inspired coinage of the term "omnivores" to characterize the ecological profligacy of the Indian elite. I should here acknowledge that the ideas that are original in our own coauthored books are all his. Much of the historical research contained in them is mine. But the analytical frameworks are, in essence, Gadgil's.[23]

Third, there is the courage he has shown, quietly rather than polemically (in this he and I are complete contrasts!), in opposing intellectual fashion. He was one of the first Indian scientists to do field research. His left-wing tendencies notwithstanding, he was one of the first Indian environmentalists to recognize that blind opposition to the market would only play into the hands of inefficient producers and an undemocratic state. He is an agnostic and secularist who can yet see a role for sacred groves in the practice of modern conservation.

Fourth, there is the unity, in his mind and work, of the intellectual and practical agendas of environmental research. Gadgil is both a scientist and a practical social reformer who conducts original ecological research but also seeks to use it to improve the lives of people and the health of the natural environment. He has done basic research on forests and biodiversity, and in ecological anthropology and environmental history. He has also contributed to the reform of public policy in these realms. Like Radhakamal Mukerjee, the man who first coined the term "social ecology," Gadgil sees this as both a methodological

[23] Madhav Gadgil and Ramachandra Guha, *This Fissured Land: An Ecological History of India* (Berkeley: University of California Press, 1992); *Ecology and Equity: The Use and Abuse of Nature in Contemporary India* (London: Routledge, 1995).

as well as moral imperative. Like Mukerjee, he would argue that "applied human ecology is the only guarantee of a permanent civilization."

A late illustration of this practical bent is Project Lifescape, started by Gadgil to mark the birth centenary of the ornithologist Sálim Ali. This aims at publishing an illustrated account of some 2500 species of micro-organisms, plants, and animals to create wide popular interest and a stake in the conservation of India's biological heritage. Although directed by an internationally renowned scientist, the project rests on the willing participation of a network of students and college teachers patiently built up over the years.[24]

Sálim Ali was himself one of Gadgil's early mentors.[25] His example animates Project Lifescape, as does the work done with students and teachers of the Kerala Sastra Sahitya Parishad (KSSP). In the early 1980s, Gadgil worked alongside the KSSP in the campaign to save Silent Valley, one of the last remaining rain forests in the Western Ghats, from being drowned by a hydro-electric project. There he came into contact with M.K. Prasad, a botanist of subaltern background who has been one of the KSSP's most inspirational figures. Born into a home of poor toddy tappers, Prasad rose to become a university vice chancellor. All through he remained "that rare example of an Indian scientist, a person for whom recognition from the West matters little if at all." Their friendship, now two decades old, has undoubtedly furthered this Harvard-educated scientist's efforts at making his science more relevant and accessible to his people.[26]

Fifth, there are Gadgil's deeply democratic instincts. These are expressed socially in the fact that his applied work has been on behalf of the "ecosytem people," rather than the omnivores.[27] He has consistently promoted political decentralization, transparency in governance, and freedom of information. I had originally thought of

[24] Madhav Gadgil, "Deploying Student Power to Monitor India's Lifescape," *Current Science*, vol. 71, no. 9, 1996.

[25] Cf. Madhav Gadgil, "Making of a Naturalist," *Frontline*, March 6, 1998.

[26] Cf. Madhav Gadgil and M.D. Subhas Chandran, "Scientist as Social Activist: M.K. Prasad," *Frontline*, May 26, 2000.

[27] As in much of the work cited above, as also in his fascinating (yet unfortunately little-known) essay, "On Biomass Budgets," *Journal of the Indian Society of Agricultural Statistics*, vol. 38, no. 3, 1986.

calling this chapter "The *Scientific* Social Ecology of Madhav Gadgil," but then I realized the title was unduly restrictive. I think Gadgil is better understood as a thoroughgoing democrat whose lifelong endeavor has been toward democratizing science, democratizing the state, and not least democratizing the environmental movement. As he expressed it in an essay of 1997, "to prosper in this age we must once and for all abandon the bureacratic culture of control and command and embrace a new democratic culture of share and inform. Only then can we hope to vanquish the forces of environmental destruction that have been gathering strength over these fifty years of independence."[28]

I have been a beneficiary of Gadgil's democratic instincts myself. He is sixteen years older than I, an age difference that, in the Indian context, generally translates into a relationship of master and follower. But from the beginning he treated me as an equal. Early on we had a vigorous disagreement on the merits of sociobiology. As a student and friend of E.O. Wilson he was then somewhat in thrall of that then relatively novel approach. In fact he was close to being what Wilson could never be, a *socialist* sociobiologist, probably the only such specimen anywhere in the world.

As for myself, I was from the first repelled by sociobiology's imperialist pretensions, its bid to take over the social sciences and the humanities with it. I had read Wilson and also critiques of his work. This convinced me that while it might indeed be possible to separate sociobiology from a right-wing political agenda, it remained a theory with limited applicability outside the natural world. In particular, Indian history and culture were too diverse and too unpredictable to fit into a model which assumed that social behavior was, in the ultimate instance, driven by an individual's genes.

My reading led to arguments that persuaded Gadgil to restrict sociobiology to the study of insects and animals. This set the precedent for our relationship, based on mutual respect for the other person's ideas and a willingness to change's one mind based on evidence. Gadgil's democratic instincts greatly impressed me, not least because I was coming into his terrain after five years in Calcutta, where Marxist egalitarian beliefs do not come in the way of professors treating their

[28] Madhav Gadgil, "Indian Environmentalism: The Emerging Paradigm," in *The Hindu Survey of Environment 1997* (Chennai: Kasturi and Sons, 1997).

students somewhat like the Bengali (usually Hindu) landlord once treated his (usually Muslim) tenant.

Finally, there is his wholesale absence of cynicism. When I first met Gadgil he had not yet turned forty. He is now past sixty but retains still that slim, spare frame, that sprightly walk, that love of nature, that interest in (especially young) people, that determination to put science in the service of humanity, that deep and abiding faith in the future of his country. As I write this, he is engaged in crafting a curriculum for "habitat learning" for the schools of India, following a mandate from the Supreme Court of India that "awareness of the environment and its problems . . . should be taught as a compulsory subject" in all the schools in the country.

Asked by the National Council of Educational Research and Training (NCERT) to devise such a curriculum, Gadgil and his co-workers have drafted a document steeped in experience, understanding, wisdom, and hope. Environmental education, they point out, cannot mechanically reproduce what textbooks say; it must "emphasize continual inquiry," on the teachers and among students as well. Its guiding principle should be "empowerment, rather than indoctrination;" its main focus the exposure of students "to the real-life world, natural and social, in which they live;" its main aims to help them "learn about the environment" and "learn through the environment" as well as "for the environment."

The NCERT document shows how students can complement laboratory experiments with field observations on soils, vegetation types, bird and animal diversity, and the human use and abuse of nature. All this information could then be uplinked to a website which would be a "publicly accessible and transparent database on India's environment," continually updated and adequately reflecting the social as well as ecological diversity of India. What we have here is a new paradigm of education—the words that follow can only be Gadgil's— "embodying the spirit of science, of democracy, and of caring for the environment."[29]

Viewing Gadgil's career in the round it is tempting to make the criticism that he has not written enough, or at any rate not enough books.

[29] "Draft Report of the Focus Group on Habitat and Learning," New Delhi: National Council of Educational Research and Training, April 2005.

Here the contrast with his Western contemporaries is noticeable—with scientists such as Stephen Jay Gould, Jared Diamond, E.O. Wilson, Robert May, and others. As it happens these men are all Gadgil's friends, not to say admirers, but who, unlike him, have distilled their knowledge in a series of hugely popular books for the general market. In terms of intellectual range Gadgil matches the best of them; in terms of field experience he probably exceeds them. He can write a clear and direct, though not always evocative, English prose. And he too has worked on themes of compelling ecological and human interest. Why then has he not published more books?

One reason could be the difference in cultural milieu. India is altogether a more sociable place to live in than the USA or Britain. It is far less oriented toward the protection of privacy, far less sympathetic to the withdrawal from human intercourse that the writing of books requires. Add to this the fact that the intellectual culture of India is more oral than written; more conducive to ideas being discussed in seminars and informal gossip sessions than via the medium of print. To these structural factors might be added aspects of personal orientation. Gadgil is, like his father and many other Indians, a *public* intellectual for whom the claims of a scientific career have often—too often?—been subordinated to the claims of social activism and social reform. Asked to join a Western Ghats march or draft a comprehensive curriculum for Indian schools, Gadgil finds it impossible to turn his back and write away in his office instead. Finally, this scholar of biodiversity so glories in the diversity of his culture that he would hardly want to pass up the chance to deepen his acquaintance with it. If one gives Gadgil a choice—would you rather spend the next fortnight on a boat with fisherfolk you have never before studied, or write a chapter of a book?—there is little doubt in which direction his heart and feet will take him.

This said, I still think that the criticism is fair. Too much of Gadgil's best writing is hidden away in fugitive documents—official as well as non-official—rather than in a more systematic and public distillation presented in the shape of published books.[30] On the other hand he has

[30] Apart from the various documents cited already in this chapter there is a never published 137-page-long document on large dams and their ecological problems inspired by the Silent Valley project. This bears rereading today,

had a significant influence on Indian science, not least through the creation of a first-class center of ecological research, now in the capable hands of a group of outstanding younger scientists.[31] And he has had a still more significant influence on public policy and public debate, on the ways in which the Indian people and the Indian state have come to interpret, understand, and act upon the natural environment. I have already made the claim that Chandi Prasad Bhatt was the first environmentalist of the poor. To now claim that Gadgil has perhaps had more practical influence within his own country than any other scientific ecologist would open me to the charge of being an Indian chauvinist. So let me only say that he has had a wider social impact than some who have written more—and better—books. And that he would have it this way.

Let me, in the end, recall what Wassily Leontief told Madhav Gadgil when he was a young boy. The son may have chosen early to depart from his father's profession, but he retained a profound respect for his father and for the tradition that nurtured him. For, always excepting Gandhi and Tagore, the most original as well as most influential thinkers in modern India have come from Pune or the Pune region. In most ways that matter, then, Madhav Gadgil is his father's son, and the child of a city to which he, on his retirement from the IISc, now returns. But while he might retire to Pune, he does not belong to Pune alone.

Like his father, and like Gokhale and Ambedkar before him, Madhav Gadgil belongs also to the Western Ghats, to India, and to the world.

---

more than twenty years after it was written. Madhav Gadgil, "Conservation of Catchment Areas of River Valley Projects on the Western Ghats," Bombay: Bombay Natural History Society, January 1985.

[31] On which see Michael Lewis, *Inventing Global Ecology: Tracking the Biodiversity Ideal in India, 1945–1997* (Hyderabad: Orient Longman, 2003), chapter 5.

CHAPTER 9

How Much Should a Person Consume?

The United States is presiding at a general reorganization of the ways of living throughout the world.—**André Siegfried (1932)**[1]

Having surveyed and analyzed some of the key aspects of environmentalism in India and the USA, and having discussed some of the neglected founding fathers and exemplars of environmentalism in these two vast countries, let me now hone the thrust of this book down to a single, and singular, question: the one posed by the title of this final chapter (and of the book itself). To answer the question, I take as my point of departure an old essay by John Kenneth Galbraith, an essay so ancient and obscure that it may very well have been forgotten even by its prolific author. It was written in 1958, the year in which Galbraith also published *The Affluent Society*, a book which wryly anatomized the social consequences of the mass consumption age. Galbraith highlighted the "preoccupation with productivity and production" in post-war America and Western Europe. The population in these societies had for the most part been adequately housed, clothed, and fed; now they expressed a desire for "more elegant cars, more exotic food, more erotic clothing, more elaborate entertainment."

[1] André Siegfried, quoted in David M. Potter, *People of Plenty: Economic Abundance and the American Character* (1954; rpnt Chicago: University of Chicago Press, 1973), p. 135.

When Galbraith termed 1950s America the "affluent society" he meant not only that this was a society in which most people were hugely prosperous when reckoned against other societies and other times, but also that this was a society so dedicated to affluence that the possession and consumption of material goods was its exclusive standard of individual and collective achievement. He quoted the anthropologist Geoffrey Gorer who had remarked that in modern America "any device or regulation which interfered, or can be conceived as interfering, with [the] supply of more and better things is resisted with unreasoning horror, as the religious resist blasphemy, or the warlike pacifism."[2]

The essay I speak of was written months after the book which made Galbraith's name and reputation. "How Much Should a Country Consume?" is its provocative title and it can be read as a reflective footnote to *The Affluent Society*. In the book Galbraith had noted the disjunction between "private affluence and public squalor," how the single-minded pursuit of wealth had diverted attention and resources from nurturing true democracy, which he defined as the provision of public infrastructure, the creation of decent schools, parks, and hospitals. Now the economist turned his attention, all too fleetingly, to the long-term consequences of this collective promotion of consumption, the "gargantuan and growing appetite" for resources in the USA. The American conservation movement, he remarked, had certainly noted the massive exploitation of resources and materials in the post-war period. However, its response was to look for more efficient methods of extraction, for the substitution of one material for another through technological innovation. There was a noticeable "selectivity in the conservationist's approach to materials consumption." For,

> if we are concerned about our great appetite for materials, it is plausible to seek to increase the supply, or decrease waste, to make better use of the stocks that are available, and to develop substitutes. But what of the appetite itself? Surely this is the ultimate source of the problem. If it continues its geometric course, will it not one day have to be restrained? Yet in the literature of the resource problem this is the forbidden question. Over it hangs a nearly total silence. It is as though, in the discussion of the chance

[2] John Kenneth Galbraith, *The Affluent Society* (Boston: Houghton Mifflin, 1958).

for avoiding automobile accidents, we agree not to make any mention of speed!³

A cultural explanation for this silence had been previously provided by the great Berkeley geographer Carl Sauer. Writing in 1938 Sauer said "the doctrine of a passing frontier of nature replaced by a permanent and sufficiently expanding frontier of technology is a contemporary and characteristic expression of occidental culture, itself a historical-geographical product." This frontier attitude, he went on, "has the recklessness of an optimism that has become habitual, but which is residual from the brave days when north-European freebooters over-ran the world and put it under tribute." Warning that the surge of growth at the expense of nature would not last indefinitely, Sauer—speaking for his fellow Americans—noted wistfully that "we have not yet learned the difference between yield and loot. We do not like to be economic realists."⁴

Galbraith had identified two major reasons for the silence on con-sumption. One was ideological, the worship of the Great God Growth. The principle of Growth (always with that capital G) was a cardinal belief among the American people; this necessarily implied a conti-nuous increase in the production of consumer goods. The second reason was political: widespread skepticism of the state. For, America in the 1950s had witnessed the "resurgence of a notably oversimplified view of economic life which [ascribed] a magical automatism to the price system . . ." Now, Galbraith himself was an unreconstructed New Dealer who would tackle the problem of overconsumption as he would tackle the problem of underemployment, that is, through pur-posive state intervention. At the time he wrote, however, free-market economics ruled the ideological roost, and "since consumption could

³ Idem, "How Much Should a Country Consume?," in Henry Jarret, ed., *Perspectives on Conservation* (Baltimore: Johns Hopkins University Press, 1958), pp. 91–2. Even if Galbraith has not forgotten this essay, it has certainly escaped the attention of his hard-working biographer: see Richard Parker, *John Kenneth Galbraith: His Life, His Politics, His Economics* (New York: Farrar, Strauss and Giroux, 2005).

⁴ Carl Sauer, "Theme of Plant and Animal Destruction in Economic Hist-ory" (1938), in idem, *Land and Life* (Berkeley: University of California Press, 1963).

not be discussed without raising the question of an increased role for the state, it was not discussed."[5]

Four years later Rachel Carson published *Silent Spring* and the modern American environmental movement gathered pace. Should not this new voice of civil society have spelled out what the market would not? But no: consumption continued the great unasked question of the conservation movement. The movement focused principally on two things: threats to human health posed by pollution, and threats to wild species and wild habitats posed by economic expansion. The latter concern became, in fact, as we have seen in earlier chapters, the defining motif of the movement. The dominance of wilderness protection in American environmentalism has from the start promoted an essentially negative agenda, namely the protection of parks and their animals by freeing them of human habitation and productive activities. As the historian Samuel Hays points out, "natural environments which formerly had been looked upon as 'useless' waiting only to be developed, now came to be thought of as 'useful' for filling human wants and needs. They played no less a significant role in the advanced consumer society than did such material goods as hi fi sets or indoor gardens."[6] While saving these islands of biodiversity, environmentalists paid scant attention to what was happening outside them. In the American economy as a whole the consumption of energy and materials continued to rise.

A perceptive home-grown critic of this selective environmentalism was the poet Wendell Berry. In an essay published in 1987 he rejected "an assumed division or divisibility between nature and humanity, or wildness and domesticity." In his view, "conservation is going to prove increasingly futile and increasingly meaningless if its proscriptions and forbiddings are not positively answered by an economy that rewards and enforces good use." He was convinced that "the wildernesses cannot survive if our economy does not change."[7]

In the American context Berry was—the metaphor seems rather

[5] "How Much Should a Country Consume?," p. 97.

[6] Samuel Hays, "From Conservation to Environment: Environmental Politics in the United States since World War Two," *Environmental Review*, vol. 6, no. 1, 1982, p. 21f.

[7] Wendell Berry, "Preserving Wildness," *Wilderness*, Spring 1987.

ironically apposite—a voice in the wild. The growing popular interest in the wild and the beautiful not merely accepted the parameters of the affluent society but tended to see nature itself as merely one more good to be consumed. The uncertain commitment of most nature lovers to a comprehensive environmental ideology is illustrated by the paradox that they were willing to drive thousands of miles, using up scarce oil and polluting the atmosphere, to visit national parks and sanctuaries, thereby pursuing anti-ecological means to marvel at the beauty of forests, swamps, and mountains protected as specimens of "pristine" nature.

The selectivity of the conservationist approach to consumption was underlined in the work of biologists obsessed with the "population problem." Influential American scientists such as Paul Ehrlich and Garret Hardin identified human population growth as the single most important reason for environmental degradation. This is how Ehrlich began the first chapter of his bestselling book, *The Population Bomb*:

> I have understood the population explosion intellectually for a long time. I came to understand it emotionally one stinking hot night in Delhi a couple of years ago. My wife and daughter and I were returning to our hotel in an ancient taxi. The seats were hopping with fleas. The only functional gear was third. As we crawled through the city, we entered a crowded slum area. The temperature was well over 100, and the air was a haze of dust and smoke. The streets seemed alive with people. People eating, people washing, people sleeping. People visiting, people arguing and screaming. People thrusting their hands through the taxi window, begging. People defecating and urinating. People clinging to buses. People herding animals. People, people, people, people.[8]

Here, exploding numbers seem at fault for increasing pollution, stinking hot air, and even technological obsolescence (that ancient taxi). Through the 1970s and 1980s, neo-Malthusian interpretations of this type gained wide currency. Countries such as India, and especially Bangladesh, were commonly blamed for causing an environmental crisis. Not surprisingly, activists in these countries were quick to take offence, pointing out that the USA consumes, per capita as well as in the aggregate, a far greater proportion of the world's resources.

[8] Paul Ehrlich, *The Population Bomb* (New York: Ballantine Books, 1969), p. 15.

Table 1 gives some evidence of this: only some because, apart from its overuse of nature's stock, which the table documents, American society has also placed an unbearable burden on nature's sink (which the table ignores). Thus the atmosphere and the oceans can absorb about 13 billion tons of carbon dioxide annually. This absorptive capacity, if distributed fairly amongst all the people of the world, would allow each human being to have the right to emit about 2.3 tons of carbon dioxide per year. At present, an American discharges in excess of 20 tons annually, a German 12 tons, a Japanese 9 tons, an Indian a little over 1 ton. If we look at the process historically, the charges mount, for it is the industrialized countries, led by the USA, that have been principally responsible for the build-up of greenhouse gases over the past 150 years.

These figures explain why scholars of the world's South argue that the real "population problem" is in America, where the birth of one child has the same impact on the global environment as the birth of, say, seventy Indonesian children. A Bangladeshi made this case whenever he could, in the United Nations and elsewhere. But, after a visit to an American supermarket, he was obliged to modify his argument, claiming instead that the birth of an American dog or cat was the equivalent, ecologically speaking, of the birth of a dozen Bangladeshi children.[9]

Table 1: The USA's Share of World Consumption of
Key Materials, 1995 (figures in million tons)

(1) Material	(2) World Production	(3) US Consumption	(4)* 3 as % of 2
Minerals	7,641	2,410	31.54
Wood Products	724	170	23.48
Metals	1,196	132	11.03
Synthetics	252	131	51.98
All Materials	9,813	2,843	28.97

* The USA's population is approximately 4.42 percent of total world population.
Source: Computed from *State of the World 1999* (New York: Worldwatch Institute and W.W. Norton, 1999).

[9] See Satyajit Singh, "Environment, Class and State in India: A Perspective on Sustainable Irrigation," unpublished PhD dissertation, Department of Political Science, Delhi University, 1994.

Arguments like this, when presented or published in the USA, lay one open to the charge of being anti-American. So let me make it clear that I consider America to be, in many respects, a model for the world. Within its borders it is far and away the most democratic of all countries that claim membership of the United Nations. Over the years I have often been struck by the dignity of labor in America, by the ease with which high-ranking Americans carry their own loads, fix their own fences, mow their own lawns. This, it seems to me, is part of a wider absence of caste or class distinctions that is unthinkable in Europe and India. In the USA one can actually travel from the log cabin to the White House, as evident not just from Honest Abe in the nineteenth century but also from Dishonest Bill in the twentieth.

Left-wing intellectuals have tended to downplay these American achievements—respect for the individual, the remarkable social mobility, the searching scrutiny to which public officials and state agencies are subjected. They see only the imperial power, the exploiter, the bully, the invader of faraway lands, the manipulator of international organizations to serve the interests of the American economy.

On the world stage, America is not a pretty sight. Even in between its various wars of adventure its arrogance is on continuous display. It has disregarded strictures passed against it by the International Court of Justice and defaulted on its obligations to the United Nations. It has violated the global climate change treaty and the global biodiversity treaty. It has not signed the agreement to abolish the production of land mines. The only international treaties it signs and honors are those it can both draft and impose on other countries, such as the agreement on Intellectual Property Rights.

Liberals and libertarians, whether American or not, salute the USA's robustly democratic traditions. Socialists and anti-imperialists, whether American or not, castigate its bullying and overbearing instincts. Neither side is willing to see the other side of the picture. The truth about America is that it is at once deeply democratic and instinctively imperialist. This curious coexistence of contrary values is certainly exceptional in the history of the world. Other democratic countries, such as Sweden or Norway, are not at the present time imperialist. Scandinavian countries honor their international obligations, and, unlike the USA, generously support social welfare programs in the poorer parts of the world. Other imperialist countries, such as France and Great Britain, were not properly democratic in the past. In the heyday of European expansion men without property and women without exception did not have the vote. Even after suffrage was extended, British governments were run by an oligarchy. (The imagination boggles at the thought of a Ken Starr examining the sexual and other peccadilloes of a Benjamin Disraeli.)

My view is that the clearest connection between democracy at home and imperialism abroad is provided by the American consumer economy, its apparently insatiable greed for the resources of other lands. Contrary to what Wendell Berry thought, wildernesses at home continued to be protected only because the ecological footprint of the American consumer grew, and grew, and grew. The freebooting instincts of the pioneer, which were once set loose on the lands of the Wild West that were formally part of the nation, now found play in lands and waters East, South, and North regardless of whether these belonged to America. To cite only the most obvious example, the USA imports well over 50 percent of the oil it consumes.

This link seems to have escaped American environmentalism and, more surprisingly and regretably, American scholarship as well. In the rich and growing field of environmental history, as I suggested in Chapter One, scholars in other parts of the world have drawn much inspiration from the work of American exemplars, from their methodological subtlety and fruitful crisscrossing of disciplinary boundaries. For all this, there is a studied insularity among the historians of North America. There were, at last count, more than 300 professional environmental historians in the USA, and yet few of these have seriously studied the global consequences of consumerism, the impact on land, soil, forests, and climate, of the American way of life.[10]

One example of this territorial blindness is the Gulf wars. In that prescient essay of 1958 Galbraith remarked that "it remains a canon of modern diplomacy that any preoccupation with oil should be

---

[10] An honorable exception is Richard Tucker's *Insatiable Appetites: The United States and the Ecological Degradation of the Third World* (Berkeley: University of California Press, 2000), which addresses the question directly. Cf. also Thomas Princen, *et al.*, eds, *Confronting Consumption* (Cambridge, Mass: MIT Press, 2002); and John R. McNeill, *Something New Under the Sun: An Environmental History of the 20th Century* (New York: W.W. Norton, 2000): these also allude to the ecological footprint of the American consumer.

concealed by calling on our still ample reserves of sanctimony."[11] There have been Americans such as Galbraith who have helped tear apart the veil of this hypocrisy, pointing out that it was the US government that backed and armed Saddam Hussain, the dictator it later overthrew. Yet the essentially imperial imperatives of America in the Middle East have remained unexamined within the dominant discourse. It was the left-wing British newspaper, *The Guardian*, which claimed that the first Gulf War was carried out to safeguard "The American Way of Driving." No American historian has to my knowledge taken to heart the wisdom in that throwaway remark, to reveal in all its starkness the ecological imperialism of the world's sole superpower.

II

Let me now contrast the American case with the German. Environmentalists in Germany have been more forthright in their criticisms of consumer society: "The key to a sustainable development model worldwide," writes Helmut Lippelt, "is the question of whether West European societies really are able to reconstruct their industrial systems in order to permit an ecologically and socially viable way of production and consumption." That Lippelt does not include the USA or Japan is significant as an expression of his movement's willingness to take the burden upon itself. West Europeans should reform themselves rather than transfer their existing "patterns of high production and high consumption to eastern Europe and the 'Third World' [and thus] destroy the earth."[12]

From the viewpoint of the German greens economic growth in Europe and North America has been made possible by the economic and ecological exploitation of the Third World. The philosopher Rudolf Bahro is characteristically blunt: "the present way of life of the most industrially advanced nations," he remarks, "stands in a global and antagonistic contradiction to the natural conditions of human

[11] Galbraith, "How Much," p. 90.
[12] Helmut Lippelt, "Green Politics in Progress: Germany," *International Journal of Sociology and Social Policy*, vol. 12, nos 4–7, 1992, p. 197.

existence. We are eating up what other nations and future generations need to live on." He argues:

> The working class here [in the North] is the richest lower class in the world. And if I look at the problem from the point of view of the whole of humanity, not just from that of Europe, then I must say that the metropolitan working class is the worst exploiting class in history . . . What made poverty bearable in eighteenth- or nineteenth-century Europe was the prospect of escaping it through exploitation of the periphery. But this is no longer a possibility, and continued industrialism in the Third World will mean poverty for whole generations and hunger for millions.[13]

Bahro was a famous "Fundi," a leader of the section of the German greens which was uncompromisingly antagonistic toward modern society. But even the most hard-headed members of the other— "Realo"—faction, acknowledged the global unsustainability of industrial society. The German parliamentarian (and future Foreign Minister) Joschka Fischer, when asked by a reporter where he planned to spend his old age, replied: "In the Frankfurt cemetery, although by that time we may pose an environmental hazard with all the poisons, heavy metals and dioxin that we carry around in our bodies." Or, as a party document more matter-of-factly put it: "The global spread of industrial economic policies and lifestyles is exhausting the basic ecological health of our planet faster than it can be replenished." This global view, coupled with the stress on accountability, has called for "far-reaching voluntary commitments to restraint by wealthy nations." The industrialized countries, which consume three-fourths of the world's energy and resources, and who contribute the lion's share of "climate-threatening gaseous emissions," must curb their voracious appetite while allowing nations of the South to grow out of poverty. Green theorists ask for a cancellation of international debt, the banning of trade in products that destroy vulnerable ecosystems, and most radically for the freer migration of people from poor countries to rich ones.[14]

[13] Rudolf Bahro, *From Red to Green: Interviews with New Left Review* (London: Verso, 1984), p. 184.

[14] This paragraph is based on Werner Hülsberg, *The German Greens: A Social and Political Profile* (London: Verso, 1988); but see also Margit Mayer and John

These elements in the green program were, of course, forged as an alternative to policies promoted by the two dominant political parties in Germany which are committed to the Great God Growth. Between 1998 and 2005 the greens found themselves sharing power at the federal level—junior partners but partners nevertheless—in a coalition dominated by the Social Democrats. Being in power tamed them. They now worked only for incremental change instead of a wholesale restructuring of the consumption and production system which some of them had previously advocated.

The critique of overconsumption made manifest by the German greens is not absent in other European environmental traditions. A few months prior to the Earth Summit of 1992 the Dutch Alliance of Sustainable Development invited four scholars from the South to write a report on the Dutch economy and environment. A Brazilian anthropologist, an Indian sociologist, a Tanzanian agronomist, and an Indonesian activist (two men and two women) spent six weeks in Holland talking to a wide cross-section of citizens and public officials. Their report focused on the Dutch "addiction to affluence" as revealed in over-reliance on the motorcar, dependence on the lands and resources of other countries, and high levels of pollution. The four foreign critics posed the sharp question, "Can Dutch society put limits to itself?" They thought, optimistically, that the developed democratic culture of the Netherlands offered possibilities of self-correction. For that to work, political action had to be accompanied by technical change, by the exercise of individual restraint, and by a wider social resolve to share wealth with the less-advantaged societies of the South.[15]

It says something about Dutch environmentalists that they extended this invitation in the first place. At the risk, once more, of being called anti-American, it must be said that one cannot easily imagine the Sierra Club initiating such an examination.

Ely, eds, *Between Movement and Party: the Paradox of the German Greens* (Philadelphia: Temple University Press, 1997); and Saral Sarkar, "The Green Movement in West Germany," *Alternatives,* vol. 11, no. 2, 1986.

[15] Mercio Gomes, Chandra Kirana, Sami Soganbele, and Rajiv Vora, *A Vision from the South: How Wealth Degrades the Environment—Sustainability in the Netherlands* (Utrecht: International Books, 1992).

III

Fifty years before the founding of the German Green Party, and thirty years before the article by Galbraith with which this chapter began, an Indian visionary had pointed to the global unsustainability of the Western model of economic development. "God forbid," he wrote, "that India should ever take to industrialization after the manner of the West. The economic imperialism of a single tiny island kingdom (England) is today keeping the world in chains. If an entire nation of 300 million took to similar economic exploitation, it would strip the world bare like locusts."[16]

So said Mahatma Gandhi in December 1928. Two years earlier he had claimed that to "make India like England and America is to find some other races and places of the earth for exploitation." Because Western nations had already "divided all the known races outside Europe for exploitation and there are no new worlds to discover," he pointedly asked: "What can be the fate of India trying to ape the West?"[17]

Gandhi's critique of Western industrialization has of course profound implications for the way we live and relate to the environment today. For him "the distinguishing characteristic of modern civilization is an indefinite multiplicity of wants," whereas ancient civilizations were marked by an "imperative restriction upon, and a strict regulating of, these wants."[18] He also spoke in uncharacteristically intemperate tones of his "wholeheartedly detest[ing] this mad desire to destroy distance and time, to increase animal appetites, and go to the ends of the earth in search of their satisfaction. If modern civilization stands for all this, and I have understood it to do so, I call it satanic."[19]

[16] "Discussion with a Capitalist," *Young India* (hereafter *YI*), December 20, 1928, in *Collected Works of Mahatma Gandhi* (hereafter *CWMG*; New Delhi: Publications Division, 1958–), vol. 38, p. 243.

[17] "The Same Old Argument," *YI*, October 7, 1926, *CWMG*, vol. 31, p. 478f.

[18] "Choice Before Us," *YI*, 2 June 1927, *CWMG*, vol. 33, pp. 417–18.

[19] "No and Yes," *YI*, March 17, 1927, *CWMG*, vol. 33, p. 163. This was part of an exchange with the British Communist parliamentarian of Indian origin, Shapurji Saklatwala.

For the individual willing to heed his advice, Gandhi's code of voluntary simplicity offered a sustainable alternative to modern lifestyles. One of his best-known aphorisms—the world has enough for everybody's need, but not enough for everybody's greed—is in effect an exquisitely phrased one-line environmental ethic. This was an ethic he himself practiced; resource recycling and the minimization of wants were integral to his life.

Gandhi's arguments have been revived and elaborated by the present generation of Indian environmentalists. As explained in Chapter Two, India is in many ways an ecological disaster zone, marked by high rates of deforestation, species loss, land degradation, and air and water pollution. The consequences of this abuse of nature have been chiefly borne by the poor in the countryside—peasants, tribals, fisherfolk, and pastoralists who have seen their resources snatched away or depleted by powerful economic interests. For, over the past few decades, the men who rule India have attempted precisely to "make India like England and America." Without access to resources and markets enjoyed by those two nations when they began to industrialize, India has perforce had to rely on exploiting its own people and environment. The natural resources of its countryside have been increasingly channelized to meet the needs of the urban–industrial sector; the diversion of forests, water, minerals, and so on to the elite has accelerated the processes of environmental degradation even as these processes have deprived rural and tribal communities of their traditional rights of access and use. Meanwhile, the modern sector has moved aggressively into the remaining resource frontiers of India—the North-East, and the Andaman and Nicobar islands. This biased "development" has proved Gandhi's contention that "the blood of the villages is the cement with which the edifice of the cities is built."[20]

The preceding paragraph brutally summarizes arguments and evidence provided in a whole array of Indian environmentalist tracts.[21] Simplifying still further, one could say that the key contribution of the Indian environmental movement has been to point to inequalities of

[20] *Harijan*, June 23, 1946.

[21] See especially the two Citizens Reports on the Indian Environment, published in 1982 and 1985 by the New Delhi-based Centre for Science and Environment. Also chapter 2 above.

consumption *within* a society or nation. India's North-East has been for metropolitan India what Iraq and other such countries have been for imperialist America. By implicitly pointing out such analogies, Indian environmentalists have complemented the work of their German counterparts, who have most effectively highlighted the inequalities of consumption *between* societies and nations.

The criticisms of these environmentalists are strongly flavored by morality, by the sheer injustice of one group or country consuming more than its fair share of the earth's resources, and by the political imperative of restoring some semblance of equality in global and national consumption. I now present an analytic framework that more dispassionately explains these asymmetries in patterns of consumption.[22] Derived in the first instance from the Indian experience, this model rests on a fundamental opposition between two groups, termed *omnivores* and *ecosystem people*. We met these two groups via Madhav Gadgil in Chapter Eight; now we can look at them more closely. Both groups are distinguished above all by the size of their "resource catchment." Thus omnivores, who include industrialists, rich farmers, state officials, and the growing middle class based in cities (estimated at in excess of 100 million), have the capability of drawing upon the natural resources of the whole of India to maintain their lifestyles. Ecosystem people, on the other hand, who include roughly two-thirds of the rural population or about 400 million people—rely for the most part on the resources of their own vicinity, from a catchment of a few dozen square miles at best. These are small and marginal farmers in rain-fed tracts, landless laborers, and miscellaneous resource-dependent communities of hunter-gatherers, swidden agriculturists, animal herders, and wood-working artisans, all stubborn pre-modern survivals in an increasingly post-modern landscape.

The process of development in independent India has been characterized by this basic and massive asymmetry between omnivores and ecosystem people. A one-sentence definition of such economic development over the last sixty years would read: "Development is the channelizing of an ever-increasing volume of natural resources, via the state apparatus and at the cost of the exchequer, to serve the interests

---

[22] The following paragraphs expand and elaborate upon some ideas first presented in Gadgil and Guha, *Ecology and Equity*.

of rural and urban omnivores." The central features of this process have been:

1. The concentration of political power/decisionmaking in the hands of omnivores.

2. The use of state machinery to divert natural resources to islands of omnivore prosperity, especially through the use of subsidies. Wood for paper mills, fertilizers for rich farmers, and water and power for urban dwellers have all been supplied by the state to omnivores at well below market prices.

3. The culture of subsidies has fostered indifference among omnivores to the environmental degradation caused by them. This has been compounded by their ability to pass on most costs to ecosystem people and to society at large.

4. Projects based on the capture of wood, water, and minerals—such as eucalyptus plantations, large dams, and open-cast mining—have tended to dispossess ecosystem people who previously enjoyed ready access to such resources. This has led to a rising tide of protests by the victims of development: to Chipko, Narmada, and the dozens of other protests that we know collectively as the Indian environmental movement.

5. "Development" has also *permanently* displaced large numbers of ecosytem people from their homes. Some 20 million Indians have been uprooted by steel mills, dams, and the like; countless others have been forced to move to cities in search of a legitimate livelihood denied them in the countryside, sometimes as a direct consequence of environmental degradation. This has created a third class of people, namely, *ecological refugees*, who live in slums and temporary shelters in the towns and cities of India.

This framework, which divides the Indian population into three socio-ecological classes—omnivores, ecosystem people, and ecological refugees—can help us understand why economic development has destroyed nature while failing to remove poverty. It distinguishes social classes by their respective resource catchments, by their cultures and styles of consumption, and by their widely varying power to influence state policy.

Our "social ecology" framework is analytic as well as value-laden, descriptive and prescriptive. It helps us understand and interpret nature-based conflicts at various spatial scales: from the village community upward through district and region to nation. Originating in the study of the history of modern India, it throws light on the dynamics of socio-ecological change in other large and rapidly industrializing countries such as Brazil and Malaysia, where too conflicts have erupted between omnivores and ecosystem people, and where the cities are likewise marked by a growing population of ecological refugees. At a pinch, this framework explains asymmetries and inequalities globally too. It was in the middle of the nineteenth century that a German radical proclaimed: "Workers of the World, Unite!" Another German radical recently reminded me that the reality of our times is very nearly the reverse—a process of globalization whose motto might very well be "Omnivores of the World, Unite!"[23]

IV

What, then, is the prospect for the future?

There are, at present, two alternative answers to this question. One answer is the one that guides the institutions that constitute the so-called "Washington Consensus." It also informs the economic policies of most national governments. The other answer animates the activism of the environmental and anti-globalization movements.

The first alternative is what I'd like to call "the fallacy of the romantic economist." The fallacy here is that everyone can become an omnivore if only we allow the market full play. When, back in 1972, resource scientists had raised the question of "limits to growth," the economist Wilfrid Beckerman claimed there was "no reason to suppose that economic growth cannot continue for another 2500 years."[24] The optimism was wholly characteristic of a profession mistakenly dubbed the dismal science, unless of course we see things from the

[23] The radical who reminded me of this is the environmentalist and social critic Wolfgang Sachs.

[24] Wilfrid Beckerman, "Economists, Scientists, and Environmental Catastrophe," *Oxford Economic Papers*, vol. 24, no. 3, 1972, p. 332.

viewpoint of ecosystem people and recognize how dismal such optimism really is for the bulk of the world's population. With the fall of the Berlin Wall the romantic economist's optimism has been reinforced and renewed. Economists everywhere are now the cheerleaders for processes of globalization, processes which, in their view, promise the universalization of American styles of consumption.

My opinion is that aspects of economic globalization are welcome. These include the free flow of information, inducements to innovation, and encouragement to entrepreneurship. In countries like China and India the retreat of the state from the economy has led to much faster rates of economic growth. All this has greatly augmented human welfare in the short term. The long-term prospects are more worrying. One problem, foregrounded by left-wing critics, is that the fruits of economic growth have been very unevenly distributed. Although aggregate poverty has substantially reduced in both India and China, there remain large and possibly growing pockets of deprivation.

The problem of *equity* can perhaps be mitigated by purposive social policies: by spreading education and health across the board, by nurturing opportunities for growth among communities and regions which appear to be falling behind. Less tractable is the problem of *ecology*. Consider the spread of personalized transport in China where—as once in America—the possession of a car is the one true sign that a human being has become properly modern. As *The Economist* magazine approvingly reports, the car is seen by middle-class Chinese as the "symbol of freedom and status." In 2002 the demand for cars in China increased by 56 percent, in 2003 by 75 percent. In 2004 the Chinese state news agency *Xinhua* proclaimed that "China has begun to enter the age of mass car consumption. This is a great and historic advance." Shanghai has a Formula One racetrack now, costing $320 million. The city will soon have a $50 million car museum.[25]

There has been, as this chapter's epigraph suggests, a general reorganization of ways of life in the past century, which the Americans have led, the rest of the world panting behind them. The Chinese, relative latecomers to this race, are striving hard to catch up with the leaders. In Beijing one in six residents now has cars. But for the country as a

[25] "Special Report: Cars in China," *The Economist*, June 4, 2005.

whole the proportion is 1 in 125, way below the USA's average, 6 in 10. But we know from *Xinhua* that the popular desire is for China to become in this respect exactly like America. And in the cities of modern India the feelings are the same. The motorcar has multiplied at the rate of bacteria and the sentiment among young professionals is that not to possess at least one is to be left out in the cold.

Consider the impact on the environment of the spectacular recent growth in the economy of my own home town, Bangalore. Within a generation a once sleepy cantonment has been transformed into a city of 8 million, an industrial and commercial hub. Although the growth has been led by a relatively dematerialized industry, information technology, the income generated and the desires spawned have had strikingly material effects. Bangalore now has an estimated 2 million motor vehicles. A little over half of these run on two wheels: scooters and motorcycles. About a quarter are cars; the rest are buses, trucks, and utility vehicles. These take metals to build and oil to run and roads to drive on, and—difficult to forget if you live and breathe there—emit toxic chemicals into the air. The massive influx of population has also caused a building boom. Large offices made of cement and glass and larger apartment buildings all consume vast amounts of energy and materials.

A question never asked by economists, or by *The Economist*, is this—can the world as a whole achieve American levels of car ownership? Can there be a world with four billion cars, a China with 700 million cars, an India with 600 million cars? Where will the oil and gas to run them come from? The metals to build them with? The tar to drive them on? I take the car here as merely indexical of a certain style of consumption. For with its use also come demands for other resources, for other goods. In China and India now, as in the America of the 1950s, with the wish to possess more elegant cars has come the desire for more exotic food, more erotic clothing, more elaborate entertainment.

In a recent series of articles the *New York Times* columnist Thomas Friedman writes with alarm about threats to the global environment posed by Chinese economic development. The billion-strong population of China, he says, uses 45 billion pairs of chopsticks every year. These account for 25 million full-grown trees. Should they not move to eating with their fingers or with steel utensils instead? Speaking of the increasing energy consumption in China, he notes that a single shop in the city of Shenzen sold 1000 airconditioners over a single hot weekend. "There is a limit to how long you can do that," Friedman warns.

"What we don't want," writes the *New York Times* columnist, "is for China to protect its own environment and then strip everyone else's in the developing world by importing their forests and minerals." He points out that "China's appetite for imported wood had led to the stripping of forests in Russia, Africa, Burma, and Brazil. China has just outsourced its environmental degradation." This, says Friedman, "is why the most important strategy the US and China need to pursue, in concert, is one that brings business, government, and NGOs together to produce a more sustainable form of development—so China can create a model for itself and others on how to do more things with less stuff and fewer emissions."[26]

Friedman might have added that China has only been doing for the past decade what his own country has done for the past century: that is, protect its woods and forests while devastating environments in other countries. Even now, it would help if the original sinner confessed and promoted a more sustainable form of development within its own borders. We know the USA still does more things with more stuff causing massive emissions, facts which make American preaching to other countries hard to swallow. That said, the industrialization of India and China does pose special problems caused by the weight of sheer numbers. Gandhi understood as early as 1928 that if the most populous nations sought to emulate the ecologically wasteful ways of the most powerful, they put in peril the very conditions of human survival. So, by the time the Indians and the Chinese reach American levels of consumption, will they have stripped the world bare, like locusts?

I once posed this question in a seminar at the University of California at Berkeley. A biology professor answered that the solution lay within developments in modern genetics. It would soon be possible, he said, to engineer adult human beings who were two feet tall and

---

[26] Friedman's articles were reproduced in *The Asian Age* on October 27 and 29, 2005.

weighed, on the average, a mere twenty kilograms, but who had the brains and techniques to outwit and dominate the rest of creation. This new race of Super (Small) Men would drive smaller cars on narrower roads to tiny offices from tiny homes. In other words, they would live more or less like the average American today while consuming a fraction of the resources he did.

That prospect is, for the moment and perhaps for a long while yet, in the realm of fantasy. In the world we know and live in, what we see is India and China simply trying to become like England and America, and thus, as Gandhi predicted, trying to "find some other races and places of the earth for exploitation." Chinese interest in the Sudan and Indian interest in Central Asia exactly parallel America's interest in the Middle East. We see the leaders of these "emerging" economies emulate the leaders of the already emerged, traveling to obscure parts of the world, sniffing the air for oil. Both countries are also, like America, expanding their military. And both are, like America again, refusing to endorse international agreements that would bind them to the more responsible use of natural resources.

Forget the rest of the world, then. All the Chinese and all Indians cannot become omnivores. The attempt to chase this fallacy will lead only to bitter social conflict and greater environmental degradation.

V

The alternative to the fallacy of the romantic economist is what I call "the fallacy of the romantic environmentalist." This fallacy holds that ecosystem people want to remain ecosystem people. The fallacy comes in two versions: the *agrarian*, and the *primitivist* or *deep ecological*. Let us take them in turn.

In 1937, soon after he had moved to a village in Central India to devote himself to rural reconstruction, Gandhi defined his ideal village:

> It will have cottages with sufficient light and ventilation, built of a material obtainable within a radius of five miles of it. The cottages will have courtyards enabling householders to plant vegetables for domestic use and to house their cattle. The village lanes and streets will be free of all avoidable dust. It will have wells according to its needs and accessible to all. It will have houses of worship for all, also a common meeting place, a village common for grazing its cattle, a co-operative dairy, primary and secondary

schools in which [vocational] education will be the central fact, and it will have Panchayats for settling disputes. It will produce its own grains, vegetables and fruit, and its own Khadi. This is roughly my idea of a model village . . .[27]

In many respects this is an appealing ideal: it stresses local self-reliance, a clean and hygienic environment, and the collective management and use of those gifts of nature so necessary for rural life—water and pasture. The problem is that Gandhi wanted this generalized. That is, in the India of his conception there would be 700,000 such villages run on ecological and moral lines. As for cities and factories, it was not clear what would happen to those that already existed; certainly, new ones were not to be encouraged. A certain stasis was also implied in the Gandhian utopia: India was, and would always remain, a land of villages and villagers.

The Mahatma's anti-urban orientation was shared by his followers, such as J.C. Kumarappa (whom we met early in this book), and has been emphatically affirmed by his modern-day admirers. Contemporary Gandhian environmentalists such as Medha Patkar and Sunderlal Bahuguna see cities as corrupting and factories as polluting—morally as well as ecologically. The opportunities the city offers and the commodities it produces are regarded as ephemeral, unconnected with the good life. The peasant must remain a peasant; indeed, they would say, he *wants* to remain a peasant.[28]

The ecosystem person of the deep ecological vision is more likely to be a hunter-gatherer than a subsistence farmer. Still, like the agrarian, the committed deep ecologist is resolutely opposed to the artifacts of modernity, whether technological, social, or aesthetic. Some elements of their preferred utopia have been described in Chapter Three; to which let me now add a contemporary effort to create such a utopia in practice. This is the handiwork of Douglas Tompkins, an American

---

[27] "A Humble Villager of Birbhum," *Harijan*, January 9, 1937, in CWMG, vol. 64, pp 217–18.

[28] See, for example, Sunderlal Bahuguna, *Walking with the Chipko Message* (Silyara, Tehri Garhwal: Navjivan Ashram, 1983); cf. also Nandy, ed., *Science, Hegemony and Violence: A Requiem for Modernity*; Shiva, *Staying Alive: Women, Ecology and Development*.

billionaire who had a midlife conversion experience and became a deep ecologist. Selling his clothing business for $150 million, he bought a thousand square miles of Chilean forest and resolved to save it for posterity—save not just the forest but also its inhabitants. He had a home built for himself by local workmen using local methods and employed local folk musicians playing timeless, or at least unchangeable, tunes. No electricity was allowed in the campus and no cars. An exception was made for the helicopter which brought the owner in and sometimes took him out. Otherwise, Tompkins kept out "the global economy which was a threat to their traditional culture." As a visiting journalist put it, Tompkins did not merely seek to save the land and forests, he planned "to freeze the people in place."[29]

Strikingly, the environmental activist's rejection of modernity is being reproduced in and by influential sections of the academic world. Anthropologists, in particular, are almost falling over themselves writing epitaphs of development in works that seemingly dismiss the very prospect of directed social change in the world outside Europe and America. They imply that development is a nasty imposition on the innocent peasant and tribal, who, left to himself, will not willingly partake of Enlightenment rationality, modern technology, modern consumer goods.[30] This literature has become so abundant and so influential that it has even been anthologized in a volume called (what else!) *The Post-Development Reader*.[31]

The editor of this last volume is a retired Iranian diplomat now living in the south of France. The authors of those other demolitions of the development project are, without exception, tenured professors at well-established Western universities. I rather suspect that the objects of their sympathy would cheerfully exchange their social and

[29] Patrick Symmes, *Chasing Che: A Motorcycle Journey in Search of the Guevara Legend* (New York: Vintage Books, 2000), pp. 85–92.

[30] See, for instance, Arturo Escobar, *Encountering Development: The Making and Unmaking of the Third World* (Princeton: Princeton University Press, 1995); James Scott, *Seeing Like a State: How Certain Schemes to Improve the Human Condition Have Failed* (New Haven: Yale University Press, 1998); Wolfgang Sachs, ed., *The Development Dictionary: A Guide to Knowledge as Power* (London: Zed Books, 1992).

[31] Majid Rahnema, ed., *The Post-Development Reader* (London: Zed Books, 1998).

financial positions with those of their chroniclers. For, if it is impossible to create a world peopled entirely by omnivores, it is equally fallacious to suppose that ecosystem people want to remain as they are, that they do not want to massively enhance their own resource consumption. I think the tenured critics of "development" and "modernity" need to be reminded of these words by Raymond Williams when speaking of his boyhood in Wales:

> At home we were glad of the Industrial Revolution, and of its consequent social and political changes. True, we lived in a very beautiful farming valley, and the valleys beyond the limestone we could all see were ugly. But there was one gift that was overriding, one gift which at any price we would take, the gift of power that is everything to men who have worked with their hands. It was slow in coming to us, in all its effects, but steam power, the petrol engine, electricity, these and their host of products in commodities and services, we took as quickly as we could get them, and were glad. I have seen all these things being used, and I have seen the things they replaced. I will not listen with any patience to any acid listing of them—you know the sneer you can get into plumbing, baby Austins, aspirin, contraceptives, canned food. But I say to these Pharisees: dirty water, headaches, broken women, hunger and monotony of diet. The working people, in town and country alike, will not listen (and I support them) to any account of our society which supposes that these things are not progress: not just mechanical, external progress either, but a real service of life.[32]

This point can be made as effectively by way of anecdote. Some years ago, a group of Indian scholars and activists gathered in the southern Indian town of Manipal for a national meeting to commemorate Mahatma Gandhi's 125th birth anniversary. They spoke against the backdrop of a lifesize portrait of Gandhi, their hero clad in the loincloth he wore for the last thirty years of his life. Speaker after speaker invoked the mode of dress as symbolizing the message of the Mahatma. Why did we all not follow his example and give up everything to mingle more definitively with the masses?

Then, on the last evening of the conference, the Dalit (low-caste) poet Devanur Mahadeva got up to speak. He read out a short poem in Kannada written by a Dalit woman of his acquaintance. The poem

[32] Raymond Williams, "Culture is Ordinary" (1958), quoted in Christopher Hitchens, *Unacknowledged Legislation* (London: Verso, 2000), p. 30.

spoke reverentially of the great Dalit leader B.R. Ambedkar (1889-1956), especially of the dark blue suit that Ambedkar invariably wore in the last three decades of *his* life. Why did the Dalit woman focus on Ambedkar's suit, asked Mahadeva? Why, indeed, did the countless statues of Ambedkar put up in Dalit hamlets always have him clad in suit and tie, he asked? His answer was deceptively and eloquently simple: if Gandhi wears a loincloth, he said, we all marvel at his *tyaga* (sacrifice). The scantiness of dress is, in the Mahatma's case, a marker of what the man gave up. A high-caste, well-born, English-educated lawyer had voluntarily chosen to give up power and position and live the life of an Indian peasant. That is why we memorialize that loincloth.

However, if Ambedkar had worn that same loincloth, it would not occasion either wonder or surprise. Ambedkar is an untouchable, we would say—what else should an untouchable wear? Millions of his caste fellows wear nothing else. Mahadeva brilliantly argued that it was precisely the fact that Ambedkar had *escaped* this fate, and the fact that his extraordinary personal achievements—a law degree from Lincoln's Inn, a PhD from Columbia University, his drafting of the Constitution of India—had allowed him to *escape* the fate that society and history alloted him, that were so effectively symbolized in his blue suit. Modernity, not tradition; development, not stagnation, were responsible for Ambedkar as sartorial inversion of Gandhi, for his successful yet all-too-infrequent storming of the upper-caste citadel. Raymond Williams or B.R. Ambedkar: take your pick. The point remains the same. Ecosystem people want to be omnivores.

Finally, it should be said that the aspirations for a better, or at least different, life among the disprivileged or disadvantaged are not restricted to financial prosperity. The journalist who visited Douglas Tompkins' Chilean estate found that his folk musicians employed to preserve their music listened on the sly to American rap.[33]

VI

Let me now attempt to represent the story of Ambedkar's suit in more material terms. Consider these simple hierarchies of fuel, housing, and transportation:

[33] Symmes, *Chasing Che*, pp. 93–4.

Table 2: Hierarchies of Resource Consumption

Fuel Used	Mode of Housing	Mode of Transport
Grass	Cave	Feet
Wood, Dung	Thatched hut	Bullock cart
Coal, Kerosene	Wooden house	Bicycle
Gas	Stone house	Motor scooter
Electricity	Cement house	Car

To go down any of these lists is to move toward a more reliable, more efficient, and generally safer mode of consumption. Why then would one abjure cheap and safe cooking fuel, for example, or quick and reliable transport, or stable houses that can outlive the monsoon? To prefer gas to dung for your stove, a car to a bullock-cart for your mobility, and a wood home to a straw hut for your family is to move toward greater comfort, well being, and freedom. These are choices that, despite specious talk of cultural difference, are desired by all and ought to be made available to all.

At the same time, to move down these lists is to move toward a more intensive and possibly unsustainable use of resources. Unsustainable at the global level, that is, because while a car expands freedom there is no possibility whatsoever of every human on earth being able to possess a car. As things stand some people consume too much while other people consume far too little. There is an intimate though not often noticed overlap between *ecological entitlements* and *economic status*. Not only do the rich and powerful consume more than their fair share of the world's resources, they are also usually better protected from the consequences of environmental degradation. It is these asymmetries that a responsible politics would seek to address. Restricting ourselves to India, for instance, one ought to work toward empowering ecological refugees and ecosystem people, strengthening their ability to govern their lives and gain from the transformation of nature to artifact. This policy would simultaneously force omnivores to internalize the costs of their profligate behavior. Such a new, green development strategy would I think have six central elements:

1. A move toward a genuinely participatory democracy with a strengthening of the institutions of local governance at village,

town, and district levels. This is mandated by the Constitution of India but has been aborted by successive central governments in New Delhi. The experience of exceptional states, such as West Bengal and Karnataka, which have experimented seriously with the panchayat or self-government system, suggests that local control is more conducive to the successful management of forests, water, and other natural resources.

2. The creation of a process of natural resource use which is open, accessible, and accountable. This would center around a properly implemented Freedom of Information Act enabling citizens to be better informed about the designs of the state and making officials more responsive to the public.

3. Greater political decentralization to stop the widespread undervaluation of natural resources. The removing of subsidies and the putting of a proper price tag to make resource use more efficient and less destructive of the environment.

4. Encouraging a shift to private enterprise for producing goods and services while making sure that there are no hidden subsidies, and that firms properly internalize externalities. There is at present an unfortunate distaste for the market among Indian radicals, whether Gandhian or Marxist. But one cannot turn one's back on the market; the task rather is to tame it. People and the environment in India and other countries similarly placed have already paid an enormous price for allowing state monopolies in sectors such as steel, energy, transport, and communications.

5. Outline sustainable policies for specific resource sectors. Chapters Four and Five summarize ways in which the management of forests and the wild can be made consistent with the twin—if sometimes competing—claims of ecological integrity and social equity. Likewise, scientists and social scientists with the relevant expertise need to design sustainable policies for transport, energy, housing, health, and water. These policies must take account of what is not merely desirable but also feasible.

6. This development model can only succeed if India becomes a far more equitable society than it is at present. Three key ways of enhancing the social power of ecological refugees and ecosystem

people (in all of which the Indian state has largely failed) are land reform, literacy—especially female literacy—and proper health care. These measures would also help bring population growth under control. In the provision of health and education the state might be aided by the voluntary sector, paid for by communities out of public funds.

The charter of sustainable development outlined here applies, of course, only to one country, albeit a large and fairly representative one. Its *raison d'être* is the persistent and grave inequalities of consumption within the nation. What then of inequalities of consumption within nations? This question has been authoritatively addressed in a study of the prospects for a "Sustainable Germany" sponsored by the Wüppertal Institute for Climate and Ecology.[34] Its fundamental premise is that the North lays excessive claim to the "environmental space" of the South. The way the global economy is currently structured—

> The North gains cheap access to cheap raw materials and hinders access to markets for processed products from those countries; it imposes a system (World Trade Organization) that favors the strong; it makes use of large areas of land in the South, tolerating soil degradation, damage to regional eco-systems, and disruption of local self-reliance; it exports toxic waste; it claims patent rights to utilization of biodiversity in tropical regions, etc.

Seen "against the backdrop of a divided world," says the report, "the excessive use of nature and its resources in the North is a principal block to greater justice in the world . . . A retreat of the rich from over-consumption is thus a necessary first step toward allowing space for improvement of the lives of an increasing number of people." The problem identified, the report goes on to itemize in meticulous detail how Germany can take the lead in reorienting its economy and society toward a more sustainable path. It begins with an extended treatment

[34] See Wolfgang Sachs, Reinhard Loske, and Manfred Linz, *et al.*, *Greening the North: A Post–Industrial Blueprint for Ecology and Equity* (London: Zed Books, 1998), on which the rest of this section is based. Also see F. Schmidt-Beek, ed., *Carnoules Declaration: Factor 10 Club* (Wuppertal: WIKUE, 1994), which sets a target of 90 percent reduction in material use by industrialized countries. For a brave recent attempt to apply these ideals to America, see Thomas Princen, *The Logic of Sufficiency* (Cambridge, Mass.: MIT Press, 2005).

of overconsumption, of the excessive use of global commons by the West over the past two hundred years, of the terrestrial consequences of profligate lifestyles—soil erosion, forest depletion, biodiversity loss, air and water pollution. It then outlines a long-range plan for reducing the "throughput" of nature in the economy and cutting down emissions.

Table 3 summarizes the targets set by the Wüppertal Institute. The report also outlines the policy and technical changes required to achieve these, including the elimination of subsidies to chemical farming,

Table 3: Some Environmental Objectives for a
Sustainable Germany

Environmental Indicator	Target set for the year 2010
Energy	
Energy consumption (overall)	at least −30%
Fossil fuels	− 25%
Nuclear power	− 100%
Renewables	+ 3 to 5% per year
Energy efficiency	+ 3 to 5% per year
Materials	
Non–renewable raw materials	−25%
Material productivity	+ 4 to 6% per year
Substance release	
Carbon dioxide	− 35%
Sulphur dioxide	− 80 to 90%
Nitrogen oxides	− 80% by 2005
Ammonia	− 80 to 90%
Volatile organic compounds	− 80% by 2005
Synthetic nitrogen fertilizers	− 100%
Agricultural biocides	− 100%
Soil erosion	− 80 to 90%
Land Use	
Agriculture	Extensive conversion to organic farming methods
Forestry	extensive conversion to ecologically adapted silviculture

Source: Sachs, Loske and Linz, *et al.*, *Greening the North*.

the levying of ecological taxes (on gasoline, for example), and the move toward slower and fuel-efficient cars while shifting the movement of goods from road to rail. Some concrete examples of resource conservation in practice are identified—such as the replacement of concrete girders by those made with steel, innovative examples of water conservation and recycling within the city, and a novel contract between the Munich municipal authorities and organic farmers in the countryside. Building on examples such as these, Germany could transform itself from a nature-abusing society to a nature-saving one.

The Wüppertal Institute study is notable for its mix of moral ends with material means as well as its judicious blend of economic and technical options. More striking still has been its reception. The original German book sold 40,000 copies, with an additional 100,000 copies sold of an abbreviated version. It was made into an award-winning television film and discussed by trade unions, political parties, consumer groups, scholars, church congregations and countless lay citizens. Several German towns and regions have begun to put some of these proposals into practice.

Admittedly, to reduce consumption even in a green-conscious rich society like Germany will take great skill and dexterity. On the one hand, as the Wüppertal Institute has demonstrated, the affluent economies of the West might easily limit material consumption without a diminution in individual and social welfare. On the other hand, if the economy does not "grow" at, say, 3 percent to 4 percent per annum, this will lead to unemployment. Which is precisely what happened during the SPD–Green coalition of 1998–2005, leading to its removal from office in the German elections of 2005. Of course, one might still aim for a "steady-state economy" and address the problem of unemployment by following policies of internal redistribution, but that would then place a great strain on the welfare state.

Governments are compelled to pursue policies which are popular enough to win or retain office. This considerably complicates what is already a deeply complicated relationship. The social needs and demands of the economy have to be made consistent with the natural constraints of ecology; and both have to be harmonized with the political imperatives of democracy.

To effectively and sustainably resolve these conflicts requires us to truly think through the environment: think through it morally and politically, historically and sociologically, and—not least–economically and technologically.

The challenges that this poses are formidable indeed. Yet they have to be met. Inequalities of consumption must be addressed at national and international levels: the two are, as we have seen, completely interconnected. Juan Martinez-Alier, the Spanish economist whose work I discussed at the start of this book, provides one telling example. In the poorer countries of Asia and Africa, firewood and animal dung are often the only source of cooking fuel. These are inefficient and polluting, and their collection involves much drudgery. The provision of oil or LPG to the cooking stoves of the Nigerian or Nepali peasant woman would greatly improve the quality of their lives. This could very easily be done, says Martinez-Alier, if one very moderately taxed the rich. He calculates that to replace the fuel used by the 3000 million poor of the world—our ecosystem people and ecological refugees—we require about 200 million barrells of oil a year. Now this is less than a quarter of the USA's annual consumption. But the bitter irony is that "oil at $15 [or even $50] a barrel is so cheap that it can be wasted by rich countries, but too expensive to be used as domestic fuel by the poor." The solution is simple—namely, that oil consumption in the rich countries should be taxed, while the use of LPG or kerosene for fuel in poor countries should be subsidized.[35] This would allow the poor to ascend one small step up the hierarchies of resource consumption, and it actually requires a very moderate sacrifice by the rich. In the present climate, however, any proposal with even the slightest hint of redistribution would be shot down as "socialist."

But things do change, they don't always remain the same. And change they will when conflicts over consumption begin to sharpen, as they assuredly shall. Within countries, access to water, land, forests, and mineral resources will be fiercely fought between contending groups. Between countries, there will be bitter arguments about the "environmental space" occupied by richer nations.

---

[35] See Juan Martinez-Alier, "Poverty and the Environment," in Ramachandra Guha and Juan Martinez-Alier, *Varieties of Environmentalism: Essays North and South* (London: Earthscan, 1997). Also Juan Martinez-Alier, *Ecological Economics: Energy, Environment, Society* (1987; new edn, London: Basil Blackwell, 1991).

As these divisions become more manifest, the global replicability of North Atlantic styles of living will be more directly and persistently challenged. Sometime in the middle decades of the twenty-first century, Galbraith's great unanswered question "How Much Should a Country Consume?"—with its Gandhian corollary, "How Much Should a Person Consume?"—will come finally to dominate the intellectual and political debates of the time.

Index